Rosie Blythe lives in London (hence all those crazy British spellings) and when she's not writing, works as a stylist in television and film.

The
Princess Guide
to Life

Rosie Blythe

Hallsworth Press

A catalogue record of this book is available from the British Library.

ISBN: 978-1-910285-00-8

Cover Design by Beckalicious

Hallsworth Press LTD
Suite 5003
PO Box 6945
London

If your response to being called a Princess is "Damn right I am, and don't you forget it" – this book is for you.

"The woman is the fibre of the nation. She is the producer of life. A nation is only as good as its women." Muhammad Ali

CONTENTS

INTRODUCTION

"The thing women have yet to learn is that nobody gives you power. You just take it." Roseanne Barr

How would you define a "Princess"?

Some people imagine the kind of entitled bimbo who makes crazy demands to prove how special she is. Others think of frothy pink dresses, diamond tiaras and passive damsels in distress; a dangerous combination to be idolised by little girls. Whether they're considered bolshy divas or simpering doormats, Princesses get a bad press.

But we're going to change all that.

It's time to rebel against the old rules: being a Princess is a state of mind. It's about being self-possessed, poised, and dignified; forging your own path instead of following the herd, and unashamedly using all of your feminine wiles. We might not always achieve our goals of regal sophistication, but the important thing is being motivated to try again tomorrow.

It's said that well-behaved women rarely make history, but "exciting" isn't synonymous with "obnoxious". Dip into any book about what it means to be a member of the fairer sex and you'll be informed that "Women have always been taught to be good girls; to be nice, quiet, and modest..." Maybe this was true in the past, but now? What planet are these writers living on? I don't see any suggestion in today's society that it's desirable for girls to be demure, sweet, or even polite. It's far more likely that the women presented to us as role models will be lauded for their seductive moves in a music video, their assertiveness in feuding with fellow celebrities and their business chutzpah in producing a sex tape. The press raves about them, but why would we want to emulate anyone so self-obsessed and shallow? Their money and fame give them the opportunity to make a difference, but they're too busy tweeting about "haters" and fighting with family members and ex-boyfriends. (Occasionally they'll put their own relationship dramas aside to preach to the rest of us about "peace" – oh, the irony.) Being "too nice" is the least of their problems.

Look at the ladies who *have* become legends – leading revolutions, breaking down gender barriers, creating art, literature and music – none of them won the world's admiration by downing tequila shots or being rude to strangers on the internet. There's nothing wrong with being feisty, but a Princess shrewdly combines her boldness with a cheeky smile and a genuinely kind attitude, creating a charm offensive nobody can resist.

This idea that women are all brainwashed to be docile and agreeable has become a mantra that everybody repeats without bothering to question whether or not it's true (just like the "fact" that no older actresses get decent parts – tell it to Sigourney).

So *are* we ladies too submissive? When it comes to anxiety about our looks and sex appeal, maybe. It's here that the notion of women being meekly compliant begins to make sense. What could we achieve if we stopped wasting time comparing our thighs to Rihanna's?

Here in the 21st century, we women are in an entirely new place. We've come a long way, but in between taking control of our destinies and fulfilling our dreams we've somehow managed to keep all our old insecurities and even find some new ones. We're saturated in advertisements and onscreen visions of what's expected of us, and given "rules" to follow: fitting the shape that's been chosen for us this season, getting the right clothes and using the right beauty products. (The worst part is that we happily buy into this and put more pressure on ourselves than anyone else could.) Then there are the insidious messages about how many people we should have sex with and how we should feel about it. Whatever we do, we'll be judged. (Which would you prefer: "frigid bitch" or "worthless slut"?)

Certain aspects of being female are dismissed or ridiculed, but is it because they're genuinely raw deals, or because they're "feminine" and that's enough for them to be considered demeaning? Some girls proudly announce that they hate romance novels involving vampires, love movies full of explosions, and would rather go fishing than get a facial. That's all fine and dandy if it's the way they really feel (for the record, *Die Hard 2* is my favourite), but if they're intentionally trying to distance themselves from "all those other girls" you have to wonder; what's wrong with being female?

Women are powerful creatures, and sometimes we forget just how much influence we have. As Orson Welles once said: "If there hadn't been women we'd still be squatting in a cave eating raw meat, because we made civilisation in order to impress our girlfriends." (Strictly speaking, if there were no women, civilisation would have died out in one generation – but let's not split hairs.) Men with high-status careers often claim they only entered politics, music or sport because it was a great way to impress the ladies; I even met a guy who dropped his plans to work in IT and trained as an architect for six years because a girl in his class laughed at him for being a computer geek. (He has *no interest* in architecture. True story.) So tread carefully, because you have no idea of your own force.

Being a Princess means recognising the advantages given to us by nature, and choosing to enjoy the perks of being female.

It's not a sin to like pink, baking, or shoe shopping.

It's OK to feel out of step with the rest of the world. Being normal is overrated.

Women can buy their own diamonds, flowers, and Valentine's Day gifts.

Not everyone has sex on the first date. Or second, or fifteenth, or eighty-seventh...

When someone says you have "balls", inform them that the word they're looking for is "ovaries" and yes, you have big ones.

Letting a man pay for the date doesn't mean you owe him anything – he's getting the pleasure of your company.

Flirting can be a way to get what you want and brighten someone else's day in one fell swoop.

If you can live without needing anybody's approval but your own, you have total freedom.

And when you discover your inner Princess, you can light up the world.

Part One

Princess Style

"Be faithful to your own taste, because nothing you really like is ever out of style."
Billy Baldwin

LOOKING LIKE A PRINCESS

"Taking joy in living is a woman's best cosmetic." Rosalind Russell

From supermodels to precocious 8-year-olds, nearly everyone has *some* anxiety about their looks. I realised how utterly pointless this is when I was a nerdy schoolgirl and had a friend called Bella who was smoking hot: luminous skin, great hair, big brown eyes, and gleaming white teeth. Everyone either had a crush on her or wanted to BE her. (She was so nice, too. The cow.) One day we were in the ladies' room, brushing our hair and primping, and she said: "Yuck, I'm having SUCH an ugly day today. I look awful." She wasn't fishing for compliments – she genuinely felt insecure. I thought "What a waste of time, for *Bella* to think she's ugly." And from that point on, I tried really hard to ignore that little voice in my head which encouraged me to focus on my weakest points, because that little voice is delusional.

Ideally, we'd all live by the maxim of Maria Montez, a Hollywood actress known as "The Queen of Technicolor" in the 1940s; she told reporters "When I look at myself, I am so beautiful I scream with joy!" Well, it's a bit extreme, but it's better than nitpicking. Maybe such self-love isn't as rare as we think it is; despite all those "body confidence" campaigns run by cosmetics companies, it's still strangely taboo for a woman to *admit* that she likes herself just as she is. Sadly, women bond by commiserating over cellulite or non-existent flab. When everyone is moaning "Ugh, I hate my legs!" it would seem kind of impolite to say "Oh well, I think mine are pretty great." Even celebrities are obliged to tell us how they dislike their lopsided smile or knock-knees. (Which is silly of them, because as soon as they point it out, it's all I can see.)

When a celebrity does have something a bit quirky about her appearance, internet trolls (who may not look like Greek gods themselves) make helpful suggestions like: "She'd be good-looking if only she didn't have wrinkles / got her teeth fixed / lost some weight." But try imagining that person with those changes, and you get a picture of every other averagely pretty model – the result is BLAND. Jennifer Grey is a poignant example; as "Baby" in *Dirty Dancing* she had a distinctive long nose. She decided to get it changed to a standard Hollywood button – and promptly ruined her career. She'd lost the very attribute that made her unique, and she fell back into the blurred mass of wannabes who all look the same.

Francis Bacon said "There is no excellent beauty that hath not some strangeness in the proportion" and it's true – the women we consider real stunners always have something striking about them. Imagine if a young Angelina had felt self-conscious about her lush lips and had them changed. Would Anna Paquin be so memorable without her gap-toothed smile? Where would Nicole Kidman be without her milky white skin? And THANK GOD nobody ever convinced Audrey Hepburn to get a boob job. The "flaws" which make us different from everyone else are often what other people envy most. (Which explains why they tease you about them.)

Not everyone can accept their unusual features; while some people are vehemently against cosmetic surgery, others are so blasé it's as if they equate a nose job with a haircut. Personally I get nervous at the thought of someone making irreversible changes to her body, especially if the "imperfection" exists largely in her mind. If you've ever seen one of those undercover documentaries where an investigator asks surgeons about getting procedures, you'll know that some unscrupulous doctors will agree very quickly that the person "needs" a slimmer waist, a tighter neck or a more defined chin. Nobody's going to discourage you when your operation means money for them. Also, cosmetic surgery is rarely a one-shot deal – breast implants don't last forever and will need replacing, and botox needs to be topped up every three months. A vulnerable woman who keeps finding new areas of her body to change is a cash cow to a quack with no morals.

On the other hand, some people hate a feature for so long that when they finally pluck up courage to go under the knife, they wish they'd done it years ago. The problem is when someone believes "If only I could change X, my whole life would be different" then after she's had the operation realises she's still the same person, and ends up chasing an impossible dream by making more and more changes until she's unrecognisable. (We all know the celebrities I'm thinking of, right?)

Is there anything sadder than a formerly classy-looking star with a trout pout, strangely puffed-up cheeks, or cat eyes? They often deny having anything done, of course. If it's way too obvious for them to get away with, they'll admit to having "tried" Botox at some point in the distant past, with a promise never to touch the stuff again. What really scares me is that a) they're deluded enough to assume they can lie about it and nobody will notice, and b) even a person

17

with millions in the bank and access to the best surgeons in the world can end up with horrifically unnatural-looking results.

So to avoid a downward spiral of image-paranoia ending in a frozen face at the age of thirty, what are the secrets of Princess confidence?

Ignore Commercials

We're bombarded with them every day. Mascara ads with a tiny disclaimer about lash inserts and CGI being used for the final picture. A hunky man featuring in every commercial, as if we're guaranteed male adoration if we use the right brand of shower gel. Miracle zit creams which leave ravaged skin looking immaculate in mere hours. It's *all* manipulative nonsense.

First of all: beauty doesn't come in a jar. True radiance comes from within – cheesy but true. It can be seriously debilitating to have acne when everyone around you has pure, unblemished skin, but nobody who cares about you will be judging the state of your face. We love people for their essence, not their looks. (Would you swap your mum for a glossier model?) The sparkle in your eyes and the friendliness in your smile will always be more enticing than high cheekbones or a line-free forehead. Whether someone is breathtaking or plain, their looks become less visible as we discover all their other characteristics and our initial appraisal of their attractiveness is forgotten. This is why the skinny, short dude with nerdy dress sense can sometimes win you over with his sweet nature and hilarious jokes, while the hot jock with the attitude problem stops being eye candy when the very sight of him is irritating.

Inner loveliness aside, another reason that angelic good looks can't be applied with a brush (unless it's an airbrush) is that your skin, hair and nails reflect your *health.* If you smoke, use sunbeds, keep exercise to a "walking-to-the-car" minimum and live on bacon and donuts, you're not going to reach your optimum level of gorgeousness, even if you do radiate joy. If you eat a balanced diet, boost your blood circulation with a booty-shaking workout, and get quality sleep, your body will reward your clean-living ways by glowing with health.

Commercials deliberately prey on our anxieties, and shamelessly make empty promises to entice us to buy their products. The truth is:

THERE IS MONEY TO BE MADE FROM MAKING A WOMAN HATE HER APPEARANCE.

I swear they must give a prize to the advertising executive who can come up with a new area of the body for women to feel self-conscious about. ("I've got it! Arm pits!") We spend our hard-earned cash on a never-ending quest to eliminate perceived "faults" – carefully constructed by an industry which thrives on body dysmorphia.

The trend for having completely bald nether regions is now more or less over, but for a while even young girls were getting their first pubic hairs waxed away because they'd been told they were "disgusting". (If anyone had expressed this opinion back in the 1970s, they'd have been ridiculed for their prudish attitude to the human body.) Bizarrely, the porn industry has managed to dictate how we look in the privacy of our own homes, with some girls even undergoing intimate surgery to make sure every body part conforms to what they've seen on screen.

Society has some strict guidelines about the way women are expected to look, but ultimately we own our bodies and we can shave our heads if we want to, dress like post-apocalyptic pirates if we want to, or spend hours painting our nails and highlighting our hair if we want to. Princesses make their own rules and ignore everyone else's.

Never Compare Yourself to Others

If you want a fast track to insanity, start measuring yourself up against the latest face of a cosmetics company. In these media-savvy times, we're all aware that nobody looks like that all the time, and a little digital tinkering is involved in creating those sublime photographs. From my experience in styling TV commercials, I've seen first-hand that the dazzling model skipping around on TV arrived at the studio looking completely different. For starters, what looks good on screen can look fairly odd in real life – it's a rare woman who's 6 feet tall and has a 22-inch waist, and models can have an elongated-to-the-point-of-stretchiness look about them. (If they weren't earning thousands for a few hours work, you'd almost feel sorry for them, or at least hope they were good at basketball.)

It's said that designers choose ultra-thin models because they want a "clothes hanger" look, which is astoundingly stupid. What kind of pinhead makes clothes that look great when they're hanging up, but terrible when you put them on? A truly skilled craftsman could create outfits which look equally alluring whether they're draped over soft curves *or* a lithe, athletic body.

In reality, willowy models are used because it makes organising a catwalk show simpler and cheaper. Samples are made in only one size – "tiny" – because it's easier to fit clothes on boyish figures. Once you start introducing breasts and hips and bums into the equation, alterations will be necessary to tailor the clothes to each individual. Straight-up-and-down women have little variety between them, so models are hired to suit the clothes rather than the other way around.

By the time a cover girl is seen by the public, she'll have been through several hours of hair and (full-body) makeup, possibly had hair extensions to give her a more luxuriant mane, and had touch-ups *literally* every time the camera stops clicking. The image this produces bears so little relation to everyday life, it's not worth our time to worry about how we measure up. The photographs are art – they're a fantasy designed to look as aesthetically pleasing as possible. Likewise, runway fashion isn't meant to be seen as ordinary clothing; it's not intended to be accessible to the general public.

Magazines often print unflattering pictures of stars looking their worst to "make us feel better", but instead it reminds us of the impossible standards women are supposed to live up to, even when they're only popping out to buy milk. It's also pretty mean-spirited; I resent the implication that all women are so envious and spiteful that we delight in seeing others look bad. Even if we'd love to believe that the Hollywood glamourpuss only looks so good because she applies makeup with a trowel, the truth is that some people are naturally stunning. (That's kind of how they got to be famous, duh.) We're encouraged to boo and hiss when a star loses weight after having a baby, because her personal choice "makes it harder for everyone else" to live up to the same standard. The same goes for anyone who achieves too much while also looking ravishing. Instead of feeling intimidated, let's see it as inspirational – and think "If she can do that, I could too." Gloating over lousy photos of celebs doesn't benefit you in any way, so let's stop wasting our time making comparisons, and start enjoying ourselves...

The Raw Materials

You might pride yourself on being intellectual and seeing straight through all those brazenly exploitative adverts; you embrace your individuality rather than trying to look like everyone else, and know that ultimately it's what's inside that counts. That's awesome and you are a true Princess. However, it's not a crime to want to look pretty; preening may be superficial, but it's satisfying. Once you've learned to cheerfully ignore the urge to scrutinise yourself for weaknesses, why not revel in the pleasure of feeling beautiful? Why shouldn't it be a delight, rather than an endless treadmill of maintenance? The best kind of grooming routine is a relaxing daily ritual involving plenty of sleep and fresh air, lavish baths, and gentle products. If it involves sitting down at your dressing table in a fur-trimmed silk peignoir and slathering your face with cold cream, so much the better.

The basics are skin, hair and teeth. Once you have these looking good, everything else is the icing on the cake. The ultimate goal of a Princess is to look and feel great *naturally*, so she can roll out of bed in the morning and go, without feeling obliged to apply a full face of slap. (This is why I'm not interested in light-reflecting makeup which promises to "blur imperfections". What am I supposed to do when I'm not wearing it, huh? I want my skin to be so flawless that I don't NEED to cover it up.)

Rather than overwhelming my face with lots of different products, I've found that keeping my routine simple makes my skin happy. Everyone is different, so you'll learn through trial and error what works for you and what doesn't. The one rule everyone should stick to for a peachy visage is using a good sunblock *every* day, to avoid the sun damage that can occur all year round.

Hair is easy to fix: get it cut regularly to eliminate split ends and keep the style looking fresh. It can take a bit of research to find someone who "gets" you and understands your hair type; for instance, some hairdressers don't have a clue what to do with curly or afro hair. Always bring a photo of what you want to show the stylist, because her idea of a "sleek bob" may be different from yours. Adding curls, waves or straightness can be done at home with heated tongs, or at the hairdressers for a more permanent solution.

Some people are put off home dye kits for fear of creating an artificial-looking block of one colour rather than the multi-tonal head of highlights you'd get in a salon. However, these days you can buy a range of sophisticated formulas which will look just as good as anything your hairdresser could do – the skill is in choosing the best shade to suit your skin tone. Although everyone recommends that you go to a pro if you're after a more drastic change, I confess that I've taken the DIY route when colouring my blonde hair everything from chocolate brown to vermillion red, and I've had no disasters (so far).

Teeth may seem less mutable than hair and skin, but with cosmetic dentistry growing in popularity, there's generally a solution to any problem. If you like your wonky teeth, good for you. However, if you always try to cover your mouth when you're speaking and avoid smiling in photographs, please do whatever it is that's going to make you feel confident about your gnashers. One day, the pain and cost of orthodontic treatment will be a distant memory, and the resulting straight white smile will increase your attractiveness by about a million percent.

And if I may give you an anti-tip? DON'T SMOKE. It's a given that cigarettes are horrible for your health, but if you suffer from "It Won't Happen To Me" syndrome, at least let me appeal to your vanity. Smoking ages you. It gives you wrinkles and fills your body with toxins. It makes your teeth yellow and your breath smell. It's GROSS. I suspect that female smokers imagine themselves resembling a sophisticated 1930s Greta Garbo type, when in fact the ever-present fag makes them look like a stereotypical chav.

It's incredible to me that women scour the shops for rejuvenating face creams or sexy clothes when all they really need to do to upgrade their looks is to give up a harmful and expensive habit. The same goes for sunbeds – when you can get a realistic tan from a bottle, why waste time with something that not only makes your skin as crinkly and dried-up as a crocodile-skin handbag, but will massively increase your chances of getting skin cancer?

Keeping it Affordable

If you go to a salon for haircuts, manicures, pedicures, facials or massages, it's worth knowing that they often have a low-cost option if you're willing to be used as a practice dummy for trainees. Colleges that run beauty courses also have dirt-cheap offers and students will always have a tutor on hand to supervise them, so the results are generally great. The downside is that it takes much longer than it would with an experienced pair of hands, and it may not be the most glamorous of venues (I had my hair cut at the local college and was surrounded by little old ladies getting their perms).

Another luxurious yet economical idea is the DIY spa day with your friends. Get the house to yourself (it's less fun if there are men around to laugh at you) and don fluffy towelling robes and slippers for that authentic health club feeling. Then you can exchange relaxing foot massages, apply face masks and oil treatments for your hair, and finish with mani / pedis. Add some new age whale music and you're good to go.

There are also lots of spas that advertise bargain vouchers for specific things, like massages or facials. If you spot one that's local to you, nab it for when you're in need of a treat.

Tattoos

This form of body art has become so ubiquitous I sometimes think I'm the only person left without one (which I kind of like because it makes me feel like the last unicorn).

Some tattoos are spectacular, and they can have emotional resonance and provide a lasting happy memory. Unfortunately, there are some truly untalented tattoo "artists" working today (as we've all seen from crazy photos on the internet). When people get addicted to adorning their bodies with pictures, mottos and dates, they can sometimes end up resembling old school desks covered in doodles. (If it looks bad now, it's only going to get worse when you're older and your skin starts sagging.)

If you would like a tattoo, remember the golden rules:

- Live with your decision for a year before you take the plunge. It's a long time to wait when you really want it, but it gives you time to change your mind; if you're commemorating something meaningful, you get the perspective to see if the event will still be so special to you later on.
- NEVER brand yourself with your boyfriend's (or even husband's) name or (shudder) face. This feels like the most obvious rule, but people persist in doing it all the time and it inevitably precedes a split. (Can you think of *any* celebrities who are still with the person whose name is permanently written on them?) I'd love to see some statistics

on this because there seems to be a direct correlation between tattoos and break-ups; maybe people who are already feeling nervous about their relationship get inked to convince themselves it's built to last. Whatever the reason, I've never come across anyone with a partner-immortalising tattoo who is still happy with this choice a few years later. Likewise, going for matching designs with a partner could end up being a reminder of someone you'd rather forget in a few years.

- Check the spelling. The tattoo artist will write exactly what you tell them, so it's up to you to verify the accuracy beforehand. Do you want to make grammar and punctuation purists cringe whenever you proudly show off your ink? Or to keep saying "I know..." when the 50th person informs you of the error? The same goes for Chinese symbols (or any writing in another language) unless you want people sniggering that you're a "slut" when you thought you were expressing your "freedom".

- No reputable tattoo parlour will work on you if you're drunk. If they happily get the needle out even though you're falling all over the chair and reek of tequila, run fast and run far.

- It's best to place a tattoo somewhere that *can* be hidden, to avoid severely limiting your choices of employment in future. Also, there are very few women who can look truly elegant in evening dress when they have words scrawled all over them.

- Before you go for the real thing, it's a good idea to get a henna tattoo of what you want. That way you can check that you really do like it once it's "on" and make sure there's no unforeseen weirdness (like the top of that dolphin's head being the only bit you can see when you're fully clothed, so it looks like a shapeless blob).

- Tattoos are reversible, but it's not an easy process. You can either get another, bigger tattoo on top (which could result in an ever-growing swirl of designs) or get it lasered off (which is expensive, and more painful than the original procedure).

- Think carefully before you emblazon your skin with that inspirational quote which got you through a bad patch. It might cheer you up now, but in ten years' time won't it simply remind you of the stress you went through?

Although I understand the urge to pay tribute to someone you love or the happiest time of your life, I'm staying away from the needle. I prefer my skin to be a blank canvas, so I get a fresh start each day. But for my inky Princesses – if you do get a tattoo, make it a fantastic one, OK?

How Every Girl Can Feel Like A Princess

(The formula is the same whether you're a sheep herder who won't see a human being all day, a harassed mother of toddlers, or a stern businesswoman who must be taken seriously at all costs.)

Pretty Underwear

Being a Princess means having self-respect; you treat yourself to some divine undies because even if nobody else is going to see them, YOU know what you've got on under your clothes. Throughout the day, what you're wearing is your little secret: perhaps some lacy vintage lingerie, a bright purple crop top and briefs, or soft and downy thermals? No matter what else you dress in and what your day will entail, you have the foundation of your outfit in place.

Unless you're shopping in some super-fancy corsetry place (lucky!) you may find that bra sizes vary wildly rather than conforming to universal measurements. I've given up looking at labels – I grab a bunch of bras that look about right, try them all on and buy the one that fits best. This makes me happy because according to some brands, I'm a C cup! Yay! (I'm *so* not a C cup.) Remember to bend and twist and all that jazz to see if it's comfortable – the back strap should be straight, not riding up in a curve. Stores often have ladies to help you with the fit, but the final decision is yours – the ideal bra should make you feel as if you're not wearing one, but your breasts are being magically supported by helpful cherubim.

Bright colours are great because if a strap peeps out, it looks deliberate rather than accidental. Forget about "invisible" bra straps – everyone can see that little piece of transparent plastic, but it's obviously not supposed to be seen, which makes it an epic fail. Flesh-coloured, seamless underwear is a wardrobe staple for every girl; wear it under clingy tops and spray-on dresses for perfect smoothness.

I resisted padded bras for a long time (I don't like the idea of false advertising) but after a while I found it almost impossible to find any styles I liked that WEREN'T padded, so I gave in. And you know what? Now if I try on a flimsy cotton bra, it feels very weird and insubstantial. That millimetre of foam between me and the world has also been invaluable on cold days; it might be an attention-grabbing gimmick, but prominent nipples are not an aesthetic I go for.

My grandmother always said you should wear nice undies "in case you're hit by a bus". The less morbid but equally encouraging reason to choose wisely would be "What if you unexpectedly met the man of your dreams and he were to somehow see your smalls?" (Like, if your dress flew up Marilyn-style, or you were in an action-movie kind of emergency and donated your shirt to become a tourniquet. Not for anything *sexual*, obviously. You've just met him!) If you have underwear which would make you blush in said situation, throw it out. There's no excuse to keep the ancient pair of granny pants you currently use for period days, when perfectly nice and affordable knickers are available.

Perfume

You don't have to spray on a choking haze of the latest celebrity fragrance; find some decent, unique perfumes that you love. Conventional wisdom urges us to find our "signature scent" but that sounds way too limiting for a Princess; we like wearing different clothes every day, so why not different smells, too? Crisp aquatics feel fresh on muggy summer days, chocolatey vanilla is comforting during work marathons, and rich musks and honeys feel sensual when you have a sexy date lined up (even if the date is you and a box of raspberry truffles).

One-scent wonders point out that a signature fragrance means your loverman will be reminded of you whenever he sniffs it. (This still isn't a good reason to choose a popular cologne that *everyone* wears, no matter how yummy.) If you wear a million different scents, there will be all the more potential reminders of you. The poor chap won't be able to walk past a field of freshly mown grass, a bakery, or a cherry tree in full bloom, without being reminded of you. (It's almost cruel, isn't it?)

Your perfume should only be strong enough to leave a faint, delicious whiff in the air as you swish past: if people can smell you from across the room, you may have overdone it. I use oils, which are a touch more subtle than eau de parfum. (My absolute favourite oils in the world come from Black Phoenix Alchemy Lab, who make AMAZING scents.) If you work in close proximity to other people, say as a dentist or physical therapist, I would reluctantly suggest laying off fragrance altogether – not everyone will share your taste in perfume so it's not fair to force it on your clients.

Lovely Hair

You may not be able to show off your great haircut if your job forces you to scrape it back, but at least *you* will know that come home time, your layers will be swinging prettily or your curls bouncing merrily away. Short hair can be a more practical choice (especially when it comes to drying and styling) but the sensuous feel of long, freshly washed and glossy hair falling across your skin is a constant reminder of your femininity.

If I'm having a bad hair day, life seems crappy and EVERYTHING makes me irritable – don't let this happen to you. Try different shampoos; some of the best I've used have been the really cheap ones, and often a change is all you need to give your locks a boost. Relax with a conditioning mask for extra silkiness, and add a soft hint of the aforementioned perfume for a long-lasting heavenly aroma.

Manicure / Pedicure

I feel so much better when my nails look good – even if I'm writing all day and won't see anyone. (It's much more fun to see your fingers flying across the keyboard if they're topped with a splash of vivid red.) Nail polish is low-maintenance makeup for your hands in that you don't need to touch it up throughout the day and it won't smudge if you rub your face, eat or cry. However, you do need to watch out for flaking, because a less-than-fresh paint job makes nails look scuzzy rather than sophisticated. If you're not into colour, buff them up nice and shiny instead.

A pedicure generally lasts longer than a manicure and is almost essential in summer when your toes will be displayed in strappy sandals or flip-flops. In winter, not many people will see your feet but it's still fun to have twinkly, colourful toenails to brighten up bathtime and make you feel glamorous when you're padding around barefoot.

Jewellery

OK, so maybe not everyone can wear jewellery every day. Earrings would be near suicidal for the mother of a baby, for instance, and I'm sure rings would be inadvisable for vets attending farmyard births. But for those of us in more commonplace jobs, a gold locket setting off your swan-like neck, a sparkly ring or two accentuating your pretty fingers, some dangling earrings or a jingly bracelet can add so much to your outfit and make you feel a million dollars.

FOOD, EXERCISE AND FUN

"You have to be as relaxed as possible about food and fitness and the rest of it, or you'll be a slave to your beauty habits... you may have great skin, but you'll become a robot." Audrey Hepburn

Remember when you were a kid and you ran as fast as you could for the sheer joy of feeling the wind rushing through your hair and the blood pumping in your veins? When I eat well and take the time to build exercise into my day, I actually feel like this all over again. (Then for some reason I spend entire weekends sprawled on the sofa, gorging myself on bonbons with my friends, and wonder why I've lost that vitality.)

If you eat healthily most of the time you can afford to indulge yourself occasionally, but if you eat *nothing* but junk, you'll end up not being able to run for a bus without huffing like a steam train. (The only drawback to being super-fit is that centring your life around your quinoa intake and yoga classes often results in an overdose of smugness which may cause your social circle to shrink.)

If you're overweight *or* underweight, you may feel a bit sluggish and tired all the time. Size (or your BMI number) isn't always a reliable indicator of fitness; you could be as skinny as a whippet and still get out of breath climbing the stairs. Instead of focusing on how your body looks, think about what it can *do*. Forget outward appearance and concentrate on creating a lifestyle which leaves you feeling happy, energetic and strong.

Food Fit for a Princess

While generations before us seem to have existed largely on meat pies, jam sandwiches, and macaroni cheese ("And it's never done me any harm!") it's become the height of cool to be passionate about living healthily. You probably have at least one friend who only eats food that's gluten-free, sugar-free, grain-free, dairy-free, soy-free, and prepared by mermaids bathed in moonlight. There are a million different diets out there, all claiming to be the best, "cleanest" most detoxifying eating plan known to man. I've seen enough news coverage of unnaturally sprightly 70-year-olds to accept that the secret to eternal youth is *probably* a vegan, raw food diet. Much as I'd love to be one of those paragons who lives on wheatgrass juice and chia seeds, I don't yet have the requisite discipline. Can these super-conscientious people even enjoy going to restaurants? After years of carrot sticks, a bowl of creamy carbonara followed by a serving of sherry trifle might seem alien and indigestible, and that would be tragic.

I believe that your body basically tells you what it needs. OK, so sometimes mine tells me to stuff cookies into my mouth as fast as I can shovel them down, but this is normally followed by a lust for salad and fruit, so I figure it balances out.

It's also pretty obvious which feelings are communications from your body – like a craving for iron-rich meat when your period is due – and which come from boredom, or an insatiable need for something fatty and rich because it's been too long since you last ate. There's also food-envy, eg the desperate urge for chips because you saw someone else eating them and they looked so appetising. I have to hide junk food in my "emergencies only" cupboard because if I catch a glimpse of a familiar chocolate wrapper, I'll suddenly find that I need some of that good stuff, even if I hadn't been remotely hungry.

A basic healthy eating regimen is to aim for food in its original state. Fruits, vegetables and nuts = perfect. Meat in one piece, eg a whole fish or a lean piece of steak = fine (in moderation). It's the processed rubbish we should cut back on; the ready-meals (who knows what's in them?), meat that's been chopped up and squished together (chicken nuggets, pepperoni etc) and all the sweet things made with bleached flour, refined sugar and artificial colourings. (You'll see that I largely ignore this last rule... oops!) As a side note, if the only thing keeping you from being a vegetarian is that you love the taste of bacon, burgers and sausages, check out the veggie alternatives, such as Quorn. Some of them are astonishingly convincing substitutes for the real thing; just as tasty but miles better for you.

I try telling myself that homemade desserts are superior to bought ones because I know exactly what the ingredients are, but the fact still remains that an ice cream sandwich should be an occasional treat rather than a meal replacement. (Unless of course, you're following 101 Ways to Feel Like a Princess. We all have to experience complete decadence once in a while.)

Unfortunately, sugar in all its forms is considered the devil by most nutritionists; obesity is just one of the many negative effects it can have on your body. Its only redeeming feature is that it makes food taste AMAZING, which is why you'll find it in all sorts of unexpected places: tins of soup, ready-made sauces, "healthy" yogurts and even pizza.

As food labels are often sneakily misleading, the best way to control what you consume is by cooking meals from scratch; there are so many ways to find great recipes (TV chefs, books, online) that you can literally search by ingredient and find a tempting way to use all that seaweed you bought when you were on a "superfood" kick.

Juicers are terrific for getting your daily allowance of fruit and vegetables when you don't have the time or inclination to munch huge bowls of cabbage and raw ginger. The bad news is that along with the antioxidants, you get a hit of the sugar content without any fibre to balance it out. This is why it's a good idea to mix the deliciously sweet juices (beetroot, carrot, any kind of fruit) with a hefty dose of leafy greens. If you don't have a juicer, you can make smoothies with soft fruit (bananas, melons, peaches etc) and yogurt. As a rule it's best to think of these luscious blends as snacks rather than drinks; if you're thirsty, water is the best way to go. As a Brit, I'm addicted to tea and like to start the day with a nice freshly brewed cuppa, but most other options (such as soda, squash or juice) are packed with sweeteners.

Another vital aspect to eating properly is listening to your body. If your family raised you to clear your plate (or have the leftovers for breakfast) it's a weird adjustment to simply stop when you feel full. Nobody likes waste, and it's especially tempting in a restaurant to scoff more than you can comfortably fit into your tummy. I always end up asking for a doggy bag, because eating until I'm bloated and bordering on nauseous is not my idea of fun. (Also, saving the leftovers means lunch for tomorrow is sorted.)

Portion control is even easier at home – just take what you want and remember you can always come back for more. Sometimes I absent-mindedly heat up ALL of those yummy leftovers before realising I only need half to satisfy my appetite; it's easy to get brainwashed into filling the entire plate, no matter what size it is. If you're with other people who can easily chow down more than you do, don't feel pressured to keep up – just have what you want, at the speed you like. And chew your food properly! Swallowing mouthfuls whole means you're taking in food faster than your body can say "That's enough, thanks" and can also result in digestive problems.

We all like feeling virtuous when we nourish ourselves with wholesome foods, but let's not get obsessive about it; some people treat diet with religious fervour and literally talk about nothing but what they can and can't eat. While lots of us might genuinely feel better for cutting out a particular food group, there's no need to bang on about it as if being lactose-intolerant makes us really special. Likewise there's no need to give your diet a fancy name, even though "I try not to eat any processed foods" isn't as catchy as "paleo". (Unless you're gnawing on the bone marrow of a rodent you caught, it's unlikely that you're really emulating your ancient ancestors anyway.)

Finally, there are few things I hate more in the world than the kind of magazine headlines that boast of "the diet where no food's a sin", or commercials which offer up "guilt-free snacking". Apparently people in general, and women especially, are meant to see food as some sort of moral snakes-and-ladders game, in which a piece of toffee cheesecake can only be justified by a proverbial beating with a wet birch twig (or a session at the gym). Screw that – food is fuel, it can provide us with moments of euphoria as well as essential nutrients and we can eat *whatever we choose*. So there!

The Princess attitude to food isn't about obsessively scraping the oil off your salad, saying no to crème brûlée and taking a little snack bag of spinach everywhere you go. I truly believe it's more important to consciously choose what you're going to eat and enjoy every bite – even if it's a gooey chocolate cake with extra sugary sprinkles – than to make a healthy diet such a burden that your life stretches out in front of you as a joyless, never-ending round of wafer snack breads. (Let's face it, chocolate is a divine gift to us all and should be appreciated for the mood-altering drug that it is.) But taste buds are creatures of habit, so the more you nibble on almonds, sip on parsley juice and create scrumptious dishes with sweet potato and chickpeas, the more you'll grow to love them. Good food – fresh ingredients, delectable flavours, and variety – is an everyday luxury that all Princesses can enjoy.

Exercise

So, we've established that there are so many gorgeous *and* health-giving foods available that you should never have to eat something you don't like just because it's good for you. Similarly, there are so many fun ways to get body-conditioning that nobody needs to grimly force another ten minutes on the treadmill.

As well as increasing physical fitness, exercise is a natural anti-depressant. Going for a run can get your brain into a naturally meditative, relaxed state and help you to sort through your problems. The stress of your job seems far away when you're bouncing on a trampoline, and riding a horse pushes out all your niggly little worries because you're concentrating so hard on staying upright. Finally, any kind of physical exertion will produce endorphins known as the "runner's high" – the opiate-like rush your body provides. There's something about being physically capable of running for a mile or paddling down a river that makes you feel powerful and invincible. With all these benefits, it's hard to believe that so many people will do anything to avoid breaking a sweat. So how can we get started?

Exercise in Ways You Don't Notice

Rev up your heart rate by walking or cycling to work rather than driving; take the stairs instead of the lift, and go to see your colleague in the next office instead of emailing. Pop out at lunchtime and take a walk around the block. Choose a particularly uncontrollable shopping trolley at the supermarket to strengthen your stomach muscles. Take the long way around the mall. Wear wrist and ankle weights while you're cleaning the house. After a few weeks of deliberately increasing your activity, it will become so natural you won't even be aware of it.

Short and Sweet

Try pushing yourself in short bursts rather than long sessions – there's a whole regime based on intense efforts for periods of 20 seconds at a time. (It sounds like nothing, but start spinning on an exercise bike at top speed and you'll see how that time can drag.) This "high-intensity interval training" appeals to me because it only takes a couple of minutes each day – but check what your doctor thinks of the idea before doing anything extreme. If in doubt, just boogie around your bedroom for the duration of your favourite song.

Let Someone Else Do the Thinking

You don't need to hire a personal trainer (although you can get some good deals if you shop around, so it's not a ridiculous idea). There are so many classes – in everything from pilates and zumba to wall climbing and boxing – that it's sometimes simpler to find a teacher rather than trying to devise your own exercise program. Check out your local sports centre for courses; even if you only go to one session of archery or judo, you've given it a try and broken up your usual routine. Best case scenario: you find a new favourite thing to do and become ultra-fit because of it.

Take a Buddy

It can be nerve-wracking to try a gym or class where you don't know anyone, but having a sidekick makes it less scary and more fun. Secondly, when it comes to workouts it's easy to let things slide and start making excuses about being too tired or too busy. If you're only answering to yourself, you have to be highly disciplined to show up when you don't feel like it. But if you've arranged to meet a friend, you'll be letting her down if you cry off. (If she cancels, you don't get a free pass – you can go alone.)

Having a partner also means the opportunity to play games like tennis or squash. (This is where I strongly advise taking a female friend – it's a rare man who can play a sport with a woman and not spend 80% of the time trying to "help" her perfect her game. If you want a casual knockabout this can be a tad annoying.) Having a training buddy means you can encourage each other; vital when you're on the verge of giving up because you don't believe you'll ever get rid of your bingo wings.

Dance Your Blues Away

The fantastic thing about dancing is that you don't have to be any good at it to enjoy it. There are loads of lessons which allow you to drop in whenever you feel like it – they cover a different combination of moves in every session so beginners can catch up with the more experienced members, but regulars don't get bored.

The other great thing is that you (probably) won't need a partner, because genres like street dance, tap, jazz or belly dancing are solo. If you have your heart set on gliding elegantly around a ballroom, you'll find plenty of classes where the teacher assigns everyone partners. Dances like rock 'n' roll or salsa are famous for being taught via informal get-togethers which are usually held in a bar or community hall. Everyone gets mixed up, you're partnered with a bunch of different guys, and the whole group has a good time. If you're not an extrovert it might sound a bit intimidating, but it's a fun way to meet men (with rhythm) and you'll all be learning together. When you're spinning around in a fast jitterbug, you'll agree that the few minutes of nerves were worth it.

If you have no interest in learning to waltz but you love exercising to music, try ice-skating, or check out your local roller disco for a retro night out that will be a blast as well as making your muscles ache the next day.

Teamwork

Lots of classes offer aerobic exercise, but what about getting out into the fresh air? A muddy field is so much more exhilarating when you don't have a teacher shouting instructions at you and it can be really fun to join others for a kickabout or to shoot some hoops. (Unless your experiences of being picked last for the netball team have scarred you for life – every single person I've ever met says they were picked last, so the popular kids were clearly culled shortly after graduation.)

Check out the local listings to see if anyone is advertising a game of footy / volleyball / lacrosse / whatever you fancy. The only downside is that the teams in your area will probably have been playing together for ages, so you might want to practise with a friend or two to brush up your skills before unleashing yourself on the world at large. You can also find meet-up clubs that organise activities such as group runs or bike rides – it's an awesome way to meet new friends as well as keeping fit. If you fancy a treat, grab some pals and splash out on a day of laser tag or paintballing for an adrenaline-fuelled workout.

Try Something New

If you're lucky enough to live near the coast, there are tons of things you can try in addition to splashing about in the rock pools. Surfing, kayaking, windsurfing, paddleboarding, canoeing and rowing are fun ways to ride the waves.

It might seem daunting to learn a new skill which means hiring all sorts of equipment as well as probably falling off your board in front of the hot guys who've been surfing for years. Remember they also had to start from square one: nobody's born an expert. Sign up for a one-day surfing course to join lots of other beginners; you'll be pleasantly surprised at how patient the teachers can be, and they'll have you standing up within a couple of hours. (If I can do it, anyone can.)

If water sports aren't your thing, you might enjoy martial arts (which could double up as an empowering course in self-defence), or circus skills – you'll soon be gracefully swinging through the air on a trapeze.

Whenever you try something for the first time, you're going to be clueless to begin with – that isn't a reason to avoid experimenting. I remember the first "absolute beginners" jazz class I went to; I was horrified when the teacher started using dance jargon I could only guess at. But I stood at the back, watched closely, and tried my best even though I was generally at least two steps behind everyone. (I also had trouble figuring out my left from right at times – the pressure got to me!) Then I realised nobody was looking at me anyway; they were all concentrating on their own routines. If you make up your mind that you're not going to take it too seriously, you'll get over your initial embarrassment, have a giggle and learn something new.

Top Tips

- It's obvious to anyone who's listened to the *Rocky* soundtrack while running, but now scientists have caught up with reality and confirmed that music enhances a workout: it distracts you from feeling tired and increases endurance. So whether you're dancing up a storm or watching music videos while you're on the rowing machine at the gym, the beat will keep you going.
- Do whatever suits you. I'm not really a fan of team games, so I'm better off going for a walk by myself than joining a cricket club. But if you need that team spirit to motivate you, solo pastimes will be a fast track to dullsville. Whatever bores you is the enemy.
- There's no reason why you shouldn't practise yoga and pilates at home – there are some great DVDs on the market. Look out for a guide with

real credentials rather than a celebrity jumping on the bandwagon – it's important to learn how to do the moves properly to avoid hurting yourself. If you go to a class, check out the teacher's qualifications, as some gyms will let anybody hire space and advertise themselves as an instructor.

- If you have exercise equipment such as a cross trainer or stationary bike at home, you can do a quick five minutes here and there (while you're waiting for the kettle to boil / reading a magazine / on the phone). Home workouts have the great advantage of not requiring you to mentally gear yourself up for a long session or go out in the rain.

- Focus on specific areas of your body for noticeable results; for instance, sit-ups (done correctly) can help to tone the stomach, using small dumbbells will strengthen arms, and squats target your lower half. Meanwhile, swimming and walking are good all-rounders for increasing general fitness, and they're gentle enough to make over-straining yourself unlikely.

- The best kind of routine feels like *playing*. In junior school, running around on the playground wasn't a chore, you were itching to get out there as soon as the bell rang. You can bring back this carefree attitude by exercising kid-style, with rollerblading, hula-hooping, and skipping. (If you don't have a rope for those playground tricks, skipping makes a light-hearted alternative to jogging when you're doing a circuit around the block. It feels so *joyful*.) Challenge your friends to a game of tag, run around shrieking like a 10-year-old and then tell me exercise isn't fun!

And Finally...

Remember those leaflets you got at school to inform you about menstruation, and how they claimed "you might experience slight discomfort"? Let's all take a moment to laugh at those. (To be fair, it was considerate of them to make it sound like the tiniest of inconveniences, rather than scaring us with horror stories.)

We all have to find a way to cope with our monthly visit from "Aunt Flo", and commercials telling us to enjoy our usual bungee jumping routine aren't necessarily helpful. If you have bad periods, check with your doctor to find the best way to deal with it: I used to get horrible stomach ache and the kind of nausea which left me unable to do anything but lie weakly in a darkened room sipping water (and then puking it up again). I now have prescription painkillers which I take at the first twinge to help me function like a real human being.

Gentle exercise can be beneficial for soothing your poor throbbing womb – even if you don't feel like doing much, a 10-minute stroll might be a good distraction technique. Heavy bleeding can cause an iron deficiency, so try upping your intake of seafood (such as clams and mussels), red meat, fortified cereals and nuts (especially peanuts, hazelnuts, and almonds). Diet also plays a part in controlling your body's comfort levels; celery is said to minimise fluid retention, calcium-rich food (especially dark leafy vegetables like kale and broccoli) can help to relax muscles, and high-fibre beans and whole grains contribute by absorbing the prostaglandins which cause the aching. Tuck into oily fish and walnuts for their anti-inflammatory omega-3 fatty acids, and zinc-rich snacks such as pumpkin seeds, cashew nuts and chocolate (the darker the better) to relieve the muscle contractions and limit bloating. Magnesium (found in bananas, avocadoes and plain chocolate) also helps to work against cramps. (The chocolate effect is real! It's not just a placebo!) Red raspberry leaf tea is another great comfort which can really eliminate pain (my mum swears by it for childbirth) and getting enough vitamin C and vitamin E also helps to make your week of communing with the moon less of a hassle.

You may or may not be aware that the sanitary towels and tampons advertised on TV only make up a fraction of the available options. For thrifty and environmentally conscious Princesses, you have the choice of washable sanitary towels made of cotton (and available in a range of nifty patterns and colours), reusable tampons made of lovely soft sea sponge (no nasty fibres coming off them) and of course, menstrual cups which are made of rubber, shaped like a little egg cup and inserted to catch all the blood, which can then be tipped away at your convenience. (Stop saying "ew!") Some of these alternatives are more convenient than others; the cups in particular take some getting used to, although true devotees swear there is nothing better.

I'm getting a bit tired of the ultra-modern way of thinking – that periods shouldn't affect our lives at all and we should all be out abseiling and leading conferences when we have them. You can't put your everyday life on hold, but there's nothing wrong with slowing down and treating shark week with the respect it deserves. Our ancient sisters regarded their menstrual cycles as sacred rhythms and would retreat from the world to honour them. It makes me wonder if that whole "women are unclean" idea was a rumour started by some ladies who didn't want to deal with men and periods at the same time...

DRESSING LIKE A PRINCESS

"Dress shabbily they notice the dress. Dress impeccably they notice the woman." Coco Chanel

Some people dismiss the idea that clothing can be an art form. It's true that the fashion business often appears to be a literal illustration of the fairytale *The Emperor's New Clothes*, as vacant-eyed journalists enthuse about the latest bizarrely unflattering designs to come out of Paris. The industry preys upon people who aren't happy with themselves – the kind who are easily separated from their money when offered a lifestyle choice wrapped up in their purchases. It can take years of burning through credit cards before a fashion victim realises that a new dress or handbag isn't really a passport to the kind of popularity or admiration she longs for.

However, there is a flipside, and that's the dynamite impact of a sublime outfit. The right dress can turn a woman into an icon overnight – remember the famous Versace "safety pin" dress worn by Elizabeth Hurley when she was just Hugh Grant's girlfriend? Great shoes can make you walk in a whole new way, and a stunning hairstyle can make you feel like a supermodel. When there's an endless array of perfume, jewellery, cute tops and dinky hair slides to choose from, why would anyone deny themselves the pleasure of the dressing-up box?

Your Wardrobe

If you're anything like me, your wardrobe will be bursting at the seams with old favourites, new purchases eager to make their debut, and a handful of mistakes – the things you bought in a sale even though they're a bit tight / have a button missing / are ghastly. There might be a few items you love but never wear because they need to be fixed in some way – hems taken down, straps shortened etc. (For some reason, this never actually happens, so they remain unworn.) Lastly, there could be a handful of much-loved pieces you've "grown out of" but have faithfully stored, either for purely sentimental reasons, or in the hope that one day they'll fit again.

It's said that we wear 20% of the clothes we own, 80% of the time. (Us? Wear the same jeans every day? Surely not!) With experimentation, you'll find that your collection of separates can be combined in totally different ways to make lots of new looks.

Some women swear by the "capsule wardrobe" – a downsized set of mix-and-match staples which can be worn day in, day out. This pared-down simplicity certainly eliminates any lengthy thought process while getting ready in the morning, but I imagine it also takes the fun out of it. Where else do you have the freedom to make horrible mistakes, if not in your clothing? It's far easier to change than a bad haircut or the wrong wallpaper. And while I can see the virtue in spending more on good quality gear that will last forever, I'm not averse to spending pocket money on something cheap and cheerful which may (or may not) lose its lustre after a few seasons. I'd rather wear a different outfit every day than be stuck with the same old shift dress I need to wear a hundred times a year to make it worth the price.

Forget Fashion; Stylists Know Nothing (Except For Me, Obviously)

I hate to disparage my own profession, but it doesn't take a special kind of genius to work with clothes; everyone has an (equally valid) opinion on what looks good. I saw a TV programme recently about a woman who needed help with her overcrowded wardrobe. The idiot stylist picked out certain contemporary items, telling her "Keep this, it's so *in* right now" as she threw away the flattering classics. The woman was left with stuff she hadn't been particularly enthusiastic about, but was deemed acceptable by the fashion police. How silly – the more on-trend something is, the more outdated it will be in a couple of months. Fashions change, but style remains. As long as you wear clothes you love, which suit your body and your personality, it won't matter if you're wearing a dress that was in vogue five years ago; you'll still look amazing. Also, somebody has to START new trends, and that somebody could be you.

Do you want final proof that stylists are not experts? Check out a magazine's verdict on the best and worst dressed celebrities. Notice that even without this "helpful" commentary it's obvious to you who looks nice and who doesn't. (It will have a lot to do with how they've dressed to suit their figures and skin tones.) Some unfortunate members of the red carpet glitterati will be wearing hideous – HIDEOUS – outfits. Please note, these ensembles were not put together from a selection of thrift stores and bargain basements. They involve designer garments, handpicked by a stylist and fawned over by a gaggle of assistants who will have pampered the star and spent hours smoothing every ruffle, pinning every strap and taking snapshots from every angle. Somehow, all the dollar signs got in the way of them noticing that the final result is AWFUL. Trust your own judgement; the name on the label and the price tag mean nothing. Speaking of which...

Designer versus High Street

Any time a celebrity is interviewed about where she buys her clothes, she will wax lyrical about the way she mixes designer and high street style. I always wonder, why bother with the designer stuff at all? (In the case of a bankable star, being vocal about her favourites is the secret to freebies for the next premiere.) But why would any sane person willingly spend thousands on something they could easily get for less?

Once upon a time, there was a difference in the quality of apparel offered by the "posh" traders and the cheaper, mass-produced items. Upmarket clothes were made from superior fabric which would last forever, stitched by hand and designed to fit perfectly. Even today you'll see a difference in *some* of the high-end shops and the ones which sell cheap, disposable fashion.

However, the lines have become very blurred. From my work as a stylist, I know that some of the more expensive clothes have been the first to start coming apart at the seams, dropping sequins or making the most exquisite figures look squat and lumpy. Meanwhile the shops that have been snobbily dismissed as selling "the kind of cheap clothes you can only wear once or twice" are producing hard-wearing, tasteful items copied straight from the catwalk.

For big-name designers, the jig is up. If you have a good eye for style, it's easy to create fantastic outfits without spending tons. The fact that shopaholics get sucked into buying couture in an attempt to impress other people would be funny if it weren't so sad. In the end, a shirt is a shirt – and NO shirt is worth thousands. (Reality check: it's a piece of material.) It might be tempting to splurge when the only place selling that very specific design is the expensive store – but of course, that's when it's useful to know how to sew. It's surprisingly easy, and a foolproof way to get unique, made-to-measure garments.

Buying Ethically

If you've got your heart set on that lacy tank top, being told it was probably made by a small child in a sweatshop is the last thing you want to hear. Check up on manufacturers so you know where to head for guilt-free purchases: the Ethical Trading Initiative (ETI) has a base code of standards and you can see if your favourite retailer has signed up. (If they haven't, write to them and ask them why not.) Also, www.ethicalconsumer.org rates companies for their attitude to the environment, the way they treat people and animals, and their politics.

While some people assume that anything cheap must have been produced in terrible conditions, it isn't necessarily the case. Likewise, don't fall into the trap of assuming that if something is expensive, it must have been made by well-paid workers. Plenty of big names use the same squalid workshops as the bargain stores; they just give things a much higher markup.

As a general rule, if a shop is upfront about where their merchandise was made, how the materials were sourced etc, it's a good sign. On the other hand, if they're oddly quiet about the age of their factory workers, it might mean children are involved – and if they don't shout about their cotton being Fairtrade, it probably isn't.

Shopping the Easy Way

When you're in the mood for a shopping spree, it's important to wear the right clothes (and preferably have a helpful lackey to carry all the bags). If you're in a pair of high-heeled boots which need to be laced up, or tight jeans you can barely get in and out of without the help of a maid, you'll end up irritable and exhausted and not feeling inclined to try things on. This could either result in your coming home empty-handed, or with a load of stuff which doesn't fit. (And will probably sit in a bag in your bedroom until its return-by date has passed, if statistics have been truthful about women's purchasing habits.)

For your shopping skills to be at their most effective, wear shoes which can be slipped off, a soft jersey skirt (you won't even need to take it off when you try on trousers – just scoop it up) and a similarly floppy top which you can wriggle out of easily.

For speedy sessions, don't bother going inside every shop: you can *totally* judge them by their window displays. The best stuff will always be the most visible, so if you can only see nylon nightmares, it's unlikely they're going to have some exquisite little 1920s number hidden in the back.

Much as I love the logic of buying the heaviest items last in order to avoid schlepping them around for hours, I can't wholeheartedly agree with the common tip of doing your shoe shopping at the end of the day. The theory is that because your feet will be at their most hot and swollen, it's a great time to get the sizing right and make sure you'll be able to endure long nights on the dance floor with no pinching. The selfish (and therefore un-Princessy) downside is that you'll leave sweat marks in all the shoes you *don't* end up buying. Always take a clean pair of socks and pop them on before you try out those slingbacks.

I like shopping online – lots of people are put off because you can't try anything on, but if you know which brand you're buying, you generally have an idea of what size you are in that shop. Browsing online is ingenious because you're not limited by fashion – you can literally search by description for what you want. So if I realise that the missing piece for my wardrobe is a cream cardigan (goes with everything!) I can search and see my options in moments, instead of dragging myself around the high street for something which won't be there because this month it's all about pink angora sweaters. You can also shop off-season; have a good old prowl around online auction sites and pick up coats in the summer and shorts in the winter. If nobody else is thinking about buying the stuff, you'll find fewer rival bidders.

Finally; I do believe in snapping up the items you fall in love with. We've all had the experience of walking away from a dress because it's so horribly expensive, and then being haunted by it forever afterwards. (There's no greater tragedy in the life of a young woman than returning to a shop to find the coveted item has been sold, never to return.) Even if you have no event on the horizon to justify splashing out, buying your heart's desire means that next time you do have a glamorous event to go to, you'll have a brand new, unworn dress to show off – and no last-minute panic shopping. So if the sight of it makes you break out in a cold sweat and you know you'll love it forever, just buy it. You won't regret it. (And if you do, you can sell it online. It's a no-lose situation.)

Every Princess Should Have the Following:

The Classics

- Blue jeans: for every one of us, the ideal pair of jeans exists *somewhere* on earth. The only problem is that most of us will have to spend many tedious hours searching before we discover them. Everyone finds jeans hard to buy – probably because they (and clothes generally) are made in vague, generic sizes in order to fit everyone approximately, and nobody exactly. This is why we've all experienced jeans which gape at the waist / drag along the ground / turn our legs into dumpy sausages. Now that stretch denim is widely available, we have a more forgiving option than the stiff or super-tight versions of yesteryear – but I still suggest that when you find a pair that look and feel as if they were made for you, buy as many as you can afford. (Tip: high-waisted and cut wide at the ankle is the most leg-lengthening, low-rise can produce muffin tops (discussed below) and cropped will make legs appear shorter.)
- A little black dress: it's not called a classic for nothing. No matter what your shape, size or skin tone, there will be a dress which suits you to a T. The rule is to keep it simple – that way you can jazz it up with different accessories each time you wear it. With a change of belt, shoes, makeup and hair you'll look so different that people won't even realise it's the same dress.
- Crisp white shirt: oh dahling, this is so Hepburn – and when something epitomises both Audrey and Katharine, you know it's a winner. Throw on a man's shirt over jeans and a cute camisole, or wear a fitted blouse with a pretty pencil skirt. Either way, it's clean-cut and sexy, all at the same time. The downside is that shirts are often thin enough to be translucent, so if this is the case, wear it with a flesh-coloured t-shirt bra.
- Body-con dress: when we see women wearing close-fitting dresses

which show off every delicious curve, we all look twice, right? I know I do, and I'm a heterosexual female – the average man pretty much starts drooling. Forget shapeless smocks and embrace the hourglass. My favourite online store is www.pinupgirlclothing.com; their sensational range is available in plus size as well as regular, *destroying* the myth that only slim ladies can wear beautifully flattering and sexy outfits.

Everyday Essentials

- Vests: whether you prefer frilly or smooth, plain rib or built-in bra, fancy straps or logos, you'll find vests you love from the dozens of styles available. They make a sexy alternative to t-shirts and can be used as the first layer of your winter outfits, as well as being great for hot days.
- Cardigans: also available in a huge variety of colours and textures, from the cosy warm Aran to the light summer cover-up. They're just what you need to slip over a vest or a t-shirt – unlike jumpers, they don't entirely cover up the pretty top you're wearing underneath, and they're easier to shrug out of without looking as if you're undressing in public.
- Go-with-everything-shoes: matching your shoes to your skin tone is a smart trick for elongating your legs, and as you're not really introducing another colour into the mix, it's a neutral which won't clash with anything else you're wearing. Kate Middleton is famous for her light beige court shoes, which blend "professional" with "sexy" – making them suitable for any outfit. For party looks and summer ensembles, silver or gold sandals are also fabulously versatile.
- Flat footwear: because we can't wear vertiginous heels every day. While sequinned slip-ons look cute, it's also essential to get some decent trainers which will enable you to walk or run around with no ill-effects. (I've given up on canvas sneakers with hard soles; give me nice cushiony rubber any day.) In winter, boots with just the tiniest hint of a heel are practical as well as sophisticated; the hard part is choosing your style: androgynous army, mid-calf biker, knee-high suede, or

vampy thigh-highs? If in doubt, buy them all.

- Sweater dresses: I wear these ALL the time in cold weather because they keep my middle warm – don't you hate it when you get a chilly draught because your top keeps riding up? Teaming knit dresses with tights and boots is a winter staple which can take you straight from work to drinks afterwards; accessorise with different belts, scarves and jewellery to create a new effect every time.

- Ultra-thin trousers: if you don't like to wear tiny shorts or skirts in summer, thin trousers are AWESOME. Linen will inevitably crease, but that's part of its charm, and it can still be a smart option for work. Cotton palazzo pants or harem pants are elegant but incredibly comfortable, and I also love silky pyjama trousers – I figure there's always a *possibility* that people won't realise they're supposed to be nightwear. (It helps if they're plain colours such as navy or oyster, as opposed to featuring little hearts or penguins).

- Casualwear: slouchy tops and fuzzy-soft sweat pants are also gorgeously easy to wear, which is why they have a reputation as the go-to clothing of slobs. They can actually be surprisingly chic: nothing shows off a bootylicious butt like yoga pants, and a well-fitted velour tracksuit has long been the outfit of choice for celebrities being hustled through airports.

- Knee-length skirts: if you only own two skirts, dark blue denim and sandy beige go with everything. Black is also good for a more businesslike flavour, but you might resemble a waitress if you wear it with a plain top on a night out.

- Coats / jackets: in winter, it's a good idea to have a few different jacket options, otherwise it can feel as if you're wearing the exact same outfit every day. Brighten up a dark coat with coloured gloves, hat and scarf – having a few choices in rotation is a cheap way to refresh your look.

- Sex-kitten nightwear: sleeping naked is of course the most comfortable option, but not always convenient if you live with your parents / flatmates / a morbid fear that the house will catch fire and you'll have to meet all those cute firemen in the nip. Little vests, soft jersey boy-shorts or a pretty nightgown are so much cuter than an old t-shirt; they'll also morph seamlessly into a lazy girl's guide to weekend loungewear (with the addition of a cashmere wrap-cardigan and some leg warmers). Or you could wander around the house in a silky dressing gown / sarong / chemise and feel like an alluring 1950s starlet, even with your curlers in – you'll never go back to your animal-themed onesie. (OK, maybe at Christmas.) It's an unfortunate truth that the comfiest, snuggliest items (furry bootee slippers) lack the sex appeal of the less-than-practical (fluffy pink mules à la Diana Dors). Keep your options open: invest in both for a daily choice between "seductive" and "cosy".

Princesses Should Avoid:

- Dressing in black all the time: yes, it can help you to look svelte. Yes, it's smart and goes with everything. But so many women stick doggedly to a strict diet of black, when it can be too harsh for some skin tones (not to mention unimaginative). Psychics often wear black because they believe it can absorb negative energy – which could explain why so many of us grab it when we're feeling the need for some protection from the world. Maybe we prefer the anonymity of dark colours; it takes a bold personality to wear a bright fuchsia dress to work.

- Super-fashionable stuff: apart from the fact that the skinny jeans and clumpy ankle boots which are all over the shops may not necessarily suit you, why would you *want* to look like everyone else? Some high streets are full of young women who are virtually clones of each other. Trail blazers like Coco Chanel made being different into an art form – dare to stand out from the crowd and be the one dressed in "X" when everyone else is in "Y".

- Maternity Style: empire line and babydoll dresses have been on the periphery of being in fashion for so long that I quite often find myself wanting to shake strangers on the street and yell: "Why can't you see that your clothes are making you look pregnant?" Even the slimmest girl will appear six months gone if her top is fitted on the bust and then gently drapes over her stomach. We're told "the way it skims over your tummy is really slimming" but this is a lie straight from hell. If you want to visually gloss over any wobbly bits, you're far better off in a wrap top or wearing a fitted dress with ruching or a twist-front.

- Anything too tight: if breathing is an effort, you need to re-think the outfit, no matter how hot it looks. (It sounds obvious, but I know more than one girl who's chosen a stunning corset over using her full lung capacity.) Muffin tops aren't the worst thing in the world; they can look quite sweet in a vulnerable, human way, but having your jeans digging into your stomach is never going to be comfortable. Try something a bit looser or higher-waisted, because hipsters can produce those little wodges of fat on even the skinniest people.

- Anything you don't want to: a friend of mine wears thick black calf-length leggings with pretty summer dresses or shorts. I once asked her why she was adding unnecessary layers on sweltering hot days, and she said it was because her legs were "too big and white" and she didn't want people to see them. As well as being self-conscious, she actually thinks she's doing the world a favour by covering up – perhaps she's been influenced by all those "Aaaagh! It's hurting my eyes!" captions accompanying unfortunate celebrity pictures. We all get paranoid about people seeing our least favourite features, but a) they're probably not that focused on you, and b) so what if they don't like the way you look? It's their problem! Nobody, no matter what their size, should have to cover up for the sake of hypothetical body-haters.

Dressing Like a Princess – Your Way

Standard Princess wardrobes consist of sophisticated elegance, magnetic man-bait and impeccable accessories. But anyone can wear a suit and look smart, and anyone can wear a push-up bra to get attention. The secret to being a Princess is to find your OWN style. If you're a tomboy who likes to wear combats and black vests with your desert boots, I'm not going to suggest you change altogether. (Although you could boost your allure by making the combat pants satin ones, and add a bit of glitz with some pretty rings or a necklace.) I accept that weather and lifestyle make irrefutable claims on what we wear every day; come January, all I care about is not freezing, so I'm hardly going to be skipping along to work in strappy sandals and a chiffon dress.

Nobody needs to stick to the same look every single day, and Princesses aren't afraid to change things up. Float around like a flower child in a hippy kaftan one day, be as groomed as a Hollywood wife the next, and then surprise everyone by sporting a rockabilly quiff along with your skull and crossbones t-shirt. Clothes are self-expression; as well as choosing the persona you want to project, you can dress to balance out your personality. For instance, if you're very sporty, you might want to pay extra attention to how you can add some girly touches to your image – pastel gym gear, a sweet perfume, floral-print trainers? If you know you come across as silly and giggly, counteract it with classic, tailored outfits rather than marabou feathers and plastic bracelets. If you're fading into the background, a dramatic change could bring you to centre stage; just adding a trilby or a glittery bindi adds a little interest to an everyday ensemble. When I feel stressed at work, I find myself dressing "defensively" in a leather jacket, fierce boots, and lots of black eyeliner; somehow this feels more *protective* than baby pink lips and a flimsy tea dress.

So next time someone lectures you on the frivolity of recreational shopping and dressing up, remind them of this: We all NEED clothes, so why not make them nice ones? You can take an active interest in creating an image for yourself – like a butterfly choosing the pattern of her wings – or you can see shopping as a tedious chore and spend your life buying nondescript, dull clothes. The process of scanning the store for something you like and then shelling out some hard-earned cash will be the same, so why not enjoy it?

Colours

According to the experts, pinky-peach will enhance most skin tones; it lights up your face without being as harsh as white, and gives you a glow the same way candlelight would. It's also very feminine – guys tend not to go for this particular hue. Bright colours are eye-catching and sassy; red in particular is associated with sex and power. Deep down, we're all led by our animal instincts; wearing a body-hugging scarlet dress is the sophisticated version of being a baboon showing off a big red bottom to signal "Come and get me, boys!" (Shopping for your office Christmas party outfit will never be the same again.)

Some people swear by the process of "getting your colours done" – finding out which shades best suit you by analysing the tones in your hair, eyes and skin. (The cheap version is paying attention to which colours always get you compliments.) One of my friends is Chinese and has almost blue-black hair and olive skin, and she looks extra stunning when she wears bright red or turquoise; needless to say, these turned out to be among "her" colours. Under the old system of Spring, Summer, Autumn and Winter, many people (including me) found themselves between categories. However, the new method includes descriptions such as Warm, Deep, Cool, Soft-muted, Clear and Light, so it's much easier to determine your colour personality.

You don't have to throw out all your old clothes, but it's worth changing your attitude from "Do I like this colour?" to "Does this colour like me?" before you buy anything new. You can still wear blue if that's your favourite, you just need to get the shade right. Try holding some different palettes next to your face in front of the mirror to see what makes you look radiant and lovely rather than sallow and unhealthy. You could also consider famous women who have similar colouring to yours and see if any of their outfits result in especially glowy skin and sparkly eyes. Of course, what "works" will be somewhat subjective; people really need to stop spreading the myth that shades like champagne "suit everyone". You can get away with them if you have dark skin, but if you're fair you'll resemble a corpse. I've noticed that in celebrity world a lot of pale ladies with light hair choose insipid pastel shades, so obviously *somebody* thinks this wash of colour blending looks great. But it always disappoints me, because I imagine how much more vibrant the image would be with some dramatic contrast.

Slutty versus Classy

Some religions require women to dress modestly in order to avoid "tempting" men's lascivious gazes. Schools make rules about the length of girls' skirts to "protect" the boys from distraction. So, what about the poor schoolgirls who could quite easily be flustered by the boys running around on the sports field without their shirts on? Or the lustful thoughts that a lady train passenger might have when the man opposite her sits with his legs splayed out? Until feminists take over the world, women will be the only ones held responsible for the sexuality of everyone around them.

And let's be honest – sometimes it's fun to dress like a total skank. It can be very entertaining to wear a miniskirt or cleavage-enhancing top and watch men's eyes pop out on stalks. The trouble with this look is that it's a dime a dozen, so you'll only have their attention until another girl walks past in a shorter skirt. (The bars in my town are always heaving with women who seem to have come out in their underwear.) What's more, men may check us out when we dress like this, but they don't respect us. When you present yourself as a pair of breasts on legs, that's how men will think of you.

There's a reason why nightclubs are called "meat markets" – there's nothing impressive about being a big juicy steak and having doggies pant over you. Getting male attention by wearing tight, revealing clothes is like shooting fish in a barrel – and where's the fun in that? When there's no mystery, there's no anticipation; it's like the difference between handing someone a chocolate bar, or presenting them with an exquisitely wrapped package which could contain any number of delicious surprises. Of course they'll still *like* the chocolate, but it won't have captured their imagination. As Marilyn Monroe told the troops, "You fellas down there are always whistling at sweater girls. I don't get all the fuss. Take away the sweaters and what have you got?"

The power to command attention comes not from your outfit, but the way you wear it – the way you move, your confidence and how you hold yourself. You can be covered head to toe and still have every eye on you because of your inner glow (and maybe a little wiggle in your walk). Also, if you're the only one in a modest, ladylike dress in a sea of exposed flesh and "skimplified" outfits, you WILL stand out.

Dressing with class means figuring out what's right for the situation; if you're going to a theme park for the day with your family, it's not the time to wear your hooker heels and a sheer blouse. (I know I said it was good to be "different", but this isn't one of those times.) Wherever you go, you should look as if you went shopping half an hour earlier and picked out just the right get-up. Not the most fashionable, or the most expensive, but something that suits you and is appropriate for the occasion, whether it's cheering for your little sister on the football field or meeting your boyfriend's parents.

During the summer months, you may find yourself at an evening event in broad daylight. Avoid full-on makeup, harsh eyeliner and strong lip colours, or you might be mistaken for someone doing the walk of shame after last night's clubbing session. Instead, lean towards a daytime look: softer makeup, a laid-back vibe, and no vinyl corsets.

You Don't Need Dates to Dress as if Every Day is a Special Occasion

Magazines tend to have a disproportionate number of features on full-length frocks and dramatic jewellery – how often do we really get to dress up like this? Even if you go to parties every week, you'll probably find the other guests in ultra-casual apparel – I've even seen jeans worn at weddings. No wonder people go so crazy for sweet sixteens and graduations – it's the only time they get to pull out all the stops. So, barring those once-in-a-blue-moon celebrations, when will we get to wear our Oscar-worthy ball gowns? Of course, the answer is to create the occasions yourself. So what if nobody else is wearing 1970s velvet flares and a crochet top on casual Friday? A spangly prom dress might be just the thing for beers at the local dive bar. Who makes the rules, anyway? If I were in charge, every day would be "Wear a Costume to Work" Day and our streets would be awash with pirates and fairies and cowboys. It would cheer things up, don't you think?

If angel wings and body glitter are too much for a Monday morning, start small. Make an extra bit of effort when you're hanging out with your friends – pretty camisole tops instead of baggy t-shirts, a dress instead of jeans. Try popping on some shimmery eye shadow when you're running out to the supermarket, and wearing bright ballet flats instead of loafers for work. A bit of extra bedazzling never hurt anyone, and it makes life more colourful.

It might sound strange, but it takes a lot of nerve to look fantastic, because everyone is going to stare at you. A lot. You may find that other women become cool or hostile towards you (and mutter "Show off!" behind your back). There's also the potential to cause traffic accidents, as people rubberneck at the beauty sashaying down the street with a pink parasol and a string of pearls over her dalmatian-print sundress.

But as a rule, having the confidence to be breathtaking is a kind of public service. I was waiting for a train on a Saturday afternoon not long ago and I noticed two women who were dressed in a spectacular vintage style – pencil skirts, heels, stockings, red lipstick, curls and little hats. They looked as if they were going to some sort of retro afternoon tea event. I wish I'd had the guts to speak to them, because their appearance honestly brightened up my day. They made the world a more aesthetically pleasing place in a way that the rest of us, in our jeans and hoodies, just couldn't do. It's not often I quote Paris Hilton, but she did make an excellent point when she said: "Dress cute wherever you go. Life is too short to blend in." I remember this every time I consider dressing down because I'm meeting a friend who always wears boring outfits.

A possible downside to dressing with imagination is that the slogan t-shirt or cowboy hat which is such a great icebreaker at a party will also invite attention from men in the street, whether you want it or not. Single ladies have long been advised to dress every day in readiness for meeting a potential prince, although I'm not sure how many of us really take this to heart. (I notice a distinct lack of coquettish women going about their mundane daily chores wearing flouncy skirts and kitten heels.)

Given that men will catcall even if we dress in baggy old overalls, we might as well enjoy ourselves. Walking the dog or going to the post office in your most bewitching outfit might sound silly, but you'll feel prettier, and the energy surrounding you will be lighter, happier, and more open. A friend of mine went out shopping in a snakeskin skirt, heels and lipstick, and all the attention from the menfolk converted her to dressing up. She now twirls around like Doris Day 24/7 and has men approaching her in restaurants, the mall, the street... (No wonder most of us don't bother – who has the time to stop and talk to all those guys?!) Arm yourself with a good exit line for unwanted suitors and enjoy the feel-good factor of strutting around knowing you look hot.

Dressing to Suit Your Shape

Most women don't like their bodies. This is a TRAGEDY of epic proportions. For a start, almost every woman will look back at pictures of herself from years ago and say "Why was I so worried about being fat / scrawny / spotty / ugly? I was gorgeous! I'd give anything to look like that NOW!"

We're all aware that this collective body anxiety is due in part to those aforementioned images of "perfection" fed to us by the media. The trouble is that simply knowing WHY we feel the pressure doesn't make it go away. I thought I was immune to such silliness, until I found myself watching a Sophia Loren movie and thinking "Gosh, she WAS quite chubby, wasn't she?" She wasn't. She just had the kind of magnificent voluptuousness which is now rarely seen on the silver screen, and I wasn't used to it.

Things are getting better; women with larger figures are still a rarity on billboards, but the likes of Christina Hendricks and Kim Kardashian enjoy plenty of positive attention. (Even if the "large breasts, hips and bum versus tiny waist" combo is hardly more attainable than the waif-like look which was formerly the height of fashion.) Unfortunately the pendulum now sometimes swings too far in the opposite direction, with advertising slogans suggesting that "real women have curves" as if anyone who's naturally slight is less than female. Being too thin can be depressing, especially if everyone is raving over the curvaceous goddesses with generous assets. Bigger women are "allowed" to talk about the way the clothing industry discriminates against them, but a slim woman who dares to voice a complaint will be told "You don't know how lucky you are!"

If we could see our bodies the way other people see us, I think we'd all relax and realise that washboard stomachs might look good, but so do softly rounded ones, we're all delightfully different, and women are attractive because of their confidence and joie de vivre. (And sometimes, a visible panty line is *sexy*.) Men don't even notice the little details you agonise over (they're probably too busy imagining what you look like naked, anyway).

Life's too short for bitching about what nature gave you, and worrying about how to hide your wobbly arms or flat bottom is a waste of energy. Forget the paranoia and focus on highlighting your favourite bits. I've always thought that larger ladies look amazing when they show off their smooth, round shoulders. (Emphasising your collar bone has become a fashion statement, but as a skinny teen, I hated the way mine jutted out. Lesson learned: if you don't like something about your body, just sit tight and it will probably end up being considered the last word in chic.)

Celebrate the fact that you're a woman: flaunt your legs, show off your waist and accentuate the femininity in your shape. Wear a necklace that draws attention to your chest, invest in racy underwear that pulls you in and pushes you out in all the right places... go on, wear that thigh-split skirt – be a devil!

Beauty is Ageless

It's inevitable that your image will evolve as you get older; experience teaches us about the shapes and colours that really suit us, and over the years of styling ourselves, we learn to gravitate towards clothes which do justice to our best features.

Sadly, many mature ladies seem to think that looking foxy is just for youngsters. They say "Ooh, I remember when I had a figure like yours!" and make jokes about stealing their daughters' clothes. It's true that certain skirt lengths look better with young knees, and low-cut tops are at their best on gravity-defying breasts. But more to the point, variety is the spice of life and nobody would want to be stuck in the same style groove for decades.

Magazines may pontificate on questions such as "What age is too old for shorts / leather trousers / red lipstick?" but the Princess philosophy is: "Damn what anyone else thinks!" You don't have to cut your hair when you reach a certain age; the days of blue rinses and bubble perms on your 60th birthday are over. If the worst thing anyone can say is that you're "mutton dressed as lamb", then you're doing OK. (And they're probably jealous.) Personally I plan to wear slinky leopard-print catsuits for as long as I feel like it, and if that means when I'm 80, then so be it.

Forget the "rules" on age-appropriate dressing, do what you like, and relish the fact that while others may tut and disapprove and whisper about you, nobody can STOP YOU.

Tips on Dressing for Weddings

- Consider where you're going and what you'll be doing. It sounds obvious, but lots of us forget (when we're choosing a pair of sky-high stilettos to accompany a posh frock) that weddings often involve lots of standing around (on grass) while pictures are taken. Unless you want to have aching feet for the next 48 hours (or to slowly sink into the turf) there's got to be a better option. Ballet pumps, wedge heels, or flat summer sandals all look pretty enough for formalwear.
- It's still considered rude to wear white or black. I point this out because I've come across quite a few style advisors describing white sundresses as "perfect for all those summer weddings". Not unless the bride is wearing red! Pale pastel shades are appropriate, but even when your outfit isn't remotely similar to a wedding dress, white is off-limits. Black is often worn these days (it's even become popular as a choice

for bridesmaid gowns) but for a guest it's a faux pas – it sort of implies you're thinking of the wedding as somebody's funeral.

- If you have no idea how formal or informal the gathering might be, teaming smart shoes with a simple, knee-length dress in a muted colour will work. But when in doubt, overdress.

- Remember to take a cardigan or wrap – even if you won't need it for most of the day, it's likely you'll want something slightly warmer as the evening draws in.

- If the outfit you've chosen looks good but is a bit uncomfortable, reconsider. If it's chafing when you try it on for five minutes, imagine hours in a packed reception hall, with dancing and eating and trying to catch up with old friends. We all know how a bad pair of shoes can ruin a night out if you're hobbling rather than twirling on the dance floor, and you won't exactly be oozing sex appeal while you're grimacing in pain.

Tips on Dressing for Work

- The rule used to be "dress for the job you want, not the job you're got" which was all very well in the 1980s when it meant simply wearing higher heels and bigger shoulder pads. These days it's possible that your boss rocks up to work in jeans and a logo t-shirt, and plays a few rounds of pinball before taking everyone out for pancakes. Times have changed – and while it's still a good rule to note what your boss is wearing as this will be what s/he deems appropriate, remember that it's also what's appropriate for his / her role, not yours. Eyeball your peers for a better idea of what works.

- A feminine blazer (fitted and soft rather than an oversized *Working Girl* throwback) will make any outfit look more professional. One in black, one in cream or white, and one in grey, fawn or pinstripe should cover all eventualities.

- When I talked about risqué hemlines and appreciating your womanly curves, I should have mentioned that such sultriness is best limited to recreational use: unless you work in a bar and hot pants get you bigger tips, it's a good idea to leave your sexuality at home. This means skirts that end just above the knee, not halfway up your thigh, and no bulging cleavage (funny as it is to see the accountant losing his train of thought, you'll have to get your kicks elsewhere). There are women who claim their "erotic capital" is getting them promotions and moolah – but an intelligent girl like you doesn't need to stroke the boss's knee and simper in order to get ahead. (In reality, telling a man that you admire whatever quality he's most proud of will do far more for you than leaning over his desk in a push-up bra.)

- When it's sunny, bright dresses – cerise, aqua, lavender – look great teamed with a white cardigan. It's fresh and spring-like, but still professional enough to wear to the office.
- Air-conditioned buildings feel glacial in the summer, so the outfit you picked especially for the sweltering walk to work is now going to be the reason you have frostbite in June: take a spare cardi.
- If you are feeling the tropical heat, remember that tip about linen trousers – they're brilliant if wearing a skirt isn't practical, and it feels like wearing *nothing*! They can be thin enough to be a little see-through, so make sure you're wearing seamless skin-tone knickers, not lacy red ones.
- Be practical. I would love to be one of those ladies who struts about in heels all the time, but I know that's unrealistic if I'm going to be on my feet for most of the day. (I also hate wearing tight clothes made from inflexible fabrics, so if I've been out dressed in fitted jeans I'll whip them off in favour of tracky bottoms the minute I get home, because I'm so glamorous.)
- Remember the words of top Hollywood costumier Edith Head: "You can have whatever you want if you dress for it."

Princess Secrets

- It's all about balance. Never a short skirt AND a low-cut top – you have to leave something covered up. Only one pattern at a time – no striped jumpers combined with paisley skirts, no siree! And consider how "busy" your outfit is; do you like a layered look with lots of frills, or the clean lines of a minimalist shirt dress? Either way, bear your clothes in mind when you choose your hairstyle and accessories. A very plain dress could be lifted with cascading curls and a few choice pieces of jewellery. The same items teamed with a floral top, multi-coloured scarf and bright makeup would be *too much*. If your outfit is vividly eye-catching, try a scraped-back hairstyle and simple makeup to create a harmonious effect and avoid frightening small children.

- Think about what other people will see of your threads. If you're going to be standing (on a red carpet, for instance) then a tight fishtail dress would be shown off to perfection. Sitting down, the same outfit might be too rigid to be comfortable. Similarly, if you're going to dinner, don't worry too much about the shoes and lower half of your outfit – your dining companion is only going to see you from the waist up for most of the evening. Why not go for a pretty neckline, sparkly earrings or striking eye makeup?

- Very few clothes really need to be ironed. Formalwear such as suits and blouses look better when they're freshly pressed, although they'll crinkle again as soon as you've leaned against the back of your chair a few times. Everything else can be worn pretty much straight from the dryer. (I genuinely don't understand people who moan that they've got a stack of ironing to do, when it's all leggings, underwear and bed sheets. Skip it! Problem solved.) For the essentials, my favourite option is a travel steamer – it's what I've always used as a professional stylist. It's much faster than ironing (the steam penetrates the garment and the wrinkles fall out) and it's easier, because you're not creating new creases the way you do when you use an iron and a board.

- When heading for a sunshine holiday, most of us get carried away and pack a zillion outfits, then spend the entire time in the same bikini and denim cut-offs. Try to be realistic – you'll probably only need one beach cover-up (a long kaftan with a belt-tie can pass for a dress) and nobody will notice (or care) if you wear the same pair of flip-flops every day. Remember to wear comfy clothes on the plane – drawstring trousers, a t-shirt layered with a soft sweater – then you can snuggle down for a snooze. To avoid either freezing or baking at either end of your flight, the key is removable layers.

- If you're going to a party and you're just not feeling it, go for high-impact items like a statement necklace, or bright lipstick. You'll look as if you've made an effort without having to spend ages delving through your wardrobe and makeup bag.

- Don't just check out your front and back view: make sure you know what the outfit looks like when you *move*. This tip was inspired by some girls wearing very short shorts on a summer day; what looks good when you stand in front of the mirror could reveal a whole lot more bum cheek when you're confidently striding around. If you're wearing a precariously brief top, hold it down with double-sided toupee or body tape (colloquially known as "tit tape") to ensure there will be no embarrassing slips.

- Along the same theme – if you're big busted, you'll probably find that blouses gape open between the buttons in an annoying and revealing way. Avoid over-exposure by either using body tape to stick the shirt shut, or for a more permanent solution, fix extra fastenings on the inside wherever needed.

- Making adjustments to your clothes will improve your look no matter what your shape – why put up with off-the-peg universal sizes when your clothes could be tailor-made for you with a few tweaks?

- Coming back to those celebs in appalling attire; you'll notice that if they have a big smile and gaze confidently into the camera, they totally get away with it. It's as if they're in on the joke, and they don't care if you love their (stylist's) fashion sense or not, because they're going to rock those baggy dungarees anyway. We're all free to wear whatever we like, even if we have terrible taste – and with a sly grin, we can make anything look good.

- "There is only one way to wear a beautiful dress – to forget you are wearing it" as French author Madame de Girardin once said. If you feel uncomfortable – and you're pulling at the hem of your skirt because you're suddenly conscious of how short it is, or you're constantly smoothing your top – it ruins the whole effect of your casually elegant pose. Fidgeting is a dead giveaway that you're very aware of how you look and you're worried it's not up to scratch; it's far better to glide about and pretend you're in a bathrobe for the ultimate in cool.

- Always dress as if you're going to meet your worst enemy.

YOUR PALACE

"Creativity is allowing yourself to make mistakes. Design is knowing which ones to keep." Scott Adams

If you're lucky enough (or should I say, financially sensible and hard-working enough) to own your own home, you're in the fortunate position of being able to do anything you like with it (budget allowing). If you're renting a flat, or a room in a shared house / your parents' home, then you'll probably have less freedom to throw paint and new furniture around.

However, it's ALWAYS possible to make your surroundings into a luxurious sanctuary, and it's incredibly satisfying to create a cosy little nest for yourself.

When You Hate Your Home

Some of you may be thinking "But I want to move out of here! I hate this tiny flat, and I'm planning to leave as soon as I can." In true New Age woo-woo style, I believe that appreciating what you already have speeds up the process which enables you to move on. So even if you have storage boxes wedged into every corner, your wardrobe is spilling over, and you can't wait to leave your current abode, there's always something positive you can do to make your time there happier.

Lots of people (myself included) have to spend years living with their parents, saving up to buy their own places and wondering just how abnormal it is to remain in their childhood / teenage bedroom. (I still maintain that the blue dolphin lampshade I picked when I was thirteen was a *superb* choice.) If you're stuck at home with your parents, try to see the bright side. You have housemates who won't think it's weird if you want to sit in your room on your own. Your rent is probably low to non-existent, your laundry and cooking may be done for you, and it's rare to find food in the fridge labelled "Hands off! Buy your own". It's unlikely that your roommates will steal your clothes / shampoo / boyfriend. You also get to spend more time with your parents – even if it doesn't feel like a blessing right now, in later years you'll cherish the memories you made while you were all under one roof.

Your Bedroom

This is your inner sanctum and your most private retreat, so the important thing is to choose carefully when inviting anyone in. If your bedroom is a meeting place and a hangout for friends of friends or guys you've just met, their energy is going to stick around long after they've left. Consider this before you open up your personal space to anyone but your close friends.

Obviously, if you live in a studio apartment, keeping your room off-limits isn't possible. There are ways to make your sleeping area more secluded, such as pretty curtains or a screen divider (ideal if you want to undress behind it, just like in the movies). You could also split up the room with storage cabinets; they're ideal for displaying pieces of art as well as your books, CDs, or plants.

Your alternative is to forget privacy and have a big daybed that everyone can sit on to chat – this works best if you use a throw and some cushions to make it look less like a sleeping zone and more like a giant deluxe sofa. After all, in the 18th century, rich ladies would have a boudoir which was a kind of hybrid bedroom / dressing room / lounge, where they'd entertain guests of both genders. They held "salons" – meetings in which everyone could exchange ideas about intellectual matters such as the arts, philosophy and current affairs. Interestingly, women would also invite guests to join them in the boudoir while they performed their long and elaborate "toilette" rituals (so it was a bit like when everyone hangs out in the loo to gossip and reapply lipstick). But the boudoir was definitely the private space of the lady of the house, so men were admitted on a strict invite-only basis. The name "boudoir" stems from the French word for "sulk" – apparently a miffed husband coined the phrase when he found himself banished from his wife's room. Of course, when men want a room of their own, it's called a "study". Those silly boys.

Decor

No matter who you live with, your bedroom is where you're most likely to have free reign over the way it looks. It should be a reflection of YOU – your individuality, your taste – whatever makes you feel good when you open your eyes in the morning. It doesn't need to fit into any stereotypes of girlishness if that's not your thing, but a little femininity can be a shortcut to feeling like a Princess.

Use splashes of colour in your favourite delectable shades: sunny yellow, baby blue, lilac, pink, turquoise. If you can't paint the walls, use accessories (curtains, cushions, and furniture) to enhance your existing colour scheme.

Your Bed

1930s star Jean Harlow is said to have had a bed made in the shape of a shell, just like the one in Botticelli's painting of Venus. I'm not saying you should go that far (although it's not a bad idea) but your bed will still be the most prominent feature of your bedroom. (Unless of course you're one of those lucky bitches with a loft space which can fit in a bed, a bath and a big open wardrobe space.) Update your room in one swift move by getting a fancy new duvet and sheets; there are heaps of eye-catching patterns for reasonable prices. If you have the cash, go for the best quality, highest thread count sheets and pillow cases you can find. Add a delicious squidgy eiderdown and a bunch of pillows and throws to make your bed a haven you sink into. Patchwork quilts are sweetly nostalgic, but even spreading a crochet blanket over your usual duvet can totally change its look and add extra cosiness.

You could also customise your bed by making your own headboard decoration. I made a removable cover to slip over mine by cutting two pieces of material to shape and sewing them together on the top and sides. I used two different fabrics, so when I get tired of purple satin, I can swivel it around to the leopard-print side. (Yes, my bedroom is somewhat ghetto-fabulous.)

Dressing Area

It's really nice to have an area in your room which lends itself to *prettifying*. For instance, a dressing table where you can sit down and take a few moments to groom yourself (rather than yanking a comb through your hair as you run down the stairs and using your bus journey to slick on a bit of lipstick). Why not create a self-indulgent space devoted to the pleasures of getting all dolled up?

Round shapes rather than sharp edges help to give the room a feminine feel. Picture the old-school sex symbols like Veronica Lake – weren't they always sitting at a kidney-shaped dressing table, rather than a big square desk? And what about those fancy perfume bottles with little round atomiser pumps? If you want real movie star ambience, add some sparkle to your dressing table with vintage-style crystal jars or bottles. Pick these up cheaply secondhand and clean them out thoroughly; using them to store your moisturiser or body lotion looks so much more elegant than the usual plastic packaging.

Storage

Wardrobes keep clothes out of sight, which is why they sometimes end up as dumping grounds for everything from your discarded sports equipment to the costume you made for your childhood nativity play. Handy as this is for hoarders, what about putting your clothes on display with an uncovered rail? It can be a great reminder of what you've actually got, and seeing that sequinned waistcoat EVERY day makes it easier to let it go; if you only see it once a year when you're having a major clear-out you might be tempted to think "I'll hang on to that, just in case..."

As well as having a row of dazzling party dresses hanging on a clothes rail like an art exhibition, you could try using your shoes as sculptures. I've been keeping a gorgeous pair of vintage sandals on my bookshelf for months – they make such nifty ornaments, I haven't worn them yet. And does anyone ever *really* print out photos of their shoes and tape them to the boxes? Clear plastic containers are a much easier option. Another solution is a large storage wheel – it takes up a bit of space but it keeps out dust. It looks especially cool if you have lots of colour variety in your footwear, not so much if you only own black court shoes.

There are tons of imaginative ways to store jewellery – no more piling all your bits and pieces on top of each other. (Nothing makes you feel as if you're wasting your life more than spending hours detangling necklaces.) If you have lots of chains to hang up, a simple pinboard works well – cover it with old magazine pictures for a quirky scrapbook background and add brightly coloured drawing pins to hang pendants from. Dream catchers also make original hangers, and if you have loads of rings or earrings, plastic ice cube trays come in really handy (especially heart-shaped pink ones).

Scientific studies tell us that we sleep better with fewer electrical items in the bedroom. Which is bad news for anyone who keeps a phone right next to the pillow, watches TV in bed and uses a laptop into the small hours... isn't that pretty much all of us? Working in your bedroom may be comfortable (I spent winter writing huddled under a duvet) but it can end up making the room feel more stressful than restful. Try switching everything off (except your alarm) for a few nights to see if you sleep more deeply.

Your Living Room (and Beyond)

Decor

If you're decorating a room from scratch, the carpet is the most important feature. You can paint walls, you can drape a throw over a sofa, but if you hate the colour of the floor, there's only so much you can hide with a rug. Shades of sandy brown, taupe and cream have been popular for so long because they go with everything, which is more than we can say for the psychedelic swirls of the 1970s. Wooden flooring looks great and is easy to clean, but it can be cold on bare feet. (Incidentally, this is why houses in hot climates often feature deliciously cool stone tiles.) Soft carpet is more comfortable, especially for people who often sit on the floor or have little kids crawling around.

If you have a small room you don't have to stick to the traditional "pale colour to make it look bigger" advice if you'd prefer something more vivid. Stencils and decals add interest to a blank space, or you could paint one or two walls a striking colour and wallpaper the others with a lavish pattern for the ultimate in dramatic design. Think "eclectic" rather than "matching" and break all the rules: your TV doesn't have to be the focal point of the room. Skirting boards and radiators don't have to be painted white. There's no reason why you shouldn't have a stair-runner made of fake fur for a gloriously squidgy underfoot experience on your way to breakfast. I suspect that people who model their style on the anonymous beige of a hotel room are afraid of expressing themselves for fear of being judged on their taste; rebelling against convention results in a far more personalised home.

Too many of us keep photos hidden away in albums or on the computer – get your favourite snaps out on display. Cheap frames can be customised with paint or glitter, and clusters of them look terrific across any wall. All those pictures make a talking point for guests as well as reminding you daily of all your good times. Kids' artwork doesn't have to be relegated to the fridge – frame it under glass and tell everyone it's the latest piece from an iconoclastic local artist (they'll all want one).

Culture

Centuries ago, courtesans would subtly advertise how smart and well-informed they were by casually adorning the room with pieces of art, books, and musical instruments. Hinting at your accomplishments and education means you won't have to do anything as crass as mentioning them out loud. So instead of talking about how awesome it is that you're in a rock band, just leave your electric guitar somewhere prominent. Rather than telling everyone you came first in the diving competition, leave the trophy on the mantelpiece. If people only find out that you have all sorts of hidden talents when they visit your home, you've just sealed your reputation as the *coolest* of Princesses.

Whenever celebrities show off their sensational homes, they always have a huge cinema-sized TV, but I've never seen any books. Do they seriously NEVER read? Their brains must be turning into mush as we speak. Piles of books can be decorative in their own right; colour co-ordinated shelves or a display in an unused fireplace can look stunning. Some brave people even use a pile of books as a table – an excellent space-saver, but strictly suitable for sturdy hardbacks, not glossy paperbacks which could create a book avalanche. Classic novels or interesting factual tomes can be good conversation starters as long as you've actually read them – leaving that copy of *War and Peace* around purely to impress people could backfire. It's nice to have some coffee table books for lazy flicking through when you're between compulsive reads; try photography, wildlife, or manga comics.

I'd suggest hiding books which could raise intrusive questions – nobody needs to know that you're reading a self-help book about a personal issue. The same goes for relationship books and ultra-girly romance novels (men should assume that you EXPERIENCE swarthy strangers asking you to dance in Cuban salsa clubs, not just read about them). If a guy checks out the contents of your shelves, you don't want him to think that your only interest is how to ensnare a husband (even if it is). Got to keep them guessing!

Lighting

Fairy lights are cheap and plentiful – use them in your bedroom (wound around your bed frame) as well as your living space to create a glittering grotto. Coloured or white, they look fabulous draped over the fireplace, around the windows or adorning the walls. It's a simple touch that can transform a room, with even the tiniest ones adding an irresistible glow and looking romantic and fun.

In the movies, people with glamorous abodes always have candles everywhere. (Of course, they also generally have a hot tub and a couple of chandeliers, but we'll bypass that). *Anyone* can do candles. If you don't have the cash to buy attractive holders for them, make your own. There are tons of craft books which tell you ways to do this but an easy one is to glue coloured tissue paper around a jam jar. This sounds like a kiddy project but actually looks brilliant, and makes a sweet mini lantern. Another option is to carefully poke a pattern of holes into a tin can for an instant Moroccan lamp, albeit the slightly studenty version.

If you have a fireplace, you're minted in the romantic Princess department. There's nothing like a warm crackling fire, especially after a bracing walk in the woods. It's perfect for creating a cosy nook when you want to curl up with a book / some knitting / a loved one. If you don't have a fire, a soft armchair, a blanket and a DVD also do very nicely. (Lounging around is a legitimate hobby...)

Quick Fixes

Making your own curtains is a fast and cheap way to change the look of a room. Just find some fabric you like and cut to size, hem both pieces at the top and bottom, and attach curtain heading tape at the top so you can hang them. They'll look more professional if you use a plain fabric to line them, but it's not strictly necessary. Alternatively, use two layers of different-coloured gauzy fabric to create a sumptuous, avante-garde set of drapes.

Raid your local haberdashery or go through your own box of scraps or discarded clothes for hidden treasures. Lampshades can be dressed up with a layer of new fabric or some glued-on embellishments such as buttons or sequins. Old clothes could be cut up for patchwork or turned into offbeat cushion covers. (It's so *tiresome* when everyone has the same style of interior design, isn't it? Sometimes making your own is the only way you can guarantee originality.) You don't have to spend a lot of money, and "upcycling" has become such a huge trend that you'll find plenty of online inspiration. Old suitcases can be transformed into pet beds, hanging bottles make great containers for plants, and crates can be painted in your favourite colours and nailed to the wall for shabby-chic storage.

When you have limited space, you have to make every inch count with great storage solutions. For instance, I have an ottoman where I keep all my craft equipment, but it has a plush foam topper covered in velvet so it doubles as a seat. You can also find patterned boxes for filing your paperwork which look good enough to serve as decoration in themselves.

Lastly – build *upwards*. One small bookcase leaves a huge expanse of upper wall bare – invest in floor-to-ceiling shelves to make use of the space above.

Creating Atmosphere

It's really lovely to bring some of the outdoors into your home: I have some seashells and smooth round stones of different colours strewn along my bedroom windowsill. Plants are pretty and therapeutic to have around, and untreated wood makes a rugged addition to a nature lover's decor. I once spray-painted a small branch that had been pruned from a apple tree, and it stayed pristine forever, making a really unusual little objet d'art. Don't even get me started on bonsai trees – I want one so badly (and not just because I plan to buy a lizard and make dinosaur films). Add flowers whenever you can; even a teacup with a couple of blooms will lift the energy in a room and add a touch of rustic charm. If you wanted to get really fancy, you could invest in one of those ultra-relaxing, tinkly water features.

Fragranced candles, an oil diffuser, or incense can all be used to scent the house, although the best way to do this, of course, is to bake something yummy.

Bathroom

Princesses spend a lot of time cleansing, scrubbing, pampering, and preening. It's essential to keep your bathroom clean in order to avoid glimpsing the grime while you're trying to unwind, so invest in a cabinet for all your products to stop them cluttering up every surface. You can always keep the prettiest on display – I buy big chunks of brightly coloured soap from Lush to scent the room, then cut off a piece at a time to use for washing. To add style to your sink, invest in a glitzy soap or hand lotion dispenser; nobody will know if you fill it with more economically priced products.

It's best to put on makeup in harsh natural sunlight whenever possible, so face your mirror towards the window if you can. For night-time glamour, the ultimate Hollywood trick is to buy one of those mirrors surrounded entirely with light bulbs.

What about entertainment? Some people like a waterproof radio to make washing more fun, but it's an unspoken truth that most of us read in the bathroom. Some people get very snobby about this (but then again, some people think that lounging around in the bathtub for hours is wallowing in your own filth). Why wouldn't you want to make use of every single minute of your life? A book which is easy to dip into can be a lifesaver at those times when you're, ahem, going to take a while. Store it discreetly and if anyone asks, it's for when you're bathing...

There's nothing cosier than a deliciously fragrant soak by candlelight; stock up on scented tea-lights, and for true hedonism keep some luxurious bubbles, bath bombs or mood-enhancing essential oils to hand.

Kitchen

Kitchens have had a makeover in the last few years. Gone are the cold steel surfaces and chrome accessories which made cooking look like a science experiment; old fashioned, chintzy tools are back with a vengeance. While we can't all afford a petal-pink food mixer or a full set of designer crockery, there are lots of ways you can make the heart of your home fit for royalty.

Totally overhauling a kitchen is not for the faint-hearted. Unless you have a big budget and a few months to spare, getting new countertops, cupboards and flooring may not be the best option. The good news is that it's relatively easy to change the feel of the room with only a few additions. Whether you're going for a country farmhouse quality (a dresser full of china milk jugs, perhaps?), a chic minimalist space (all white accessories create a clean look) or a warmly chaotic maximalist effect (eclectic colours and evidence of actual activity) there are small and affordable ways you can put your own stamp on the room.

Start with the obvious blank spaces: add sticker decals to plain kitchen tiles, paint the walls, or add funny magnets and clippings to your fridge. Then why not try pasting some swanky vintage posters onto your cupboard doors, or stringing up some more of those fairy lights to make the room more homey?

These days you can find saucepans, toasters, and kettles in bold, zesty colours; even equipment such as potato mashers and whisks can be exotic rather than mundane and utilitarian. Matching is *so* over – it's much nicer to have an array of different colours and patterns. Who wants a boring dinner party with a uniform look when you can make it a bohemian, free-spirited soirée where everyone has a different plate? The bonus is that when one or two dishes break over time, you won't have to worry about finding replacements to match, either.

Look out for sales on quirky picnicware at the end of the summer, as this is a good time to find fun cocktail glasses as well as jewel-coloured salad bowls and unbreakables with bright patterns. Another seasonal buy is Christmassy-themed crockery – I know you're only going to need it once a year, but if it's in use for one month out of twelve, it's not that ridiculous. And who could resist a teapot with merry red-capped gingerbread men on it? Not me! I also have a cake tin decorated with baby chicks for my hot cross buns at Easter...

If you find any cheap cuts of a fabric that appeals to you, you could make it into a tablecloth, napkins or even placemats (applied to a hard back with some fabric glue). I always buy mugs and tea towels if I'm visiting a souvenir shop; that way I have a *useful* reminder of the lovely trip to Cornwall without adding to a collection of "tat that will take up space".

Your Car

This is one of those unfortunate occasions where I have to suggest "Do as I say, not as I do." Because, gentle reader, my car is a piece of... work. It has little rust spots across its bonnet (I prefer to call them "freckles") and a couple of dents (one I inherited from its previous owner, one the result of an argument with a lamp post). I wash it so infrequently that at one point it actually had things growing on it. But I was once told that guys like hot chicks in crappy cars, so there is hope.

How can you add some Princessy touches to your car, which is no doubt much nicer than mine? Start with a cute key ring; it can be an expression of your individuality as well as helping you to find your keys in the mass of frivolity that is the contents of your handbag. (The ultra low-budget option is a silk ribbon.) No matter what your car looks like on the outside, you can create any atmosphere you fancy on the inside. Dangly decorations can be distracting if they swing in your face when you're attempting a 3-point turn, but a comfortingly furry steering wheel or cheerful floor mats and seat covers could make your ride feel positively palatial.

Keep some practical-yet-glamorous accessories in your car: a pocket-sized tin of mints, a spare hair clip, a packet of tissues in novelty wrapping, a glittery nail file. As a reminder to be eco-friendly it's useful to keep some cloth bags on hand so you can avoid getting more plastic ones at the supermarket. In case of unforeseen traffic or hunger emergencies, I always take a fresh bottle of water and an energy bar when I drive. For safety I also recommend storing a map, a warm blanket, a wind-up torch, a plastic raincoat, and a high-visibility jacket just in case you break down on a dark and stormy night. (Keeping your phone charged and your breakdown rescue details handy is also essential.)

Vacuuming, keeping some decent CDs in rotation, and adding an air freshener will make riding in your car a more pleasant experience for you and your guests. If you really want to go the extra mile you could even add some inviting mini cushions for the backseat – your friends will be begging you to be the designated driver.

Keeping Your Home Fit for Royalty

Much as I can sympathise with the adage "A tidy home means a wasted life", nobody enjoys living in squalor. If you're sentimental / disorganised / generally messy (*raises hand*) clutter can build up. I have a terrible habit of creating a "floordrobe" but I always feel so much better when everything is put away neatly. If you regularly clear out your home, you're guaranteed to feel wonderful afterwards, but just straightening things out in 5-minute bursts each day can help you keep it all in order. Sometimes we can get weighed down by all our junk and feel so overwhelmed that we don't know how to start sorting through it. My favourite tip when you feel helpless is to use a big box or sack – put all the mess in there and the room is instantly transformed. You'll feel much better when you can at least see the carpet. Once you've given the room a good clean you can go through the contents of the box at your leisure – if you leave it for a few weeks you'll probably find you don't even miss the items. When you cut the strings and let something go – to roam free at the dump, or live happily in someone else's home – you'll feel so liberated.

But what if it's something that "might come in handy one day"? This excuse only works if a) you could easily find it in the event of suddenly needing it, and b) it's more useful to you (languishing in a cupboard) than it would be to someone else who would actually use it NOW. My best advice is to have a big clear-out when you're in a really bad mood – you might as well put all the anger to good use, and you'll find yourself thinking "What the hell am I keeping this piece of CRAP for?" Aggression fuels ruthlessness.

If you have lots of beautiful pieces of art, take your cue from museums and galleries: display some and store the rest, then keep rotating your "stock" so you always have something new on show.

Princessify Your Belongings

You can add a touch of Princess sparkle to every part of your life – why be boringly functional when you can be delightfully dainty? Carry a handbag full of whimsical items that a man wouldn't be caught dead with; a foldable hairbrush, a zebra-print wallet, a heart-shaped pocket mirror. Don't automatically reach for a sensible black or brown leather handbag – try one in electric blue, or get something silly with cartoon deer all over it (possibly better for social activities than board meetings, but at least they'd remember you).

Invest in an elegant sun shade for hot days when you need to protect your delicate skin from the UV rays. Keep a miniature electric fan on your desk or carry an artistically patterned paper fan for Edwardian-style flirting. Cold weather brings no end of opportunities for adorable accessorising – you're never too old for fluffy ear muffs or mittens on a string.

Working doesn't mean an end to the opulence – look out for ladylike frilly aprons for baking days, stationery so shiny it makes writing a dissertation seem alluring, and any neat little twists you can add to a mundane work uniform. You could even get a dinky flower-printed trowel to brighten up those days when you're up to your knees in weeds.

Sitting in the garden (on ornate filigree chairs), eating lunch (with a kitsch plastic box and flask combo) or topping up your drink (with the discreet hip flask you keep strapped to your thigh... wait, what?); no matter what you're doing, you can be gloriously stylish while you're doing it.

Part Two

Creating a Princess Persona

"If you are always trying to be normal you will never know how AMAZING you can be." Maya Angelou

YOUR PRINCESS PERSONA

"Who is Katharine Hepburn? It took me a long time to create that creature."
Katharine Hepburn

Remember *The Princess and the Pea*? She could feel a single pea through dozens of mattresses, and that's how everyone knew she was of noble blood, even though she'd arrived looking bedraggled and scruffy.

It's supposed to be an example of the saying "breeding will out", meaning that you can always spot true royalty, even if that someone is dressed in rags. Am I the only one who thinks the moral of this story is all screwed up? You get caught in a storm and knock on a stranger's door in the middle of the night to ask for shelter... then when they ask how you slept, you COMPLAIN that you were uncomfortable?

Honey, that's not being a Princess. That's being a diva bitch.

You can have any number of luxurious lambskin rugs for your tootsies and diamonds on your fingers, but none of it means a thing if the way you relate to other people is less than regal. Princess behaviour is all sweetness and light – at least until you *have* to kick ass.

Life isn't about Finding Yourself, it's about Creating Yourself

"Be yourself" is a piece of advice suitable for anyone who has ever copied a friend's style of walking, talking or dressing, or drastically altered their opinions to fit in with the status quo. Attempting to squeeze yourself into someone else's mould is a project doomed to failure – even if you become Miss Popular, you'll have lost your self-respect.

So when is "be yourself" *not* such great advice? The obvious answer is: when you're an idiot. (You and I both know plenty of people who should try to be as different as possible from "themselves", right?) What if we're not naturally good-natured, serene, or kind? Should we just express our grumpiness and look out for number one, because that's "being true to ourselves"?

If none of us followed the social niceties expected of us, we'd all still be

76

acting like toddlers: pulling each other's hair and screaming when our sandwiches aren't cut into the right shape. (Hey, isn't that how some people *do* behave?) When we make an idol of "being ourselves", we end up with a lot of self-centred egomaniacs whose excuse for everything is "That's who I am." No wonder one of the most popular internet memes is a quote supposedly (but probably not) from Marilyn Monroe: "I'm selfish, impatient and a little insecure. I make mistakes, I am out of control and at times hard to handle. But if you can't handle me at my worst, then you sure as hell don't deserve me at my best." Apparently it never occurs to us to try to STOP displaying these negative traits, rather than demanding that everyone put up with it because we're so stupendously awesome at our best that it makes up for our behaviour the rest of the time.

So here's a radical idea: let's all work towards being the people we WANT to be, rather than settling for the first draft. This doesn't mean picking yourself apart and feeling rubbish, comparing yourself unfavourably with Beyoncé, or buying products because the commercial promised you'd be the envy of all your friends. It means making your life the best it can be; eliminating the aspects of yourself that you don't like, and disciplining yourself to reach your potential. Nobody's perfect, and every day is a fresh opportunity to polish our tiaras and try again. Of course, if you're *already* a Princess who brings a little starshine into everything you touch: just be yourself!

Accentuate the Positive

Few of us are naturally so positive that we can stay cheerful no matter what our circumstances; a lost wallet or an argument with our favourite man will result in most of us having a little whinge to anyone who'll listen. Refusing to get sucked into this kind of downward spiral takes a conscious decision and then considerable effort, but finding that little glimmer of joy even on your darkest days is the sign of a true Princess. It's a challenge most people aren't up to – not least because they find the world drags them down again. There's a story about a man who would say "Good morning" to his neighbour every day, without ever getting a response. After a while, someone asked him: "Why do you still bother, when he's never going to say it back to you?" The man replied "Why should I allow him to change the way I live?" We can't determine other people's responses to us, but we're in total control of our own mindsets; as the

US senator Al Franken once said, "It's easier to put on slippers than to carpet the whole world."

If you come across as an upbeat, carefree kind of gal, people might assume that you don't have any problems. Of course you do; everybody does. The difference is that while others bitch and moan and make no effort to crawl out of the slump they find themselves in, a Princess will confide her troubles to a select few, dry her tears and be kind to herself until she's in a better mood.

Princesses can still be serious, and post Facebook updates about politics or news stories or injustice in the world. (Unlike some girls, they won't make a token effort to look interested in current events, and then write "OMG I'm painting my nails the cutest colour" thirty seconds after lamenting the plight of starving orphans.) A Princess balances the serious with the uplifting, and is more likely to say "Hey has everyone seen this petition / charity / fundraiser to help X cause?" rather than depressing everyone with a pessimistic view of the world. Nobody likes a downer – no matter how sincere and well-meaning – and worrying doesn't help anyone.

Life becomes so much more fun when you can find the silver lining in any situation ("At least I hadn't just filled up the tank when my car got stolen. That would've *really* sucked!") and there's no greater skill than being able to see the funny side of your problems. (Embarrassing moments are especially hilarious once the humiliation has dulled over time.) This joyful attitude also has the sneaky bonus of annoying anyone who wants to see you unhappy; nobody can act as if you're a sad, pitiful creature if you're visibly peppy and exuberant.

Being Self-Possessed

Lots of people talk about "being comfortable in your own skin", but what does this phrase actually mean?

Everyone has a negative voice in their heads. It's the voice that says you're ugly, nobody REALLY likes you, and people only hang out with you because they feel sorry for you. It's the voice that says you're no good at the things you love doing and you might as well give up. In short, it's a whiny little party pooper. You can tell the voice to go screw itself, or you can ignore it, but it will always return. My solution is to inwardly respond with sarcasm. Say for instance it whispers "Everyone's looking at you, they probably think your feet look gross in peep-toe shoes and that top you're wearing is ancient." Laugh at the voice. Tease it. Retort "Oh no, people are looking at me! What will I do? They don't like my outfit? Boohoo, how awful for them! They'll have to close their eyes!" This is much more fun than trying in vain to tune it out. It's also a useful way to deal with stress generally; when your mind starts going round in circles (with all the comebacks you should have used when arguing with your sister, and all the reasons she's wrong and you're right) a sing-song "BORING!" should calm it down. Because thoughts like this *are* incredibly tedious.)

Once you've shut up the gremlin, you're free to enjoy the company of other people without over-analysing their reactions to you. When you're feeling anxious and making up things to worry about, you're not truly present in your own life. It's impossible to live in the moment while you're trying to get inside another person's head to see what they think of you – which is none of your business anyway.

Most of us gain confidence as we get older; the little things which bothered you in your teens are forgotten as you grow up and realise that the only people making critical, bitchy comments are the ones whose opinions don't matter anyway.

The Princess Attitude

The Princess attitude may be 99% sunshiny demeanour and jaunty walks, but it also includes a low threshold for other people's BS. This doesn't mean marching up to someone who's annoyed you and announcing in a screechy way "I'm not taking any more of your crap!" Why *tell* them when you can *show* them? Rather than yelling or screaming, simply walk away when you're not satisfied with the deal you're getting. Princesses ignore bad behaviour and reward the good (a reward could mean bestowing the lucky person with your smiles, praise, or even just your presence).

In soap operas and reality shows, divas come up with catchphrases like "I'm worth more than that", which they churn out when they're not getting the respect they crave. Unfortunately, these rants sound contrived and hollow, as if they're trying to convince *themselves* of their value. What makes a more powerful statement? Getting all red in the face and teary as you make a blistering attack on the person who's wronged you? Or merely gliding away from them (physically or metaphorically) in order to be with people who do appreciate you? I'm going for the graceful swan act here.

When you have confidence, you can smoothly extricate yourself from any situation which isn't making you happy – because you have faith that a much better alternative can't be too far away. I should point out here that I DON'T mean we should all be spoilt brats who demand that everyone kisses our feet when we enter the room. Arrogance and entitlement like that is not only unattractive, it also falls into that "desperate to prove myself" category. True self-love results in a quiet self-assurance and no *need* to lord it over other people.

Princesses don't bother trying to "get" something which promises lesser mortals the seal of approval – a swanky handbag, a rich boyfriend, or entry to a VIP area. You don't need to ponder advertising campaigns or chain emails about what constitutes a "real woman". You know who you are and there's no reason to beg anyone else to define you. Even on your worst day, you would rather be you than anyone else in the world, because you're *that* extraordinary.

I've been practising this most Princessy of attitudes for so long that I now have a colossal ego. I'd never buy a ridiculously expensive designer outfit – *they* should be paying *me* to advertise their stuff – and I'll never stand in line to get into a new, hip and happening club because wherever I am is where the party's at, baby.

On second thoughts, be careful with this self-love thing. You might unleash a beast...

Being Nice

Scottish writer Ian Mclaren was the original source of some wise words commonly attributed to Plato: "Be kind, for everyone you meet is fighting a hard battle." You have no idea what circumstances someone might be dealing with when you interact with them, but you can set yourself the Princess Challenge every day and try to be the reason they smile. When you're sweet and charming you'll brighten up the world, and be a good memory for people long after you've all left the same school / workplace / social group.

Being pleasant doesn't just benefit those around you; kindness lights up your features with a luminosity you can't fake. Most of what humans communicate is picked up subconsciously, which explains why you're drawn to some people and inexplicably repelled by others. It's as if all those little selfish acts – cutting up someone in traffic or snubbing someone you deem "not cool enough" – show up in your demeanour. But when you say hi to the receptionist on your way into the office, give your friend that halterneck top because it looks better on her anyway, and pick up groceries for your sister when she has the flu, that shows too. Plus you're a much happier human being as a result, because being nice is FUN and it really does warm your heart.

Don't forget the power of touch – something I discovered when I was styling a celebrity I had secretly considered a bit annoying. She seemed nice enough in person, but my opinion of her truly changed when she gave my arm a squeeze as we chatted excitedly about clothes. Instantly I revised my "silly bimbo" assessment to "Aw, she's lovely". It can be that easy; a subtle touch to emphasise a point or greet someone in an extra-friendly manner could make all the difference in the way they see you.

Some people are very huggy while others flinch at physical contact, but even the shy ones often appreciate cuddles more than they'll admit. (N.B. Some people hate being touched, so don't go around squeezing their cheeks and saying "You do like it! The Princess Guide told me so!" It won't work. I've tried it.)

Compliments

If you've ever had a real blinder of a compliment, you'll know how powerful they are. They make you glow all day. You recall the words years later when you're feeling blue and need a pick-me-up. Compliments ROCK. Now, wouldn't you like to make someone's day? And be remembered forever as that enchanting girl who told them something great about themselves? Well, do it. They'll never forget you.

This comes easily to some people – it's normal for them to tell an acquaintance "I love your bag / hair / artwork." Other people find it awkward, or they overdo it. (It's difficult to praise someone's clothes, taste in music, and eyeliner skills in one breath without sounding sycophantic.)

Stand out from the crowd by making your compliments the BEST ones. Make them specific and make them memorable. Instead of casually tossing out

"Nice outfit" try saying "That colour brings out the blue in your eyes," or "Your long legs make you look like a baby deer!" (Seriously, offbeat works: I was thrilled when someone said I reminded them of a fairy.) Instead of telling your friend that her chocolate pie is "really good" say: "I've been telling everyone about your delicious pies! You're famous in my neighbourhood!" Your compliment will still be ringing in her ears long after the others have faded.

Make sure your admiration is appropriate, rather than mindlessly repeating something you assume everyone wants to hear. I once knew a girl who would gush to everyone "You've lost weight!" which might have been gratifying for those who were trying to slim down, but everyone else spotted the insincerity, and those who had always prided themselves on their slender frames felt slighted: "When was I fat?!" Likewise, telling someone how great they look NOW (after their holiday / haircut / makeover) could be misconstrued; it immediately begs the question: "What was wrong with the way I looked before?" (As for those particularly touchy people who can read an insult into even the most carefully worded approval, the only solution is to avoid talking to them altogether.)

The best praise you can give boosts the image that person has of themselves – so if your boss prides herself on being a mother hen to everyone in the office, telling her that you love being able to come to her for advice is going to warm her heart more than honeyed words about her incredible marketing skills.

If someone surprises you with a flattering comment, remember that the accepted response is "Thank you" NOT "This old thing? I've had it for ages" or "Ooh, no, I'm terrible at this game, they were obviously lucky shots." When you brush off a compliment, you're belittling not only yourself, but also the person who kindly volunteered their admiration. You might see it as being "modest" but if you disagree with their approval you're also insulting them, saying "You're wrong" and being disrespectful of their opinions.

Be gracious: if you can't bring yourself to *agree* with them by saying "Thanks!" you can simply give them a big smile to show that you appreciate the encouragement.

We're often told we should try to remember the nice things people have mentioned and forget the criticisms (easier said than done). The flipside of noting down lovely compliments you get or listing your achievements is that you may depend on them for your sense of worth. How can you then avoid giving equal weight to the insults? Remember that your value doesn't actually depend on what others think of you, whether they have a high opinion of you or not. And what if nobody ever gives you positive feedback? It's not up to other people to make you feel good about yourself: it's up to you. Encourage yourself!

When You're Miserable

This might be a good time to point out that you don't need to worry if you're 17, or 21, or 35, and you're wondering why you're not having the most fantastic year of your life: TV shows lie to us. Life is full of blessings but it also has its tough moments, and if you're finding it hard it's not because you're doing it wrong; sometimes it's just hard.

Some young women suffer from the kind of dark depression which feels as if it will never lift; they might try to regain control of their lives by developing compulsive behaviours, eating disorders or destructive habits such as taking drugs or self-harming. Needless to say, these are very serious issues, and popping your favourite song on your headphones and going for a walk isn't going to "cheer you up". If you know that you need help in this area, it's essential to take that first difficult step and make an appointment with your doctor; there's no need to struggle on alone when there are people who really can help (even if that sounds impossible).

When it comes to ordinary bad moods, having a chat with someone sympathetic and wise can get your worries out into the open and make you feel better. However, focusing on the negative aspects of your life and constantly reminding yourself (and everyone else) of what's wrong with you is unlikely to have great results. A friend of mine has the rather radical idea that women should never go into therapy; they should save up all the money they would have spent on a counsellor and use it to go travelling instead. She isn't joking – after years of analysis she wishes she'd spent less time dwelling on her problems and more time having fun. There's no doubt that therapy does work wonderfully for some people (especially those with deep-rooted issues) but for the more common-or-garden grumpiness, there's a lot to be said for doing what makes you feel good instead of talking about why you feel bad.

Part of the reason people find depression so unfathomable is that we're raised to believe that if the external circumstances look good, there's no reason for anyone to be despondent. This is why unhelpful people will say things like "What's a pretty young girl like you got to feel down about?" The advertising industry brainwashes us to think that certain things *should* make us feel contented. Crazy nights out. New clothes. Having a boyfriend. Perfect skin. They can all help to bring us pleasure, but they're not necessarily guaranteed to provide any kind of deep satisfaction.

Forget what society has told you to pursue and go for what *genuinely* makes you light up. Personally, my eyes glaze over when people start talking about music festivals, even though we're all supposed to be falling over ourselves to get tickets. I don't *want* to camp amid drug dealers for three days and get squashed in crowds of smelly people. (When you've queued up for portaloos once, it loses its appeal.) A better option for me would be camping in some quiet woods with a few buddies and playing guitars around a campfire. Maybe your bliss will be snuggling with your dog, or walking in the country, or secretly listening to embarrassingly bad music you love.

When we're feeling fed up, most of us have the attitude: "If only X was different, then my whole life would be better." We blame our jobs or relationships for our gloom, and dream of how things will be when we're rich and live in the Caribbean. The trouble is that we take *ourselves* wherever we go, so even when we do start a new career or find new friends, the same problems will keep popping up. The first step to a more fulfilling life is to take responsibility for our happiness instead of expecting circumstances to provide it. If you choose to appreciate all the good things about your existing situation, you'll feel blessed even if it never improves. But if it's your habit to find fault with everything, you could be living on an idyllic island with your rock star husband, and still spend your days complaining about how annoying it is to get sand in your satin bedsheets.

On the other hand, sometimes a change of scenery is enough to jolt you out of the rut you're in. When I was 23, I was in a horrible relationship which looked as if it could drag on forever without improving, my skin was all broken out from stress, I hated my job and life was generally crap. (Being positive can have its drawbacks – I'd been looking on the bright side of all these things for so long that I had to hit rock bottom before realising I HAD to get out.) I decided I'd travel around the world, so I saved up, planned my itinerary, and gently broke the news to everyone. (This took some time, as my loved ones all strongly discouraged the idea.) I took my heart in my hands, boarded a plane and had the best year of my life. Frankly, I wouldn't exchange that experience for anything. (And my skin cleared up within weeks.)

This may or may not be feasible in your current circumstances, but even a short break doing something different could revitalise you when you're feeling low. (Volunteering is a fast track to getting out of your own head; it helps other people, *and* it puts the kibosh on self-obsessed navel-gazing. What's not to like?) The worst period of your life might end up triggering your greatest learning experience, and your misery could spark the creation of your favourite memories. So use your heartache to spur you on to better things; life's too short to live in stagnant sadness when it's within your power to change everything.

When there's bad stuff going on in a Princess's life, she maintains her poise in public. It might be hard to hold it all together (I had to go for secret "cry breaks" at work during my lowest point) but it's not appropriate for your boss, dates, or casual friends to know every detail. Offload on your closest, most trustworthy supporters, and show everyone else a brave face. Life as a Princess isn't all sparkles and rainbows – sometimes it means being strong and keeping your cool just long enough to lock the door behind you. As Elizabeth Taylor said: "Put on some lipstick, pour yourself a drink and pull yourself together."

And if it helps, the concept of hard times resulting in a positive transformation is repeated in nature over and over again; it's why they say that a diamond is a piece of charcoal that handled stress exceptionally well! Think about how a caterpillar has to cocoon herself in darkness and wait, in a space which becomes far too small for her expanding wings. If you were to interfere with the process and help her out, she would never develop the strength she needs to fly; it's the struggling which makes her powerful enough to break free and become a butterfly.

Reacting to Other People

The 14th Dalai Lama said; "When you think everything is someone else's fault, you will suffer a lot. When you realise that everything springs only from yourself, you will learn both peace and joy." As we've already established, you can't make other people behave the way you'd like them to. So it's your choice: are you going to let them get to you or not? Suppose you give your housemate a lift when she's running late, and she then *complains* that you don't drive fast enough and it will be your fault if she gets into trouble at work. Would this make you spitting mad? You can't force her to be courteous, and if her lack of appreciation is enough to ruin your day, what does that say about your own level of peace and serenity?

There'll be moments when you catch yourself being similarly ungrateful – like when your colleague is kind enough to water your plant, but you're annoyed because it's a cactus. Instead of yelling at him, concentrate on the silver lining and appreciate the effort he put in. (You can gently correct him AFTER you've said "thank you".) Instead of whining that the way your husband feeds the kids is all wrong and you "might as well do it yourself", count your blessings – at least he's trying to help.

If you know someone who nitpicks at everything you do, it's tempting to pull the "You're not perfect either" card and start speaking up every time they do something that irritates *you*. But then they'll have changed your behaviour, and you'll be a complainer just like them. Instead of getting even with an eye for an eye, graciously keep quiet (and smugly congratulate yourself on being so mature).

If your friend, colleague or loved one is sad and needs a friendly ear, it's natural to give them a hug and listen sympathetically. However, if someone is an expert at sulking, going off in a huff or being ostentatiously "in a mood" (the kind where their only replies are growls) the best thing to do is to ignore them. Remaining cheerfully oblivious means they can't drag you down into misery with them. Asking "What's up?" only invites more irritable answers of "Nothing!" or a rant you don't need to hear. Leave that person alone. By the time you return, they'll be over it and you won't have had the unpleasant experience of their negative energy. If they have a problem with you, they can always grow up and talk to you about it.

The unselfish bonus of turning a blind eye is that it makes it much easier for the grouch to snap out of it. I know from experience that having people compassionately ask me "What's wrong?" makes me focus on the problem as I describe it at length and possibly work myself up into an even bigger snit. Then later when I've forgotten all about it, someone kindly asks "So are you feeling better about...?" and I get annoyed remembering the original cause of my crabbiness all over again! If everyone disregards my bad mood, it gives me permission to forget it with less fuss.

Being Independent

We might equate self-sufficiency with being able to earn a crust, read a map or do our own taxes, but real independence starts on the inside. You have to be able to make your own decisions and stick by them even when nobody else believes in you. Having faith in your own judgement means that, unlike most people, you're never going to be led astray by someone who cajoles you with "It will be fine, trust me." When you rely on yourself rather than other people, you feel empowered – you'll never worry about being alone, because you already know you can handle it.

One thing many people find challenging is going out by themselves. It's not surprising when you realise we've been conditioned to see being on our own as a punishment – from solitary confinement in prison to being separated from our friends in school.

Solo public appearances can feel awkward, largely because of the fear that people will look at you, notice you're alone and think you're a loser. (I prefer to think they're looking at me and thinking "Wow, she's on her own... how brave! I wish I had the courage to do that.")

The truth is that we can only live in total freedom when we decide to *stop worrying about other people's opinions*. If "What will they think of me?" determines a lot of your behaviour, you're a slave trapped in an imaginary cage. Once you get over this fear, the sky's the limit! You'll find it incredibly liberating to do whatever you feel like doing, even if it makes you look "weird". I used to feel shy going anywhere alone and would always make sure I had a friend or a date to accompany me. But I realised I was skipping events if none of my usual crowd wanted to go – what a stupid way to miss out on all the fun. When I pushed myself to be daring and go anyway, I found I was far more sociable and met new friends easily because I wasn't huddled in the corner with people I already knew.

I built up my confidence slowly by going alone to fast food cafés or popping into art galleries, before graduating to concerts, the cinema and then international travel! Going solo is sometimes even preferable to going with a friend; there's no compromise about what to do, how long to stay, or where to eat. Never again will you miss the film you really wanted to see because your friends weren't interested. You can go to a museum and spend as much time as you like in front of each piece, instead of getting hurried along or waiting impatiently for someone else. You're not dependent on anyone else's whims; if they don't fancy that party, you'll go anyway and have a ball. When I was travelling I made friends with other people in backpacker hostels and actually ended up feeling sorry for those moving in groups – they were always pulled in so many different directions and had to debate and agree on whatever they were going to do next. I could come and go as I pleased, being utterly, joyfully selfish. It was great!

Of course, going stag can be difficult – when everyone is jumping around and singing along to your favourite rock star, you feel pretty silly doing it on your own – but a moment of self-consciousness is still only a tiny part of the totally worthwhile experience. (It's not as if being alone will make you stand out in the crowd; you can't exactly chat throughout a gig or a movie anyway.)

So be the woman you've always wanted to be: comfortable in your own skin and confident that you can handle anything. Remember; your ability to grow as a person depends entirely on how much insecurity you can handle – every time you do one little thing which takes you outside of your current comfort zone, you expand it.

Oh, and if you're single and worry you'll end up alone – don't. Not least because women live longer than men, so unless you hook up with a 30-year-old stud when you're 50, the chances are that you'll spend your twilight years on your own anyway. (Cheery, huh? You're welcome.)

Treating Yourself the Way You'd Like to be Treated

Much as I loved the decadence of pleasing myself when I was travelling, I'm realistic enough to know that most of the time family obligations, relationships and friendships do require compromise and we all have to put our own desires on the back burner occasionally in order to please somebody else. It's possible to get so obsessed with not being a doormat that you refuse to ever put others first, but being self-sacrificing occasionally is a necessary part of living harmoniously with your loved ones.

In order to do this without resentment, you must carve out time and space for yourself too. Whether you're a busy mother, a full-time carer for a sick relative, or an average girl trying to make her way in life, you have to treat yourself well. Take care of yourself the way you would take care of your most beloved friend (because that's exactly who you are). Grab a cappuccino at a sunny table outside and people-watch. Have a relaxing session of acupuncture. Notice when your hair looks good, or the way all those squats have paid off since you started working out. Tell yourself how well you're doing. (Just don't get too effusive in your affection, lipstick marks on your mirror would be embarrassing.)

If you're already feeling cherished, you'll be far less needy with the men in your life and you'll have high expectations of the way they should treat you. If they don't give you the same respect you give yourself, kick them to the kerb without looking back.

Be Smart

High IQ or not, we can all choose to be well-informed and educated. Keeping up with current events, having an opinion on various political arguments, and being curious about the world around you makes you more cultured than the average person. (Think of "interesting" as an abbreviation for "interested in everything".) Reading – anything at all – is a great way to expand your horizons. You don't need to get a degree to be knowledgeable when the entire internet is at your fingertips and there are educational books and juicy novels to get into.

Most people never really question what they think about issues, and simply offer up the same boring old knee-jerk reactions. Be open-minded (without going so far that your brain has to be strapped in). If your opinions on everything are exactly the same as they were five years ago, it might be a sign that you've always been preternaturally wise... or that you haven't made the effort to seek out people, forums or news reports which challenge your way of thinking. Make a point of reading a book or watching a film / documentary which sums up the opposite of your current views, even if you want to dismiss it within the first ten minutes. If you always gravitate towards people and things which fit in with what you already believe, how are you going to learn anything new? Instead of living in a tiny bubble like so many people do, try to get outside of your own world and find things to bring back with you.

Being book-smart is one thing; it's even more important to be street-smart and develop good judgement. Learn to read people and take note of the kind of moves pulled by bullsh*t merchants (clue: they often say "Trust me," or "I swear to God"). Be aware that you could be an attractive prospect for some dude who likes his women intellect-free and intoxicated. We all like to have a wild night out once in a while, but getting so drunk that you have no control over yourself is not a wise move. This isn't about victim-blaming; we all know that sexual assault can happen to anyone, at any time, and the only person responsible for that is the perpetrator. But we need to use our common sense: is there any other situation where you would willingly walk into a roomful of salacious strangers and then drug yourself? No? So why get falling-down drunk in a bar or a frat party? There are plenty of men who've been raised right and would never take advantage of a girl who's wasted, but there are others who'll jump at the chance. Sadly, until the world changes the way everyone is educated about consent, it's up to *us* to protect ourselves. If it's a big night out and you're determined to do shots and go home with inexplicable bruises and missing shoes, at least make a pact with trustworthy friends that you'll look out for each other.

But Don't Worry if People Think You're Dumb

Dumb like a fox, baby! I've noticed something weird: if you're a young woman, some people will automatically assume you're not especially intelligent. If you're pretty, for some reason the idea of you being brainy as well just blows people's minds. A guy once told me "You're smarter than you look" as if my features could give away anything about my IQ. He didn't look too clever with a smacked face! (Joking. I promise.) While it can be frustrating to know that someone thinks you're thick, it's better to be thought of as stupid when you're smart than the other way round. Plus, if someone's assuming you're a bit fluffy-headed, you're at a huge advantage – it's kind of like being a spy. You get to hide behind the "cute and harmless" smokescreen while your brain works faster than a speeding bullet. Bring out the razor-sharp wit when they're least expecting it and watch them choke on their tea. As Dolly Parton said, "If people think I'm a dumb blonde because of the way I look, then they're dumber than they think I am."

Live NOW

This book isn't specifically about romantic relationships, but it's inevitable that the person you're dating will have some effect on the way you live your life. So I'll just say this: don't let a man control you or make decisions for you, and don't put your dreams on hold for a man. I've met so many women who regret choices they made to please the guy they were with at the time: turning down dream jobs because they'd recently started seeing someone and didn't want to relocate, deciding which university to attend based on their boyfriend's choice, or allowing themselves to be isolated from family and friends because hubby wasn't keen on them.

Arranging your entire existence around a man puts way too much pressure on the relationship. Assuming your boyfriend *isn't* a control freak who demands to be the centre of your universe, it puts him under a hell of a lot of pressure, too. He now has to live up to an impossible ideal in order to justify your decision to put him before your own needs. No wonder I've heard so many stories about the guy breaking up with his girlfriend shortly after she's moved 300 miles away from her friends and family in order to be with him.

Get your own priorities straight – not only when you're dating someone, but before that, too. It's tempting to think "I'll wait until I'm with someone before I think about buying a house," or "I want to see Paris for the first time on my honeymoon." But guess what? You might marry someone whose job requires a city apartment, and then you'll never get to experience life in that little seaside cottage you're hankering after. The man you meet might have already been to Paris a million times, on business or (horror!) with other women.

So create the life you want NOW. Make the memories for yourself NOW – that way the hypothetical future will be pure bonus. Do that thing you always wanted to do "someday" in the future: get on a plane in your Jackie O shift dress and shades, take a train across Europe wearing red lipstick, buy that sporty two-seater car, spend your money on perfume. Otherwise you might wake up one day with a husband and kids and wonder what you did with all that free time you once had. And if you're already experiencing the domestic bliss of family life, savour every moment.

YOUR PRESTIGE

"I can walk down the street as anyone and not be recognised, but if I walk down the street as Marilyn Monroe, I am." Marilyn Monroe

Pity the poor celebrity. Not only do they have to endure paparazzi loitering outside their houses, but when they deflect nosy questions with "I don't want to comment on the guy I broke up with two years ago, I'm over it," the headline will read *"I don't want to talk about him ever again!"* as if they'd brought him into the conversation. At least they have a secret weapon; magazine interviews. You know, the ones where the journalist describes how radiantly makeup-free yet still beautiful the starlet is... and how she's so refreshingly candid compared to those other pretentious divas. And how she chose a little local café for the meeting because that's the kind of down-to-earth girl she is, but every head turns when she walks in because of her natural charisma... Sounds dreamy, right? The truth is, those interviews are screened by the star's publicist and the final version will only go to print once it's been approved. They could make Hitler sound like an offbeat, interesting guy if they struck the right deal. The mags rely on big name features to sell copies, so it wouldn't be wise for writers to be brutally honest about their impressions of the stars and risk annoying them.

It's all very well pointing out that it doesn't matter what anyone thinks of you, but the fact is, sometimes you'd rather dazzle people with your coolness than confess you spent all weekend in your pyjamas watching old episodes of *Columbo*. It's fascinating to see how a movie star or politician works to control their image, and we can pick up some of their best tips.

Your Public Princess Persona

When you were a kid, there was probably someone in your class who was a total fantasist. You know the type – whatever you had, she had something better. Your dad was a pilot, her dad was an astronaut. You went shopping at the weekend, she went to The Ivy and hung out with movie stars. This kind of lying is really obvious and screams "Please like me! I can be whatever you want me to be!" Keep this in mind while you create your Princess persona.

Being a Princess ISN'T about lying, trying hard to impress people, or living in a fantasy world because it's so much better than your reality. It IS about putting a positive slant on everything, and being so relaxed and self-confident that you're perfectly happy to be seen doing the "nerdy" stuff you enjoy rather than trying to fit in with what everyone else is into.

However, there will be occasions when you really don't feel like telling someone how you've spent your downtime because you know they'll jump at any opportunity to pick you apart. You can always give stories a bit of spin, just like any good PR executive would do. For instance, "I stayed in on Friday night and didn't really do anything" sounds a bit dull. "I chilled out with a box set of fascinating David Attenborough documentaries" is still the truth, but it instantly sounds more interesting and suggests a much-needed respite from the hassles of going out and rubbing shoulders with all the plebeians in the seedy local nightclub. With a bit of gloss, any story can be re-framed to sound more appealing.

Show, Don't Tell

It's said that men tend to exaggerate their talents, while women undervalue their own. No matter what their gender, there's no bigger bore than someone who's always banging on about how terrific they are in every way. Subtle hinting is a more palatable way to let people know about your brilliance without appearing to brag. If you're good at playing the ukulele, organising meetings, or making your own clothes, you don't need to be all faux-coy and say "Ugh, I'm rubbish at it really." Just be matter of fact about the level you're at, volunteer to give someone some helpful pointers, or show off your stuff in a competition. Why talk about your prowess when you can demonstrate? Likewise, never *tell* people how smart you are, it might frighten them (and it's very boring to listen to). And there's no need to talk about how attractive you are; people have eyes.

In our culture, being quiet is often seen as a weakness; we have an unfortunate habit of describing someone as having a "strong" personality because it's more polite than saying "overbearing and obnoxious". There's nothing wrong with being confident, but a lot of people seem to be confused by how "confidence" is defined. It DOESN'T mean being the loudest person in

93

the room and always making yourself the centre of attention. Most people will see straight through this act and realise that you're covering up a *lack* of confidence. Do you think Steven Spielberg walks into rooms saying "Woohoo, look at me, I'm a big movie director! Hey, over here! Wanna hear about my bank balance?" Of course not; he's Steven Spielberg. He doesn't need to. And neither do you.

However, you can *show* people that you're a sassy, savvy young lady without saying a word. Wherever you go, walk in as if you own the place – literally. I vividly remember one time I was working in an office while job candidates arrived for their interviews. Some sat nervously, twisting their hair and biting their nails. One woman acted as if it were already her workplace, sitting casually with her legs crossed as if she had just grabbed a seat during a rest from her duties. She confidently greeted my boss as if he were an old friend, chatted to him as they entered the interview room, and walked out alongside him. Guess who got the job?

The Handicap Principle

The "handicap principle" was the brainchild of biologist Amotz Zahavi back in 1975, when he noticed that animals sometimes evolve to attract mates or put off rivals in some rather odd ways. The idea is that if you clearly have something "wrong" which should be holding you back, but you're still thriving, then you must be incredibly tough and resilient. A prime example is the peacock's tail – it's big and beautiful and he uses it to attract females, but it's also a bulky, inconvenient thing to drag along behind you. It's a huge weakness to flaunt in the face of a predator, so the fact that he's still strutting about with his tail in pristine order proves that he's skilful at avoiding trouble.

So, how can a Princess like you use this concept to your advantage? Go against type once in a while, and choose *not* to use your greatest asset. If you're known to be book-smart, let people see you being silly and playing around too: if you can goof off and STILL get great results from your work, that speaks volumes about your abilities. (Note: this works best if you do it only in front of your peers, not your teacher / boss...)

If you're always groomed to within an inch of your life, hang out with your friends occasionally with a baseball cap and sweats on. Because you CAN.

Why make an effort when you're naturally stunning? (The envy you get from other girls is the downside of being a Princess, although it's kind of fun, too.)

You'll notice that models and movie stars often do this kind of subtle gloating about what they can get away with. They love telling interviewers how they never do anything special with their skin or hair – the implication being that they look gorgeous with no effort whatsoever. (The best / most ridiculous line I've heard: "I never go to the hairdresser, I just hack away at it myself.") Talking about how they pig out on junk food all the time, but "never do any exercise" (yeah, right) sets them apart from the rest of the population, who couldn't eat like that without going for a workout to make up for it. Claiming to be lazy and greedy, yet still somehow managing to look incredible – these girls have got the handicap principle down to a T. (Unfortunately some still struggle to get the hang of the humblebrag: "Oh, at school they called me 'goggle eyes' because I had such HUGE baby blues, and 'bee-sting lips' because I always looked as if I'd been punched in the mouth!" or "It's so hard when you have a curvy, hourglass figure. I wish I was scrawny like everyone else so I could get clothes to look good on me...")

Done right, admitting a weakness can make people warm to you; we all love a successful beauty who admits she has insecurities like the rest of us. The problem is that this strategy only works if your target already thinks highly of you – if they believe you're awesome, your imperfections will merely seem cute and quirky. But if someone currently thinks you're a loser (I know, it sounds impossible), admitting those faults will merely confirm their suspicions. So don't attempt a cosy heart-to-heart with your boss in which you confess you've never had a head for figures...

BEING A LADY

"A lady is a woman who never shows her underwear unintentionally."
Lillian Day

It sounds very old-fashioned to talk about being a *lady*. It triggers an angry response in some women because they associate it with negative restrictions. To them, "ladylike" means women being controlled and forced to behave in a certain way while men are free to do as they please.

Thankfully these days girls can play sport, climb trees and get muddy like the boys without anyone criticising them for not being "feminine" (unless they're living in a particularly backward town). You're no less of a lady if you like tinkering with engines or playing rugby, or more of one if you wear pearls and a satin skirt. The Princess knows that the real business of being a lady is about keeping your cool when everyone else is getting into a flap, putting others at ease, and looking damn classy while you do it.

Social Graces

Assuming you've never been to finishing school, it's up to you to cultivate your own refinement and behave with poise. Don't you hate that awkward moment when you meet someone and don't know if you're going to hug, or kiss, or shake hands? Ugh, me too. One way to avoid it is to be the person who initiates contact. Just *decide* what level of proximity you want, and go for it: extend your hand to shake, or grab them for a hug (advancing slowly so they have time to see where you're going with it). With this method, you avoid that hesitant, wavering, "Do I step forward or smile from a distance" gawkiness.

You can add enthusiasm to casual encounters with acquaintances by adding "Nice to see you!" when you say hello, and "It was great talking to you" when you leave. When introducing two strangers, it's always best to give a little snippet of information to boost the small talk: "Rachel, this is Ben, he's studying psychology at Leeds university." It's also useful to remind friends of someone's name if they've only met once or twice before: "Jenny, you remember Paul, don't you? You met at my birthday party."

You might live in a small town where everybody chats to everyone else, but if you live in a city, this will be far less common (and pretty much labels you as a loony if you try it on public transport). Yet a little extra effort will make everyday interactions more warm and fuzzy: eye contact and AUDIBLY saying "Good morning" and "Thank you" when you're buying coffee makes all the difference to the person you're interacting with and leaves them with a bit of your Princess sparkle. If you're shy and have a hard time looking people right in the peepers, remind yourself to make a mental note of the person's eye colour.

You can also do your bit to encourage good manners in others: whatever your feelings on feminism versus chivalry, be courteous enough to accept any kind gestures presented to you. If a man opens a door, offers you his seat, or otherwise shows you a level of gallantry that isn't expected in the current generation, please smile sweetly at him, say "Thank you" and allow him the great favour of doing something nice for you. If you refuse, then you may be the reason that man decides to give up on gentlemanly gestures and shoves me aside to get the last seat on the bus. It's the circle of life, ladies.

Telephone Etiquette

These days, everyone has a mobile phone; they're amazing inventions and they've revolutionised our lives, not least because internet access, apps and games mean you need never be bored in a waiting room.

However, some people take their technology dependence too far. Answering your phone when you're with someone has become so commonplace it barely raises an eyebrow. If you're in a group and you excuse yourself to take a call, you're still within the realms of good manners. However, if you're alone with a friend and you ignore her in favour of your mobile, what is she supposed to do while you chat away? Stare into space? Use her own texts for entertainment? Curse your ill-breeding? Letting calls go to voicemail might FEEL impolite (and your friends will complain that you never pick up) but they'll see the benefit of this when they're with you and have your undivided attention. (It's easier to let the call go than to pick up and quickly try to explain that you can't talk right now, especially if this would hurt the caller's feelings.)

Some people don't even wait for a call or a text to come through – they start fiddling around during any lull in the conversation. This is BEYOND rude. When people do this, they're letting everyone in the vicinity know that they're so socially inept they need a little gadget to fill every second so they won't have to wrack their feeble brains for small talk.

Using a machine as a security blanket is not just bad-mannered, it's counterproductive. If you're on your own at a party and trying to look less awkward by texting, people who might have approached you will think "I won't disturb her right now while she's obviously in the middle of something." To avoid discouraging potential pals, put the phone away and busy yourself with pouring a drink or offering snacks around.

If your friends' smartphone addictions have got you sympathising with your parents' old "no phone calls at mealtimes" rule, try this: everyone places their handsets in the middle of the table and the first person who succumbs to the temptation to check their messages has to pay for dinner... Alternatively, send them a text saying "Pay attention to ME!" – at least you know they'll get the message.

We all know it's rude to put someone on speakerphone without telling them, but there are more subtle pitfalls of protocol. Whether you're telephoning someone in a professional or social setting, always find the info you need before you dial. It's so annoying to be stuck on a call with someone who says "Hang on..." and insists you wait on the line while they search through their computer for that address they promised to send you.

And when the conversation comes to a close, don't say "I've got to go" – it's sweeter to say "Well, I'd better let you go," as if that person has done *you* a favour by taking time out from her busy life to chat to you, rather than the other way round.

Elegant Words

I have a horrible habit of swearing in my head. My first reaction to any minor inconvenience – getting stuck behind a slow walker on a busy street, a dropped glove, an overly loud radio – is a silent curse. This is marginally better than letting the expletives loose on an unsuspecting world (I stopped saying words out loud years ago when I was working with children) but it's still a distinctly un-Princessy habit and I'm working on eliminating it altogether. It's become common for people to boast "I have such a potty mouth!" as if it's something to be proud of. Why would anyone aspire to this? It's not as if it takes any particular talent, considering we all have access to the same vocabulary. What exactly are they trying to prove?

People who swear frequently come across as:

a) Trying to be cool. Talk about sad! Grown adults need to leave this is in the playground where they found it.

b) Vocabularily-challenged. There are *other* words. Use them.

c) Classless. Sorry. There is just something really trashy about a constant stream of foul language.

And it *is* foul; it sounds ugly and aggressive. In my pre-Princess days I noticed that boys would sometimes apologise for using bad language in front of me, to which I would simper "Oh, don't worry, I swear all the time!"

Nowadays I find that if I don't use profanities, then men I'm with will notice this and either a) amend their own language to match mine, or b) apologise for their cussing. Some women find it sexist if a man apologises for swearing in front of them, but I love it. It suggests that they think I am a delicate lady of noble blood who cannot soil her ears with nasty words. (Which is absolutely true, of course.) Nobody feels cherished by some guy who is always using vile language around her; and if you think I'm being anti-feminist, I should stress that the observations above apply to men, too.

Of course, there are exceptions; sometimes a naughty word has a comic effect that wouldn't be the same with a kiddy-rated substitute. There's a difference between using certain phrases because they're funny, and making your everyday speech sound relentlessly grim. We're not crack whores, so why would we talk like them?

If you'd like people to stop treating your shell-like ears as sewers, lead by example and keep your words clean. If they don't get the hint, a wrinkled-up-bunny-nose-of-distaste or an elegant eyebrow raise should let them know that their bad language isn't acceptable in front of you. You're a LADY!

Words are powerful. If you use one swearword per year, people will realise that when YOU bring out the obscenities, you mean business (and they'd better run for cover). In the meantime, you can pepper your conversation with more imaginative and entertaining exclamations: "Zut alors!" "God Bless it!" and "A thousand curses!" won't get you thrown out of a tea party at Buckingham Palace.

Getting What You Want

If you've ever had a job at a call centre, as a waitress, or as a shop assistant, you'll have noticed that some people save up their rudeness especially for workers in the service industry. What's the betting they do this because it's literally the only time in their lives when they feel a heady surge of power?

Sometimes people believe they're far too busy and important to bother being pleasant to the people "under" them. What an anti-Princess move! Little do they know the reason that potential client never takes their calls is because they were rude to her secretary. Or that their order went astray purely because they yelled at the store clerk. Or that they might have had an upgrade if only they'd made a respectful enquiry instead of an entitled demand. They've forgotten the first rule of getting what you want: you catch more flies with honey than with vinegar. (And being nice to people only if you think they're "important" means that your attitude sucks.)

A Princess has beautiful manners no matter who she's dealing with. She would never stoop to being brusque when giving a burger order, or shouting at the barista who forgot her syrup shot. When we behave like true Princesses, people enjoy serving us, because they're more likely to get a sympathetic smile instead of a complaint about the long wait.

As well as being the decent way to behave, working your charm on people benefits you as well as them. It means you can get what you want *and* leave the other person happy they were able to do a favour for such a nice lady. (If you've ever worked in hospitality you'll know what a pleasure it is to give extra-special treatment to the people who deserve it.)

Always make polite requests rather than strident orders; that way it's less embarrassing if anyone dares to defy you. If you're in the wrong – say for example you've been stopped for speeding – it would make sense to be super-sweet and apologetic ("I'm sooo sorry, officer, I had no idea how fast I was going...") rather than aggressive or defiant ("I was only just over the limit! Why aren't you chasing real criminals?"). There's always a chance you could smooth-talk your way out of it. As Tallulah Bankhead put it: "I'll submit to wheedling, but never to bulldozing. The man doesn't live who can bludgeon me into a contract."

You have to find a way for people to be able to give you what you want without making them feel they've lost face. This could mean being so nice that they'll willingly bend the rules for you, offering them a compromise, or as a *very* last resort, bringing out the big guns and weeping pitifully. Another useful trick is to ask for something outrageous – when you get turned down, you could gaze at them with your most innocent expression and ask "Well, could I at least have..." and your associate will happily agree, thinking he has cleverly avoided having to comply with your crazy first request.

A note on crying: it might be *effective* when used on a loved one but they could end up feeling manipulated by your waterworks. Some of us are naturally prone to tears (I've been known to sob at commercials featuring especially sweet, rosy-cheeked old people) so it's annoying when someone assumes you're "putting it on" to get your own way. However, I can see why it's frustrating; if you're having a heated discussion and someone starts snivelling, all bets are off. Tears always outmanoeuvre logical arguments.

If you need to say something that your listener isn't going to like, be sure to serve it up in a sugar sandwich:

Sugar: "Julie, you've been working really hard and I want you to know that I appreciate the effort you've put in..."

Your message: "But you've been late three times this week and that's a problem. If you can't improve your timekeeping, I'll need to replace you with someone I can rely on."

Then another sprinkling of sugar: "Because even if you don't realise it, you're an important person to have around. If you're not here for the first twenty minutes of your shift, we can't get by without you. And I know that's because when you're here, you're one of the best workers."

If you need a favour from someone, make it easy for them to help you out. For instance, if your faithful buddy has agreed to help you wallpaper a room, it's really tedious for them if they arrive at your place and you say "Oh, so we have to go to the hardware store now, I've got to buy lining paper too. Which kind of paste do you think I should get?" You need to have everything prepared so they just walk in, start the work and then finish the day with the pizza and cold beer you've thoughtfully laid on. Make sure you offer a reward for a job well done, rather than making their favourite brownies then jumping them with "So, I was going to ask you a favour" as they take the first bite.

Even if the only answer you can possibly accept is a "Yes", try to make it sound as if you're offering a choice. For instance, tell your toddler he can have sandwiches in the shape of dinosaurs *or* bunny rabbits – with any luck he'll be so intrigued by the prospect of apparent autonomy in the matter that he'll forget he swore off sandwiches altogether yesterday...

And if in doubt, it's better to ask forgiveness than permission. If you make an urgent request and the person in authority says no, you're stuck. If you don't ask but go ahead and do it anyway, you may have to grovel afterwards, but at least you've done what you needed to do.

Being Gracious (Even When Things Go Wrong)

So what if everything is going awry and it's almost enough to send you flying off your pedestal into an enraged tantrum on the floor?

Even in situations where you're totally in the right and feel justified in getting angry, start out gently. If you go in with all guns blazing, it doesn't leave you any wiggle room and it makes people less inclined to do you any favours. It's far more effective to do your big-eyed fawn act and get them to sympathise with your point of view. Suppose a restaurant has screwed up your reservation and you're feeling suitably annoyed. Instead of unleashing a full hissy fit, convey that you're upset BUT you're a naturally sweet-natured person and will happily agree to the fantastic arrangement they're bound to come up with... a reservation tomorrow night with some bonus freebies, perhaps? Put the onus on them to fix the problem with a phrase like "How can we move forward with this?" rather than letting them shrug their shoulders and expect you to come up with a solution. If you start threatening them with official complaints and letters to their management, you've got them locked into self-preservation mode and they'll be thinking from their point of view ("How can I save my job and make this psycho go away?") rather than yours. If you start by being pleasant, you can always bring out the full force of your diva power when niceness has failed to get you what you want. In most cases, however, you won't need to do that.

Speaking in a low, even-toned voice goes a long way towards keeping things civil. Once people start yelling, order breaks down quickly – and you may find yourself accused of being "shrill" (still the number one "let's undermine women when they argue" word) or "hysterical" (second most popular). If you're the one who's cool and calm, your antagonist can't get away with this kind of nonsense.

Having social finesse means wanting the best resolution *for everyone* in every situation. So for instance, if you carefully ordered a chocolate cake with an inscription for your grandfather's birthday and ended up with a batch of pig-themed cupcakes, you'd be pretty mad. But while you would be in the right, is there any reason to drag the bakery through hell and back? In situations like this you're likely to be taking out your anger on the person with the least power (the store frontman) who probably wasn't even responsible for the mistake. Letting rip and giving staff the hairdryer treatment won't solve the problem, but it will humiliate them and quite possibly give an innocent person a terrible day at work. If you make the choice to be gracious and accept their apologies – perhaps even pointing out that you're very upset but still decent enough not to shoot the messenger – they'll probably not only give you a free cake, but free coffees for life and extra care with every future order. It will be a win-win situation, and YOU have the power to make it happen. (If someone who's made a serious booboo isn't adequately sorry, of course, you should totally sue them. Princesses may be exceptionally serene and polite, but they have a steely inner core.)

The same goes for any arguments. You know you're right, but there's no need to *crush* the poor soul who's been unfortunate enough to cross you. If you've made a killer point in the debate and they're lost for words, don't crow about it. End it with "Let's agree to disagree" and they'll be forever grateful for the lifeline you threw them. Just as shouting and making personal insults prove that you have no valid arguments, being charitable to your opponent instantly puts you on the high road.

Please, Thank You and Sorry: The Three Pillars of Civilisation

In junior school, if you said "Give me that!" your teacher would have reminded you sternly "*Please*" before handing it over. But somewhere between kindergarten and adulthood, some of the basics of good manners are often forgotten. Whether you're opening your birthday presents, being offered a cup of tea, or stepping through a door someone's holding open for you, saying "thank you" is vital. The older generation (who all grew up slavishly penning thank-you letters for the slightest thing) are shocked when their children or grandchildren don't bother to acknowledge a gift. Even if you don't write in your best handwriting on gilt-edged notelets (and this *is* the ideal scenario) a quick text or phone call is the very least you can do. Elderly people often worry that packages haven't arrived, because they can't think why else they would have heard nothing from the recipient. (The best advice I have for Grandma Princesses is to send your cheques unsigned – you might then find that your generosity gets a response.)

Big-hearted folk often take the time to acknowledge other people's birthdays even when they get no thanks for it (or reciprocal gifts and cards). If you're happy to do this, fine; your kindness doesn't have to depend on the feedback you get. But don't feel obliged to keep sending to your nephew if his lack of response is starting to make your blood boil – you'll only end up resenting him. It sounds churlish to say "people only get presents if they make a big enough fuss of them" but ultimately, if your gifts are appreciated, the recipients will let you know. Silence surely indicates that the pressies are unnecessary or unwanted, doesn't it? As a last-ditch attempt to squeeze some appropriate etiquette out of your ill-mannered beneficiary, you could always try sending them a gift of thank-you cards – including one addressed to you.

As they become a rarity, thank-you notes may be your secret weapon. A friend of mine got her entire deposit back when she moved out of her flat, despite there being some wear and tear. (Hardwood floors and a scrabbly-clawed dog – not the best combination.) However, she sent the building owner and the maintenance staff a thank-you letter when she left, and she credits this with her mysterious good fortune. Nice manners really can pull strings.

Some people are over-apologisers – they say sorry when they bump into an inanimate object, they beg forgiveness if they burst into tears during a horrible day, and they excuse themselves when someone else gets their name wrong. At the other end of the scale, there are the people who have a great deal of trouble with the word "sorry" and will do anything in their power to avoid saying it. ("Oops" doesn't cut it, I'm afraid.) You don't want to be a cringing wimp who assumes everything wrong is your fault, but there is power in taking responsibility for your actions. Apologising when you're in the wrong oils the wheels of society, and (bonus!) it makes you the grown-up in every situation. Apologising when the *other* person is in the wrong (you know it and they know it and they know you know it) makes your kindness positively cruel...

Princess Manners

My sister-in-law was once placed at the top table at a very upmarket "do", and naturally she remained standing along with the rest of the room while everyone arrived. She couldn't understand why nobody made a move to sit, until the man next to her hissed "You're the only woman at the top table – the rest of the room can't sit down until we sit down, and nobody at this table can sit down until you sit down, so SIT DOWN!" Next time she was in this position she remembered the lesson and smoothly led the room in taking her seat.

But who had bad manners? Not my sister-in-law, who was going by the usual etiquette of waiting for others to be seated first. It was far ruder of those who were experienced in posh protocol not to let her know the drill. A discreet "By the way, when we go in..." would have been far preferable to leaving it until she was shown up by not knowing "the rules". Good manners are about making other people comfortable, not highlighting lapses in etiquette to make yourself feel superior. A snob might say it's impolite to use the wrong fork for your fish; a Princess wouldn't dream of pointing out such a mistake. A real lady can make conversation with a queen or a beggar, and make both feel at ease.

The key to good manners can be summed up by putting the other person above yourself. So you pass the bread rolls around before taking one, top up your neighbour's glass before your own, and don't bore people with rambling anecdotes about yourself. When you can respond with impeccable composure to even the most uncivil oaf, you know that you're a real Princess.

BEING MYSTERIOUS

"Never trust a woman who tells you her real age. A woman who would tell you that would tell you anything." Oscar Wilde

A true Princess has an alluring, inscrutable air about her. Nobody needs to know all your business, and keeping some details discreetly to yourself makes you an intriguing enigma. Social networking has created an abundance of overshare, with many of us tippety-tapping out details of our lives which would have been unheard of in previous generations. We all need confidantes, but unless someone is very close to you, they're probably not interested in the minutiae of your life. For instance, food intolerances seem to have skyrocketed in the last few years and it's often the first thing I learn about a new acquaintance. "Hi, I'm Amy and I'm wheat intolerant." Why would anyone think this was their most fascinating feature?

When we're not yawning over the long-winded stories about the genius of someone's child, we're being grossed out from hearing specifics which belong firmly in the "Too Much Information" vault. Have you ever heard a guy say there's nothing sexier than a woman who talks openly about which foods make her gassy, or the way she bloats up when her period's due? Yeah, there's a reason for that.

It's not your job to provide people with gossip fodder. What would you gain from spilling the beans about your personal life? Nothing. What could you lose? Prestige, privacy, the delicious feeling of knowing a secret. A Princess has a sphinx-like smile and a little bit of feminine mystique which marks her out as different from the rest of the girls.

The Elusive Social Butterfly

Much as you love your friends, there's no reason to hang out with the same crowd all the time. Why not meet an old school pal for lunch, ask the girls from yoga to go for a drink, or join a local book club? Mixing with different groups means you never have to worry about falling out with someone and being left friendless and alone. When you miss an event and don't tell people what you're doing instead, you'll have them wondering what else you're up to: let them assume it's something exciting and glamorous. If you're turning down a date, the poor guy's imagination will be focused on you the whole time he's with the gang at the barbeque. What *could* she be doing?

Another fun trick is to do a circuit of a party being your usual gregarious, entertaining self, and then leave without saying goodbye to all the men who have basked in the warmth of your flirtatious charm. They'll spend the rest of the night saying "Hey, has anybody seen (Princess)? Where did (Princess) go?" You'll become the belle of the ball without even being there.

Keeping Your Private Details Private

Sometimes you really need to get something off your chest – but if you don't want it spread around, be careful who you confide in. In theory your best friend should be a safe bet, but unfortunately some people are completely incapable of keeping a secret. Actually, forget that; MOST people can't keep their mouths shut. It doesn't mean they're not a good friend in every other way; it just means you should think twice before telling them all about your visit to the STD clinic, who you have a crush on, or who you're trying to avoid inviting to your party. (As a side note, even a friend who's tight-lipped 99% of the time will probably share news with her boyfriend, so treat couples as a unit; if you tell one of them something, the other will end up knowing about it.)

You can roughly judge how trustworthy a person is by how many times they say: "Now don't tell anyone I told you this..." or "I'm not supposed to say anything, but..." Obviously if they tell you secrets, they'll tell YOUR secrets! I'm sure some of my casual acquaintances would be quite horrified at how much I know about their love lives / salaries / family feuds, due to the gossip of mutual friends.

If you're the one having a hard time handling confidential information, remember that you only need to let the cat out of the bag ONCE to get a reputation as a bigmouth forever. So not only will you have upset the friend whose secret you told, but you'll never again be the first to know about the latest scandal.

It's also worth taking into account that people are more closely linked these days, so even if you confide in someone who's totally outside of your usual circle – say, your cousin on the other side of the country – she might have local connections you don't even know about. One of my colleagues was excited about being pregnant but couldn't say anything at work, so she told a geographically-distant pal – who promptly congratulated her on Facebook, letting the entire world know her news. If it's a really important secret, you can't afford to tell ANYBODY.

Now, here's a controversial piece of advice I'm only giving because I've seen such disastrous results from people being 100% honest. If you're ever in the position of knowing something bad about your friend's boyfriend – say for instance he's cheating on her – think very carefully before you tell her. It might seem like the right thing to do, but more often than not, it will cause a rift in your friendship. We all know the first break-up never "takes", which is why you should also never let slip what you really think of someone's recent ex, no matter how much they claim to hate them now. If your friend stays with the cheater despite his misdemeanours, you're almost guaranteed she'll never speak to you again. (Assuming theirs is a serious relationship, not a 2-week fling.) Reasoning that *you'd* want to know in her position doesn't take into account the strong pull of denial; for some, ignorance really is bliss. Keeping your lips zipped and feigning ignorance if the truth ever comes out is less honest (and will make you feel terribly guilty) but it will probably save your friendship in the long run.

Talking about Work

If you love your job and enjoy talking about it, that's great. It's refreshing (and rare) to meet people who are bursting with joy at the thought of Monday morning. For most people, work is a mixed bag, and for some it's misery. I somehow manage to meet lots of people who take my polite interest in what they do for a living as a cue to tell me every boring detail about their bitchy assistant, the 3-year training programme they're on, or why they hate their boss (complete with a blow-by-blow account of every stupid thing said boss has done in the last six months). It can get dull for people if you talk a lot about a workplace they have no connection with, so when you're chatting about your job try to keep the details light and frothy rather than in-depth and dreary. As well as potentially boring them, if people know exactly where you are and what you do all day, any fascination you held for them is quickly eroded. If you have an intriguing-sounding job, there's no need to disillusion people with tedious details of the drudgery that's actually involved.

When your career is high-powered and exciting, it might be tempting to toot your own horn and let everyone know what a big shot you are. But as we know, bragging is never attractive, and it may even intimidate men (or other potential friends) who could feel inadequate in comparison. Without downplaying your achievements like the poster girl for low self-esteem, use a little finesse in social situations; a touch of modesty goes a long way in the sophistication stakes. You can be non-specific, eg "Yes, I work in the media / construction / medicine" (when in reality you're a hotshot journalist / architect / brain surgeon). When that new man or friend finds out later that you're actually kind of a big deal, they'll be impressed with your well-mannered lack of boasting.

If you're dating a colleague, keep the mood upbeat with something like "Oh, I'm not in work mode right now... have you tried the piña coladas here?" – otherwise you'll become one of those boring couples who spend candlelit dinners talking about your workmates, basically inviting them along with you.

How's Your Love Life?

When people enquire "How's your love life?" it's acceptable (if not essential) to be discreet. You don't even have to answer; give them a cat-like smirk (purring optional). Otherwise, "Great, thanks!" is an airily cheerful answer which lets them know it's not up for discussion. If they persist (and they will), gently evade with a wink: "That's for me to know and you *not* to find out!" or "Ooh, I really can't talk about it right now!"

If the questioner knows *who* you're dating but not the exact nature of the relationship, you don't need it getting back to the guy that you've been talking about him. Either gushing about how wonderful he is *or* sounding lukewarm could bounce back on you in a negative way, but if all you've said is "Great!" then you're fine.

If a man is doing the asking, tell him: "I never talk about men with other men, it's bad manners." That way he still knows nothing about who else you might be seeing – and he also knows that if he's added to the rotation, you won't be giving detailed reports all over town. No man wants to think that his girl-friend might be analysing their dates with her male friends. (Or gal pals, for that matter.)

If your attached friends are bugging you about being single (favourite accusation: "You're too picky!") turn it around on them. "Do *you* know any gorgeous single men I could meet?" (This could backfire if they're keen to set you up and their idea of "gorgeous" is vastly different from yours. And it will be.) Alternatively, be super-sweet and tell them you're waiting for your ideal partner "just like you did". (It won't work if you snigger at this point.)

Answering the Question You Want to Answer

It can feel quite confrontational to have questions fired at you, but remember the ball's in your court and you can respond any way you want to. Politicians are masters of not giving a straight answer to what they've been asked. The classic technique they use is known as "bridging" and it's taught in media training to help people take control of press interviews; note how celebrities direct questions away from their personal lives and back onto the movie they're promoting.

Essentially, you choose which part of the question you want to focus on – even if it's only one word – and you centre your reply around it. This takes the conversation in an entirely new direction, making it harder for anyone to continue their original line of interrogation. For example, if someone asked you "How long are you planning to live with your parents after graduation?" You could pick up on the word "planning" and run with it. "Planning? You know I'm not a planning person! I'm all about flying-by-the-seat-of-my-pants spontaneity, ha ha!" If you're going for the full-on politician answer, say whatever you want to say, regardless of how it fits in with the question: "Hey, when I graduate I'll have a degree, yay! I can't wait to get these exams over with." (Then swiftly change the subject). Top tip: phrases like "Well, the real issue here is…" or "I'm focusing on..." make the perfect "bridge" to something completely different.

A final suggestion from the celebrity-watching skill set is learning to use silence. Famous interviewer Michael Parkinson advises reporters to keep their mouths shut after the star has finished answering a question, in the hope that she'll babble on purely to fill the awkward silence. This ploy works both ways

– there's no reason why the celebrities shouldn't have spun it back on Parky. If you've replied and no further questions are forthcoming, it's not your job to fill the void; it's not even your "turn" to speak. Let the questioner do any gap-filling, or use the silence to change the subject to something *you're* interested in talking about.

Never Explain

So you're keeping all the juicy details to yourself, while giving away just enough to be fascinating. One more thing to remember is that you don't HAVE to tell anyone anything. Ronald Reagan said "If you're explaining, you're losing", and it's true that going into details about your own reasoning can sometimes feel an awful lot like defending yourself.

Some people just like snooping, but others have an agenda. Have you ever felt as if someone is leading you down a particular path of conversation? They start to ask about what kind of partner you're looking for, then suddenly you're being quizzed about whether you'd ever date someone older / younger / with different religious beliefs, and being chastised if your views don't fit in with those of your questioner. It's as if they've tricked you into what seems like small talk before catching you out and verbally slamming you against the wall for daring to have your own opinions. So why waste time having these conversations?

Explaining yourself leads to more explaining. Using a brief, simple answer and shifting onto a different topic is actually more effective than attempting to reply in a defensive, elaborate way. It stops people short and can even unnerve them a little if they're expecting you to justify your thought process. It's the opposite of "fighting back" with your words and getting drawn into an argument and is therefore the epitome of Princess-like Zen.

Why?

When people ask you awkward or probing questions that you don't want to answer, you can deflect them with a single word: "Why?" This points out in a subtle way that their prying is not considered well-mannered. (They already know this of course – which is why they often throw in "If you don't mind me asking...") They now have to come up with a polite-sounding reason for their curiosity, and even if they manage this feat, you can still leave the question unanswered and float away. For instance:

Rude person: "So why did you split up with your last boyfriend?"
You: "Why?"
RP: "Um... I was interested to know what happened between the two of you."
You: "Oh."

End of conversation...

It works for enquiries about your finances, your marital status, potential children, and pretty much anything else you can think of. Alternatively, a coquettish "I can't tell you that, it's a trade secret" also works for any intrusive question.

Off-limits to Everyone But Your Closest Confidante

- Your love life. Good or bad, it could reach the ears of the wrong person. You don't need to be the hot gossip, even if you like the idea of being the centre of attention. And NOBODY needs to know about your sex life or what kind of contraception you use.
- Your health. This includes the details of your menstrual cycle and what you weigh. If you need to take time off work, or use medication, it's nobody's business. Tell them the pills are painkillers for your broken nail or top-ups for your inner supply of awesome.
- Your finances. I'm stunned at how many people think it's fine to ask what someone earns, how much they paid for their home, or what they have in savings. In the past I've accidentally blurted out details of my wages because I was so taken aback at being asked. To avoid getting caught out like this, prepare for questions with a stock answer like: "I'm sorry, but I never discuss my personal finances." If they want to know about house prices in your area or average salaries in your industry, they can find out online.
- Anything else you don't feel like sharing.

SOCIAL NETWORKING

"Every morning we are born again. What we do today is what matters most."
Buddha

We all have at least one mode of social networking, right? Whether you use it for chatting, dating, sharing photos, promoting your political views or building your own business, you have a web page somewhere with your name and face displayed on it. This online representation shapes people's impressions of you; even if they've met you in person, they might be surprised at how different you seem when you're at a keyboard.

Your online presence is a good way to gauge what kind of aura you're projecting into the world. Do all of your friends know exactly what you're doing, 24/7? If so, you might want to dial it back a bit. If you log every location you visit and post pictures of every meal you eat or person you hang out with for five minutes, how much mystery can there be? Life online is often deceptive – the general rule is that we all think everyone else is having a much better time than we are. But we're in control of the information we post, so those people whose lives seem to be a constant whirl of parties and exotic holidays have chosen their words and pictures carefully.

Some sites have a history that goes back FOREVER. If you don't want something made public to the world, don't post it online, even if you're on a private message board and you have a secret username – IP addresses can be traced and once it's out there, it's out of your control. It's no good just deleting stuff – it will remain in a cache for some time, and anyone can download pictures or take a screenshot of what you've added. The internet never forgets...

Your Privacy

Firstly, who has access to your page? Most sites have various degrees of privacy settings: use them. It's risky leaving everything open for the whole world, whether it's alerting strangers to a party at your place or letting slip that you've popped out for a coffee while you're meant to be home sick. Not to mention the way "journalism" has now come to mean "trawling social networking sites for gossip". Reporters wait like salivating dogs to pounce on famous people saying stupid things online. If you suddenly find yourself in the public eye because you left a nightclub at the same time as Prince Harry, everything you've ever posted will be up for media scrutiny.

Some people want as many followers or friends as possible, whether they know them or not. This can be a fun way to "meet" people; it can also be a way of attracting creeps who won't stop messaging you. As a rule of thumb, it's never a good idea to be "friends" with your boss or elderly relatives. You may not be able to avoid your parents following you: depending on how laid-back they are, this could potentially cramp your style as you self-censor to avoid getting horrified phone calls about your lifestyle. If someone really wants to connect and it would be too rude to ignore them, you can choose settings to reflect the little you want to reveal to them. If this isn't possible, I find that acting clueless about friend requests is pretty useful as a stalling technique. "But when did you send me that? Ooh, I'm going to have to get better at navigating my page..."

Being a Little Ray of Sunshine in a Dreary World

Some people spend most of their time online WHINGING. Please don't do this. If you saw a guy tweeting "So bored..." or "My life sucks" it's unlikely that you'd think "Wow, he sounds fun, I must get to know him." So why would *you* do it? Entitled griping (barista spelled your name wrong on your mocha, your phone battery dies sooo quickly) just makes you ripe for ridicule. Why not appreciate the fact that you live with riches unimaginable for large portions of the world? (For starters, you have access to the internet.)

We all go online to vent sometimes, but being positive in your messages makes you feel better. (It's not as if it's any fun to scroll down over the past and see all the times you were miserable.) Negativity will only bring you down, so why not try posting something uplifting? Funny animal videos are always preferable to moaning that you hate your noisy neighbours.

I've noticed a lot of girls on Twitter are weirdly aggressive – they describe how they're psychotic and hostile to everyone, don't tolerate a-holes and they don't care if you like it or not. Maybe they think it makes them look tough, but to me it suggests they must be *expecting* lots of hate because that's what they're used to; this doesn't do wonders for their prestige.

One more tip: don't make your permanent username something which is dependent on circumstances: we all know a "hisgirlforever" who abandoned her account when they broke up. Why would you need to name yourself in relation to another person, anyway? Aren't you enough by yourself?

Don't Be an Open Book

With websites for every aspect of our personalities, lots of people are addicted to answering questions about themselves and documenting every day of their lives. (My theory is that it makes us feel like celebrities, who have long enjoyed the ego-stroking experience of being asked their opinions on everything.) Why not buck the trend and be like one of those A-listers who rarely speaks out? That way, it'll be an event when you do.

When we use the internet as a confessional and let all our most intimate thoughts gush out, it's a sure sign that we've lost the art of being enigmatic. Some people make a half-hearted attempt to be discreet by posting cryptic messages aimed at some nameless unfortunate who no doubt knows who he is: "I don't even understand why I miss you" or "You don't know the hell you're putting me through..." They also use little teasers to inspire interest in their social lives: "Some of my friends are so annoying!" or "You never know who you can trust..."

Vague hints that clearly invite further questions often pop up on lists of the most hated online habits, so it's safe to say that attempting to bait the morbidly curious isn't a cute way of expressing yourself. Yet lots of people love to add a bit of melodrama to the day by bringing their private issues into a public arena.

Calling people bitches, hoes, or any other names is never necessary and it makes YOU look bad. Scientists tell us that if you're the bearer of bad news about someone – for example, "Katie's a slut!" – anyone you tell will unconsciously associate you with the news. So really it's best just to talk about how sweet everyone is; it makes you look adorable, and nobody will be able to criticise you without looking like total scum. As Audrey Hepburn said, "You can tell more about a person by what he says about others than you can by what others say about him."

Nor is there any need to draw attention to your own shortcomings: "I wish I could be pretty" or "I wish I had bigger boobs." While sometimes it might be genuine low self-esteem (attractive!) it's often a transparent attempt to get people to exclaim at your actual loveliness. I know someone who is stunning and often posts pictures of herself with the caption "Looking rough today!" As a compliment-hook, it's as obvious as it is annoying.

Lastly, I'm not a big fan of instant messaging: it can give the impression that you have nothing better to do than sit by your computer waiting for the next message to pop up. Princesses are too busy for such things!

Staying Classy

When you have a boyfriend, the temptation to sing it from the rooftops can be overwhelming. Let him take the lead in going public with your relationship: any pictures of the two of you or changes of relationship status should all come from him first. He may want to plaster your page with soppy love notes; this is fine, but there's no need to turn it into a public smoochfest. Obviously, you don't have to leave him hanging if he's initiating the romantic sweet nothings – but I've noticed it's more often the female partner who starts writing "Luv you so much Snooki Bear mwah mwah" on her boyfriend's page. It's a way of staking your territory, which is exactly why you should hold back and let him do any chasing that needs to be done. Let him be the one to write "I love this pic!" next to a photo of the two of you. You may believe other women will back off when they see (from your constant comments on everything he does) that he's "taken" – but they'll also note that you reek of desperation while he's relatively indifferent to you. Not a good look.

We all know a couple who write lovey-dovey messages to each other on an open forum; call me a cynic, but it always makes me doubt how close they really are. (If you're in the same room, you can say it in person...) Why make your conversations visible to the world when you have the option to keep them hidden? Think before you make all your friends witness messages such as "Mmmm I can't wait to kiss you tomorrow!" There's nothing wrong with wanting to tell people how happy you are, but constant protestations of love, photos of the two of you snogging and updates such as "Having such a romantic weekend away" belie the intimate nature of relationships and look like an attempt to convince yourselves that you're a passionate couple. (I'll make an exception for photos where people are kissing but trying to look at the camera at the same time, because they always make me laugh.)

Your Pictures

Ideally, you'll have a ton of pictures of yourself hanging out in interesting places, looking great and having fun. They all add to the persona you've created – that of a Princess who leads a fascinating life, knows a bunch of smiley happy people and always has a fab time. Let's avoid:

- Bathroom mirror selfies, especially if you're in your underwear or otherwise scantily-clad. You may want to show off your smokin' body, but this looks quite self-obsessed and tacky.
- On a similar theme, holiday snaps of you in a teeny weeny bikini. (I'm talking about those microscopic swimsuits that leave nothing to the imagination, not regular beachwear.) Think about who's going to see these pictures: are you online friends with your work colleagues / old school friends / boyfriend's buddies? If you wouldn't be happy parading about in front of them in your underwear, why would you let them see you on their phone or laptop? There's nothing to stop them from saving the photos to their own computer, and... ew.
- Duckface selfies. No. Just no.
- Drunk pictures where you look awful, but post them anyway because they're funny. (Oops, I am guilty of this. Sometimes the comedy value seems to outweigh the need for dignity.)
- Pictures of you *all over* some guy. You might think he's gorgeous now, but you'll cringe later.

If you get tagged in a friend's album and it's a horribly unflattering photo, you can either ask her to remove it, or quietly de-tag yourself. (It's also useful to set up your account so that you have to approve anything you're tagged in before it's allowed on your wall.) If you have lots of great pictures of yourself you want to show off, team up with a pal and share *each other's* finest moments – it looks slightly more modest than uploading all your own hot booty shots..

When it comes to the way you present yourself online, the acid test is: Can you imagine Grace Kelly doing it? If you can picture her saying "Dem hos betta watch out imma beat some ass tonite", then congratulations, you have a much better imagination than mine. Likewise, if you can't quite see her posting a snapshot of herself drunkenly pole-dancing, think twice about broadcasting *those* pictures to the world.

And Finally

There's no getting away from it – spending so much time cultivating a following and updating the world about ME ME ME is a little bit narcissistic. Maybe in future we'll be victims of a new world order in which we're all forced to "check in" online and describe what we're doing every minute of the day, photograph all our meals, etc. But while it's not mandatory, how about just enjoying the moment? When I go to a gig, I want to scream "Use your EYES!" at all the people who've paid for tickets so they can look through a viewfinder and then watch the footage on their phones later. If you're really present in the experience, you'll be focused on it, not tweeting about the fact that you're there and posting photos of yourself to prove it.

FEMININITY VERSUS FEMINISM

"Femininity is depicted as weakness, the sapping of strength, yet masculinity is so fragile that apparently even the slightest brush with the feminine destroys it." Gwen Sharp

In lots of ways, we ladies have never had it so good. If you're living in a country where education is a right and not a privilege, voting is such a non-event that you sometimes forget to do it, and you're able to earn a living and buy a home without getting a man's permission, you may wonder if we even need feminism any more. Haven't we got everything we ever wanted?

Well, not really. For one thing, not every nation offers women these privileges. No matter where you live there will probably be a gender pay gap, and women are objectified – and objectify themselves – in a million subtle ways. Little girls still listen to fairytales in which the king offers his daughter's hand in marriage as a prize. Grown women like to play a game in which they're the property of their father and men have to ask his permission to marry her. (Hmm, romantic or weird?) Naked pop stars claim that simply by acknowledging their sexuality, they're automatically empowering themselves.

If you're in any doubt that we have a long way to go, simply do an online search for "violence against women" to see a list of horrific problems causing suffering to women *today*: "honour" killings, female genital mutilation, "corrective" rape, and human trafficking are the tip of the iceberg.

Feminism

The official definition of feminist is a "person who advocates equal rights for women". Yet somehow it's become a dirty word, with women labelled "feminazis" for daring to speak up about issues that concern them, and all manner of celebrities saying "Ooh, no, I'm not a *feminist.*" (Even though they're earning their own money and enjoying the fact that they have more interesting prospects than buying a new duster. They ARE feminists, like it or not. And they need new dictionaries.) For goodness' sake, our epitome of ladylike poise Grace Kelly was proud to tell the world "I'm basically a feminist.

I think that women can do anything they decide to do" – and that was last freaking century.

It's not surprising that so many women are eager to distance themselves from the "F" word when it has such negative connotations; we don't want to alienate men, appear uptight, or be mistaken for the kind of woman who plaits her leg hair and would let her breasts swing down to her waist rather than wear a bra. (Widespread bra burning is a myth, by the way. This will be obvious to any female who has ever tried running down the stairs without one.) It's also fairly unhelpful when so-called "feminists" damage the cause by suggesting that women need extra help to do the same work as men – like the ministers who call for all-female shortlists for a particular job. Then there are the women who assume any slight against them is because of their gender – like when Miley Cyrus claimed that nobody called Elvis Presley a slut when he danced saucily "because he wasn't a girl". Apparently she's never heard of the huge controversy "Elvis the Pelvis" caused back in the 1950s.

But why are we so afraid to stand up and confess that we want equality with men? (The same pay for the same jobs, for instance. The ability to walk down the street without getting our bottoms pinched. Not being expected to do all the housework.) Is it such a dirty little secret that we can't admit it?

It's still common for a woman to be asked "What were you wearing?" if she's sexually assaulted, and the press occasionally laments the loss of a young man's promising future if he's convicted of such an offence. Porn is freely available and watched by schoolchildren. Young women finance their degrees by working in the sex trade; they brightly point out all the easy cash they can make by stripping and lap-dancing. Our idea of a badass heroine is one wrapped in skintight latex, and it's considered completely normal for a bikini-clad woman to prance around a suited-up man in a music video. Do we secretly believe that sexuality is the only currency we have?

We're living in a rape culture; the clue is when rape is a prevalent theme in jokes, song lyrics, movies and your daily newspaper. No wonder men think it's acceptable to make lewd comments to any female who walks past them on the street. Seriously, what is going through their heads? Can you imagine saying "Ooh, sexy!" to every man crossing your path, whether he was a shy 14-year-old or a father taking his kids out? Because apparently some men consider this perfectly acceptable behaviour towards women.

Are Men Afraid of Us?

It may not be very ladylike of me to point this out, so I'll whisper it: men do seem to be a little bit scared of us. They can't outsmart us. They're starting to have trouble out-earning us. They still haven't figured out a way to have babies without us (even though they're working on it.) If Freud thought women had penis envy, Erica Jong makes a good case for womb envy: "The only difference between men and women is that women are able to create new little human beings in their bodies while... doing everything men do." She has a point, doesn't she? There will be no true equality until men can match us in the ultimate power – giving birth. Some men love to boast that they can father children any time, while women have to get a move on. But while a 50-year old first-time father might have had a few more years of freedom, he also has far fewer years to see his children. Death is the ultimate "biological clock", after all.

Women were once kept at home to take care of the kids while being denied the chance to have a career, and to this day women still struggle to balance their ambitions with the desire to have a family. We're encouraged to hurriedly achieve all we can in the space between leaving school and all our eggs running out (we've been told for years that we need to get pregnant by the age of 35, although new research and the evidence of countless older mothers challenges this). As soon as we have babies we're expected to go back to work and outsource the job of bringing them up (and pay through the nose for it, too). Some women barely make enough money to cover childcare, but they continue to work in order to gain respect and not be "just" a mother. According to society's values, RAISING THE NEXT GENERATION is such an unimportant job that you could grab a random teenage girl having a gap year and get her to do it for you. (No offence to those of us who have worked in childcare, but isn't it a bit weird that an au pair or nanny is expected to provide the children with the same amount of love that their parents could offer them?) Raising babies has long been considered a thankless and menial chore, but perhaps we should start seeing our ability to create new life as the miracle that it is, instead of moaning that we're getting the fuzzy end of the lollipop.

Men and women both contribute to the treadmill of self-obsession which keeps ladies distracted from real issues; we're conditioned to seek approval for the way we look, and judge our value by how attractive men find us. Our habits of using hot wax to rip out our body hair and starving ourselves with trendy "detox" diets look relatively normal compared with some of the things we've done in the past – squeezing our internal organs with corsets, or mutilating our feet by binding them into dainty, husband-attracting miniatures. As writer Maxine Hong Kingston pointed out, "Perhaps women were once so dangerous they had to have their feet bound."

Thankfully there have always been some men who identify as feminists; they're the ones who have helped us get to the point we're at now. And by the way, I've *never* met a "man-hating" feminist, so I'm forced to accept that this is just a fictional character invented by the media.

Femininity

So, does being a Princess mean that you can't be a feminist? If we expect our dates to be chivalrous, it raises a moral dilemma: how is it "equal" to expect a man to pick up the tab, open the door and generally act like a glorified servant? Princesses don't expect men to be doormats, but watching the way they treat people gives us insight into their characters. If a man wants to buy you dinner, see you home safely, and give you his coat when you're shivering, it tells you he's a decent chap who's able to put your needs first. What's more, you're biologically wired to swoon. We have millions of years of instinct telling us that a man who can provide for us is super-sexy, and it's going to take more than a few decades of splitting the drinks bill to change that. Princesses never take advantage of a man's generosity, but we can still enjoy it. Hey, we have some way to go before women are treated with fairness, so we may as well get the perks as well as the problems.

Femininity isn't a fault. Yet as a society, we have a tendency to think that girly = bad and boyish = good. Girls are encouraged to leave the glittery fairy dolls aside and play with trucks, although boys aren't expected to make the same switch (and people get nervous if they do). But masculinity isn't "power" any more than femininity is "weakness". You don't have to become like a man in order to be strong, behave with intelligence, or gain success in your career.

Modern sexism is so insidious that many people don't even notice it. One young model I styled on a photo shoot told me she "should have been a boy" –

because she liked surfing and go-karting. One of my friends says she's glad her father raised her "like a boy" because it means that she now knows how to change a tyre and put up shelves. Isn't this being raised like... a competent human being? Would her brother say he'd been "raised like a girl" if his mother taught him the basics of cooking or showed him the best way to iron a shirt? Nope, he'd believe he was well-rounded and self-sufficient.

Equally silly is the idea that enjoying traditionally female stuff like making scented soaps, scrapbooking, or cooing over babies makes us "bad feminists". Imagine a man saying "Gosh, I'm such a bad men's rights activist, because I can't help liking beer and football." As if! We also need to avoid getting caught up in an obsession with "sisterhood" which means women are never allowed any conflict between them. Does anyone accuse men of betraying their "brotherhood" if two of them strongly disagree on a political point?

Being a feminist doesn't mean being vulgar and boorish so you can say you're "keeping up with the guys". The fact that so many girls do try to emulate men – drinking them under the table, swearing like troopers and pouring scorn on anything feminine with the words "Ew, I'm not a GIRLY girl!" hints that we still have some way to go in terms of *seeing ourselves* as equal. Quite often, female celebrities claim "If I were a guy, nobody would criticise me for being smart and assertive, but because I'm a woman, they call me a diva." Is it really true that nobody ever criticises men in power? What about Donald Trump or Kanye West? I can think of *tons* of males in the public eye whose egomaniac posturing gets them ridicule rather than a reputation as a "boss".

We're also told "Women get judged if they go out with younger men, but nobody bats an eyelid if an old guy goes out with a teenage girl." This myth has been shattered over and over again – one example that springs to mind is the horror and mirth expressed at the sight of Ronnie Wood with a series of bimbettes. The truth is, any large age gap draws attention.

The one area where the media really does give women a hard time is in reporting celebrity relationships: a single man in his forties is likely to be described as a stud enjoying commitment-free flings with glamorous ladies. A woman of the same age would be portrayed as a spinster who's had a string of "failed relationships" and can only hope to ensnare some guy and drag him down the aisle before she becomes too much of a wrinkled old crone.

What about the "sexual double standard" which means any woman who is (or just looks as if she might be) promiscuous will be called a whore? Does it still exist? In our current mainstream media, daring to criticise *any* aspect of a woman's behaviour will probably get you shot down with an accusation of "slut-shaming". (Which always seems a little illogical if someone merely comments that they don't like someone's (brief) outfit and everybody else jumps in with "Slut-shamer!" – doesn't it reveal more about *their* secret thoughts if nobody else had actually mentioned the S-word...?)

In real life, people are less politically correct and everyone has their own idea of what constitutes "healthy" sexuality. But while frat boys cling to the message that a guy who beds lots of women is a stud and his female counterpart is a hussy, they're forgetting that lots of girls will be equally judgemental towards the men of "easy virtue". Either having sex with lots of people is a good thing, or it isn't – there's no gender divide.

Ultimately, a person's sexuality is nobody's business but their own, and as we know, Princesses don't go around calling people names. But what if you know a girl who's widely considered a "tramp"? Perhaps she sends nude photos of herself to boys she barely knows, or gets sloppily drunk every time she goes out. It could be that she's desperate for love and acceptance, has self-esteem issues or problems with intimacy. Is it really going to make you feel morally superior to talk behind her back, when you could be helping her instead?

Conclusion

There are few things men can do which women can't (the only time I get penis envy is when there is a "peeing outside" situation and they can do it without squatting in the bushes). However, there are many things women can do which men can't (or won't.) We can wear feather boas and sparkly shoes, we can say "YAY!" and clap our hands when something good happens, we can bring the gym to a standstill if we let our hair flow free while we're running on a treadmill. To men, we are mysterious creatures with secrets they can never know.

Society as a whole downplays the power women have, because it's terrifying. People joke that women shouldn't be allowed to be air traffic controllers or rocket scientists or presidents because they're ruled by their hormones "once a month". This always makes me chuckle because it's fairly obvious that men are ruled by their hormones *all the time*. They can't look at an attractive lady without their thoughts getting all scrambled. A topless woman could bring Wall Street crashing down as slack-jawed men lose the ability to count. A lady at a Washington summit combining feminine wiles with a mind like a steel trap could change the world. No wonder some people prefer us to be entirely taken up with making sure our hair looks nice...

But even if they don't know it, men do want us to be their equals. Social reformer and abolitionist Frederick Douglass pointed out: "No man can put a chain about the ankle of his fellow man without at last finding the other end fastened about his own neck." How could men really be satisfied sharing the planet with a bunch of spineless, uneducated sexual servants as companions? When women are degraded, it degrades men too.

Some of us worry that we're not quite the right sort of feminist. Can you really call yourself that if you happen to like cooking and cleaning? Or if you work at home as a full-time mother? Or if you disagree with the "accepted feminist point of view" on any political debates? YES. Feminism is about being free to make your own choices. You might still shy away from using *that* word to describe yourself – but who benefits if you scoff at the tradition of women supporting each other? Our ancestors changed the world for us, and feminists continue to fight for our rights. I for one am proud to stand among them.

Part Three

The Social Princess

"People are like dirt. They can either nourish you and help you grow as a person or they can stunt your growth and make you wilt and die." Plato (attrib.)

THE PRINCESS AND HER FRIENDS

"It's the friends you can call up at 4 am that matter." Marlene Dietrich

Good friends make life worth living. They're the ones who tell you it's "his loss" when you get dumped, make you hysterical with giggles over something that seems totally unfunny to everyone else, and let you know when you've got your skirt tucked into your knickers (without uploading a picture to the internet first). You could get stuck at an airport together for hours and still find things to talk about – or feel equally comfortable sitting in silence. You might not see each other every day, but when you pick up the phone after months apart, you'll launch straight back into talking about who makes it onto your list of "ugly men I find inexplicably attractive", and it will be as if no time has passed at all.

Some friendships are short-lived and don't survive after you leave school and go your separate ways; others might start randomly at a bus stop and end up lasting a lifetime. Some people are so casual about the way they relate to their closest pals that a single argument is enough to ruin the entire relationship. What a waste! There will always be ups and downs (and probably a fight or two over boys) but really great friends are precious, so appreciate the good points rather than dwelling on every little thing your homegirls have ever done to annoy you.

With the right posse as your support system you can rule the world; celebrating each other's successes, giving pep talks when a member of the gang is on the verge of giving up, and inspiring each other with new ideas and different points of view.

Choosing Friends Wisely

It's said that you become the average of the five people you hang out with most often, so choose them carefully. Nothing good can flourish in a friendship group that focuses on picking people apart; if the chat tends to be on the malicious side, there's a high chance it will include *you* when your back's turned.

Some people might be funny, smart and entertaining, but they also make snide remarks to cut you down and are only friendly as long as you're useful to them. They might have a good *personality*, but their *character* stinks. You'll have noticed them in school; the kids with the highest number of friends weren't necessarily the nicest people in the class. They might have had a lot of charisma, or maybe they made fun of people to get a laugh (and everyone joined in to avoid becoming the joker's next victim). It's hard not to get drawn into that kind of behaviour when you see it "working" – those kids attracted quite an entourage. But true friendship isn't about impressing people, or motivating them with fear; no group of "fans" will ever equal just one good friend who really *gets* you.

The "NICE" Backlash

If you normally drink alcohol with your friends, try going sober one night. It would be reasonable to assume they would accept this without a murmur – what does it matter to them what you're drinking? But you'll be surprised at how many people are extremely eager to see you guzzling vodka. Now, boys you can understand – the poor saps think they've got a chance when you're tipsy. But girls? What's in it for them? They might complain that you're "no fun" unless you're drinking. (Thanks a bunch!) But gently peel back the layers, and someone will eventually confess: "You're making me feel bad." Yes, simply by not joining in with the boozing – without saying a word to condemn it – apparently you'll be tacitly showing your disapproval of it. Playing armchair psychologist for a moment, maybe this is why smokers / drug takers always want to share – "Go on, one won't hurt!" – because if they can get other people to indulge, they won't feel so guilty about their own unhealthy habits. (You'll also be astonished by how many people will get really angry if you *sip* a drink from a shot glass. Try it, it's hilarious.)

Similarly, being "nice" can sometimes aggravate people. Lots of friendships are based on complaining; there's a kind of unspoken agreement that we'll always be up for a good bitching session, because that's how we bond. We just love to moan about our lack of money, our crappy jobs, our colleagues, our bodies, our families, our hair, our boyfriends, our friends, and the bitchy shop assistant who sold us our mascara. Some people thrive on hearing your sob stories because it makes them feel better about the fact they're not happy with their own lives.

If you have nothing bad to say about anyone and refuse to join in with the "Woe is me, my life's a mess but it's all somebody else's fault" attitude, you're breaking the rules. It's easier to tell a whinging friend "Your boss is an idiot" rather than jolt her out of her comfortable little rut by challenging her with: "Well, if you're late three days in a row, of course he's going to yell at you." Being positive, taking responsibility for your own life and subtly suggesting that others might like to do the same is a Princess move... and it won't make you popular with the ordinary girls.

Being a Princess Surrounded by Bitches (aka "If I have something bad to say about you, I'll say it to your face...")

Everybody has at least one tactless friend; she's the one who'll observe that your new hairstyle makes you look like a 40-year-old newsreader, or that the tuna bake you made reminds her of cat food. She's not being nasty – it just doesn't occur to her that she could keep her thoughts to herself. Her insensitivity can be hurtful, but it's also useful, because you know she'll tell you the truth when everyone else is being diplomatic. We all need someone who'll be blunt enough to tell us that buttock-exposing hot pants are not our best look.

However, it's normally fairly obvious when a person is being deliberately obnoxious as opposed to cheerfully clueless. As Michelle Obama once observed, "We've come to the point where mean is a character trait that we laud. We mistake meanness with toughness." Recently I've noticed how many girls are proud to be known as "bitches". There can be a kind of power in reclaiming a word and using it yourself before it can be used against you; successful women often defend themselves against critics by saying "I know what I want and I know how to get it, does that make me a bitch?" Certainly not, and we should beware of how easily women can be *labelled* as a quick shortcut to putting them in their place. If every female boss is called names like "bitch", "prima donna" or "diva", it's a very gender-specific way of undermining them with no evidence for why they're apparently so incompetent.

On the other hand, some girls seem to think that treating people badly and gaining "haters" is somehow a fantastic thing and a source of pride. It's as if they believe that the more people they annoy, the more proof they'll have that everyone is just jealous of them.

There's also so much stock put in "being real" and telling people "I won't talk behind your back" that it's used to justify being incredibly rude. An example would be making fun of your friend's performance when she's acting in a local play, then when she gets upset, telling her: "Hey, I'm being honest with you. You wouldn't want me to be fake, would you?" Unlike the innocently thoughtless person who blurts out the first thing that comes into her head, this is deliberate nastiness. There's no merit to being "real" if it's an excuse to be hurtful. Whatever happened to "If you can't say something nice, don't say anything at all"?

We Princesses have to watch ourselves too – if you happen to know a lot of malicious people, it's easy to start thinking about them very scornfully and considering them beneath you. But if we do this, aren't we becoming just like them?

When You're the "Weird One"

A dynamic duo or a big tribe of pals is great, but pretty much any time you get *three* friends together, one will end up feeling left out. This may be completely unintentional – sometimes two people simply line up more naturally together if they have more in common or have been friends for longer. Unfortunately, it's sometimes deliberate – and will inevitably stem from somebody's insecurity. Every time I've ever been sidelined by a friend purposely leaving me out (talking about plans I'm not involved with, or creating in-jokes I'm not part of), they've later confessed it was because they felt that THEY would get left out otherwise. When someone is spiteful towards you, they're telling you plainly that they see you as a threat.

Of course, there's also the irresistible urge to compare notes and have a giggle at the life choices of your absent friends; as comedian Herb Shriner pointed out, "'Conversation' is when three women stand on the corner talking. 'Gossip' is when one of them leaves."

Everybody feels like the odd one out occasionally, and the more extraordinary you are, the more of a misfit you'll be when surrounded by people who are committed to being average. If your friends have mundane aspirations – a job where they can slack off as much as possible (because they don't care about the big picture), drunken oblivion every Friday night, and a couple of kids when they've run out of other ideas – they're going to think it's very strange if you reject this life plan and walk to the beat of your own drum. Staying in every night to practise your violin-playing in preparation for being a professional musician, volunteering instead of going for an alcohol-fuelled holiday in the sun, or appearing totally unruffled by your lack of boyfriend: this is all very bizarre to those deeply entrenched in being conventional.

When you befriend people who have a similar viewpoint to you, suddenly you'll find that you're fitting in much more comfortably. For some of us, this happens when we leave school and have a whole new world opened up to us. (Unfortunately for the teenage queen bees, scare-tactics and bullying don't work quite so well out there in real life.)

In the meantime, unless you conform to "normal" in every possible way (ugh) you're going to run into people who don't understand you. If you're gay, or like dressing in steampunk outfits, or have no interest in necking shots of whisky, certain people are going to find you so utterly perplexing and possibly threatening to their own tiny worldview, they'll have no choice but to constantly hassle you. You can either see this as an annoying attack on your character, or you can see it as an opportunity to educate them about all the many wondrous and varied ways of the world.

Drama Queens

It took me a long time to realise that certain people are not the unfortunate victims of all kinds of trouble and chaos. They create it. If you have a friend who is forever feuding with other people, is always fresh from a new disaster and likes nothing more than bending your ear about her troubles – trust me, she LIKES it that way.

People often brag about being "hot-tempered" or "fiery" when a more accurate description would be: "I stopped developing emotionally when I was a small child and therefore never learned to control my tantrums." I blame movies and soap operas: how often does the big screen offer us screaming rows with the dramatic smashing of wine glasses, and neighbours complaining about the noise? Almost every romance involves the couple confessing their love in a steamy embrace *in public*. It's not good enough to be amorous in the privacy of your own home – you need witnesses. (Preferably an entire train carriage of gawking rubberneckers.) Proposals are nothing without a restaurant full of applauding onlookers or someone filming the event. We're continually fed the idea that an exciting, passionate life means MAKING EVERYONE ELSE LOOK AT YOU.

So it's understandable that many people like being part of a real-life emotional scene – it makes them feel like superstars. Drama junkies enjoy misery. They'll ricochet from one bad relationship to the next, because they're addicted to the melodramatic quality of having those big public arguments with their partners on the street. They bad-mouth people on the internet to stir up trouble. They'll be the ones to tell you what your sister said behind your back – partly because they want to be at the very centre of "What's Going On". By actually creating the situation, they ensure they'll be the first to find out the gossip, which they'll then use as currency to attract hangers-on.

It can be entertaining to have a friend like this; boring weekends are livened up when she has a fight with her brother's girlfriend at a family wedding, sleeps with her boss, or begins a vendetta against her ex-best friend. The flipside is that your pal could just as easily turn against you one day. True to form, she'll create a big noisy fuss over nothing: a missed phone call, a perceived slight, a failure on your part to read her mind. It's all too tedious for words, and after a while you'll happily trade the "he said / she said" rubbish for time with your *nice* friends: evenings in which pleasant people have fun together. Remember them?

If you stick around you'll only end up just like her; sensitive to the nuance of every look, searching for the double meaning behind every innocuous remark, and second-guessing every throwaway comment. Don't do it to yourself – you'll have to live with the person you've become long after your friend has dropped you because you borrowed her dress and accidentally looked better in it than she does. You'll probably continue to hear news of your old buddy once in a while, because drama llamas are often the subject of gossip – and that's just the way they like it.

Introverts versus Extroverts

If you're introverted, you'll enjoy lots of time alone, with quiet days of reading or maybe meeting up with one friend for a chat. You value peace and privacy above all and people describe you as a good listener. On the other hand, if you're extroverted, you'll love getting out and about, meeting new people, having lots of laughs and chattering all night long. A weekend alone in a log cabin would be heaven for an introvert, a boring hell for the extrovert.

Most situations are tipped in favour of one group or another; an extrovert will find it difficult to get on with work quietly without talking, while an introvert may feel shy and nervous about socialising. Whether hanging out with people leaves you needing some alone time to recharge your batteries, or you thrive on company, there's no right or wrong. We're all different and we need both kinds of people. We need those who'll quietly study and write and develop art, and we need others who'll get things going, inspire people with their leadership skills, and perform to provide entertainment. We all have something unique to contribute, and when introverts and extroverts work together, we can create more than we could ever achieve by ourselves.

Friendships with Men vs Friendships with Women

Occasionally you'll meet a woman who doesn't have any female friends – she'll claim that she's a tomboy, she "thinks like a man" and "doesn't have anything in common with girls". If you've been the victim of bitchy behaviour, you might agree that men are sometimes easier to get along with. Yet it would be misogynistic to dismiss women altogether, as if girl-on-girl friendships are nothing but a seething mass of cattiness, jealousy and vicious rivalry. It's not as if men never have male "frenemies" – note the way guys will make fun of each other in front of women they're trying to impress, make spiteful comments about other men's physiques, and try to manipulate situations to their advantage.

Men's friendships with other men tend to be based on activities (playing sport, picking up chicks, drinking in bars) so when they want to get some emotion-based support, it's a woman they're going to come to. If they're not partnered-up, female buddies are ideal. But can men and women really just be friends? Ah, the age-old question! I used to hang out with lots of guys, and I would have said that yes, definitely they can be great friends. Fast forward a few years, and the answer is... more complex. While there are many males I respect and whose company I enjoy, they often fall by the wayside as they meet girlfriends and wives. Several will disappear for months, before re-emerging when they're newly single. You might argue they're bad friends for dropping their female pals, but I'd counter that this makes them better boyfriends to their partners; it's one thing to hang out with other women in a group, but if the old routine was to go out for dinner or drinks one-on-one, this cosy arrangement could cause difficulties.

I used to go to dinner à deux with my "platonic" male friends, thinking of it as no different from meals with my female buddies. I'd somewhat naively figured that, if *I* didn't have any romantic feelings towards the guy, and he didn't *appear* to like me that way, we were on the same page. However, one by one, every male friend I had would eventually "declare himself" and things were always awkward after I'd turned them down. (Some of them disappeared completely.) Since then, I've realised the universal truth of life: ALL YOUR MALE FRIENDS WANT TO HAVE SEX WITH YOU. There may be some exceptions, but it's a fair assumption that 95% of them – even if they don't have a full-blown crush on you and have no intention of ever making a move – wouldn't say no if you made a half-hearted attempt to seduce them. Of course, this isn't necessarily a bad thing – some of the best relationships start out as friendships. Getting to know each other first is a brilliant basis for romance, and works far better than picking up a random dude in a bar just because he's cute.

If you're gay, of course, men won't create the same issues (unless they're trying to "convert" you) but some women may be resistant to starting a friendship because they believe they're so irresistible you'll have no choice but to jump them. If you're straight and have a lesbian friend, don't feel obliged to keep pointedly referring to your heterosexuality – she knows.

It's really only in the last few generations that the idea of men and women being "friends" has become commonplace – in years gone by, the expectations were always about courtship and marriage. These days it's almost taboo to suggest that the sexual magnetism between males and females is so strong it can override friendship. Lots of couples are blasé about having opposite-sex buddies: it's trendy to be "totally cool" with your boyfriend going out for drinks with his old school pal (who just happens to be female), or for you to meet up with your male colleague and have a meal while you discuss a work project. I'm a little bit cynical, because I've heard so many stories about affairs that started as friendships before the lines got blurred. We can't erase millions of years of evolution in a few generations, and sex will always be a part – no matter how tiny – of the male / female dynamic. Stick to clear boundaries with your male amigos to avoid breaking their hearts and complicating your social life.

BEING A GRACIOUS GUEST OR HOSTESS

"I've learned that people will forget what you said, people will forget what you did, but people will never forget how you made them feel." Maya Angelou

Whether your current social life consists of hanging out with your sister, getting takeaway fried chicken with your buddies, or having weekly dinner parties, you can bring a little high society into the proceedings.

Being a Gracious Guest

If you're lucky, all you have to do as a guest is turn up and allow yourself to be waited on. It's always nice to offer to do the washing-up, and if it's a good friend's house you'll probably feel comfortable getting your own drink refills and curling up in an armchair. If you don't know the hosts well, it's best to hold back on taking your shoes and socks off and stretching out across the sofa, or helping yourself to anything. (Even with old friends, no matter how at home you feel, it's polite to ask before poking through the fridge for a snack.)

So, what makes you the kind of desirable guest who'll be in demand for the party season?

Going With the Flow

The best guests are the easy ones; they don't make lots of demands, try to control all the arrangements, or mess around with last-minute changes. So don't arrive half an hour early / late (unexpectedly bringing your brother because he didn't have anything else to do), object to the snacks on offer, and then try to convince everyone to forget going for a walk after lunch because you'd rather play a game. Complaints of any kind are out, so no disparaging comments about the quality of the food / entertainment / other guests (they're your host's friends too).

Let hosts know *beforehand* if you have strict dietary requirementsso they can be prepared; it's not your fault if you can't eat seafood or you're allergic to peanuts, but springing it on them at the last minute would be unnecessarily diva-like. (A good host will enquire about essential details they need to know, but if they don't ask, tell them anyway to be on the safe side.) If you don't trust them to understand what you mean by "vegan" or "gluten-free", you can always offer to bring your own meal. However, most hosts pride themselves on their ability to cater to their guests' needs, so make sure you give them plenty of warning and they'll probably be delighted to create a menu which suits you. DON'T keep quiet about something you can't eat and then pick at celery sticks all night – your hosts would be mortified that they'd failed to feed you properly (and nobody likes a martyr). If you do need to bring your own provisions, make sure everything's cooked and ready to eat; the host won't appreciate your crowding the kitchen or taking up gas rings on the stove.

Hostess Gifts

(Nobody ever talks about "host gifts" do they? Poor men don't get presents.) If you're invited to a relaxed Friday night DVD session, it's all right to show up empty-handed, although a bottle of wine never goes amiss. For anything more formal, it's a good idea to take a small gift. Flowers are lovely but they require your hosts to scramble for a vase just as they're receiving other guests. Why not go with a little potted plant such as a mini-orchid, or a bouquet of flowers which comes ready-packaged in water? If you grow your own produce, own livestock or go to a local farmers' market, something like a package of eggs (with a ribbon tied around it) or a jar of homemade jam would be charming.

Some hosts like to create a potluck meal, but if they insist they've got it covered and you don't need to bring anything, don't go against their wishes and bring a cheesecake because that's what you'd like to have for dessert. (Princesses are not control freaks.)

If you do bring booze or chocolates, emphasise to your hosts that the gifts are for *them* to enjoy, and they're under no obligation to serve them as part of the evening's offerings. Try to hide your disappointment when they say "OK then" and hide away those Belgian choccies you chose especially because you like them. (A note for hosts: it is considered de rigueur to serve up any edible gifts, rather than stashing them aside for a private pig-out later. Especially if the bottle of wine the guests brought for you is nicer than the one you'd already got...)

Don't Be Nosy

We all love the opportunity of having a poke around someone's house, checking out their taste in decor or seeing the new kitchen we've heard so much about. However, some people take this too far; when seated by their hosts in the living room, they start wandering around, saying "Can I see your bedroom?" and commenting on tidiness / cleanliness / the price of the furnishings. Non-compliments on a house are unnecessary and unwelcome; be respectful, and don't walk around picking things up and saying "What's this?" unless you want to be mistaken for an inquisitive 6-year-old.

Knowing When to Leave

It's important to recognise the signs that an event is drawing to a close, otherwise you risk that uncomfortable feeling when you look around at the end of the party and realise you're the only person still standing who doesn't live at that address. (I know this only because I'm a reformed straggler. What can I say? I like parties.)

At the end of the night, conversation will slow down and there may be some yawning. Instead of the relaxed slouching around they were doing earlier, hosts might be sitting upright, as if they're getting ready to stand up and see you out. If in doubt, go sooner rather than later – leave them wanting more.

If you can see your hosts wilting but other guests aren't picking up the hint, say to them "We'd better let (hosts) get to bed, we've been enjoying their excellent hospitality for long enough."

Thank-You Notes

Following a delightful soirée, write a little thank-you to your hostess on one of your prettiest notecards. Some people manage a text or email of thanks, but a handwritten letter posted the old-fashioned way puts you a cut above the average guest.

Being a Great Hostess

To make your house the kind of place people love to visit, remember that hospitality is making your guests feel at home, even when you wish they were...

The Art of the Invite

Be clear on what the social event is: will there be a meal? Just drinks? Snacks? Do you expect people to bring a bottle? Different groups of friends will have different routines and expectations. The last thing you want is ten hungry people showing up expecting dinner when all you're serving is cocktails.

You also need to be direct about timing: for some people, saying "Dinner party at 7:30" means that arriving any time before 8 pm would be to risk arriving when the hosts are still running around trying to find their bottle opener and place mats. On the other hand, I met one guy who insisted that an invitation worded like this would mean that food would be served at 7:30 on the dot, so guests should arrive at about 7:15. (Imagine the terror of having guests arrive fifteen minutes earlier than you expected!)

If you're hosting anything more formal than a barbecue where everyone's children and dogs are wandering in and out and it's open house from midday to midnight, you need to be ultra-specific. Something like "Arrive at 7:00 pm for dinner at 7:30." That way it doesn't matter if people are a bit late, and you can relax and serve drinks and nibbles in the meantime.

And if you have friends who are guaranteed to be abnormally early or late, feel free to adjust the invitations especially for their sense of timekeeping.

Social Graces

Take people's coats and hang them up; it always feels awkward if you arrive at someone's house and end up carrying your jacket around with you, sitting on it or slinging it over the back of your chair because you don't know where else to put it.

I've been to some homes where "shoes off at the door" is a compulsory rule. I understand that people want to keep their floors clean or protect the woodwork from stiletto heels, but it's nice to give people an option rather than an order. If you're tyrannical about your marble kitchen tiles, why not offer your guests some fluffy slippers? Not everyone will take you up on it, but those who do will instantly feel super-cosy.

Present the refreshments straightaway, and keep them coming – there's nothing worse than arriving at someone's home parched and either suffering in silence or feeling that you're being rude by asking for a drink. (Requesting a glass of water isn't impolite, but it always makes me feel as if I'm pointing out the inadequate hosting skills.)

Background music can help to create a suitably festive or laid-back atmosphere, but if you want to plan the evening's soundtrack you must keep your beady eye on the stereo, or guests might take it upon themselves to liven things up. If that means changing your carefully chosen classical chill-out to pounding hip hop, it will ruin the ambience you had in mind. Be sensitive to volume: if people are struggling to make conversation, it's MUCH too loud. This is my pet hate – you expect clubs and bars to be too noisy to do anything but dance, but if I'm in somebody's home, I don't want to be yelling or straining to hear what someone across the table is saying to me.

Guests might offer to help with the food, and sometimes an extra pair of hands is invaluable. However, if you *can* avoid it, do. When you have lots of random people bustling about in the kitchen it can make everything feel a bit chaotic, and guests should be able to relax and await the delicious feast you've provided. Also, if they help you to do the drying-up afterwards they'll put everything back in the wrong cupboards.

Use place cards to mix up your guests; it's boring if everyone sits in little blocks of friends they already know well, and it can make single people feel isolated if everyone else is in couples. (If you're a guest, make the effort to speak to someone new; it makes the evening much more interesting and you can always compare notes with your usual partners in crime later.)

If it's a cocktail party and you're expecting people to circulate rather than sit down (or you have more people than chairs) serve finger food and forget plates. It's impossible to hold a drink, a plate, *and* a fork while mingling, whereas a glass in one hand and a goats' cheese canapé in the other is manageable.

Chucking-Out Time

Some people are unaware of social cues, and will totally fail to pick up on your subtle body language as the evening winds down. (Unfortunately these people often turn out to be VERY "sensitive" when it comes to their own feelings.) With your impeccable Princess manners, you can gently take control of the situation without offending anyone.

If you stopped offering drinks half an hour ago and your guests are still wittering on, oblivious to the fact that you can barely stay awake, it's reasonable to say "Well, it's been absolutely lovely having you here, but I can hardly keep my eyes open! Would you mind if we called it a night?" and then get up and help them on with their coats.

For a daytime event, you could wrap up with: "It's been great to see you, but I'm afraid I've got some phone calls to make / chores to do / work to catch up on." If you know them well, you can simply say jokingly "I love you guys, but I need to throw you out now."

Sometimes guests will say "Well, I should get going" as a kind of test to see if you protest "Oh no, stay a bit longer!" or not. If they make noises about leaving but make absolutely no move to get off your irresistibly comfortable sofa, help them along by immediately rising out of your seat as you regretfully agree that all good things must come to an end, and you must do this again sometime.

To speed the parting guest, sometimes it helps to suggest getting up ("Would you like to see the new painting I've put in the back room?") because once people have left the relaxed and cosy lounge, it's easier to herd them to the front door. (In winter, turning the heating off might help too...)

If you have a friend who's chronically unaware that you may not want to spend 24 hours with her when she visits, you could avoid the problem by meeting outside of your home. That way, when dinner is over, you both go your separate ways. If you're meeting for lunch, you can always have something else planned for the afternoon; preferably something boring like a dentist appointment. (I have one friend who would simply invite herself along if I said I was going shopping with my mum.)

Take the Secret of Costs to Your Grave

There's a phenomenon I've noticed recently: people invite you to dinner and then bring up in conversation how expensive it was to make that particular meal. "These steaks were £7 apiece...", "This wine cost me £25 even with duty-free..." They may mean it to be casual conversation about the price of food these days, but as a guest, it's hard to know how to react. Are they bragging about how much money they can throw around, or are they expecting you to offer to pay for your meal? Either way, it's bad manners. I was once invited to dinner along with a few friends and the host made such a point of mentioning how much he'd spent on scallops that someone did offer to contribute some cash. They were turned down of course, but how embarrassing for that less-than-perfect host.

If a hosts talks about the money they spent to feed you, don't sweat it. I find in life generally, playing dumb and not "getting" hints is a very useful tool. If people want to say something crass, they have to actually say it, not beat around the bush and hope you'll do them a favour and jump in first. If they want you to pay for the meal they invited you to eat with them, they'll have to say that out loud...

The Pop-In

If you're an extrovert, you probably adore surprise visits and consider them an unexpected pleasure in an otherwise dull day. You and your friends might have a cosy arrangement of walking into each other's homes all the time, sharing the day's news and rummaging in each other's larders for snacks. See, it *sounds* lovely. I've come to the conclusion that I'm an awful, anti-social person, because I hate it when people drop by without calling first. Much as I like the idea of living in a sweet, communal area where people leave their doors unlocked and neighbours walk in saying "Anybody home?" I realise that in reality this would be my idea of hell. If I ever move to a neighbourhood where it's considered normal for people to come in and help themselves to stuff from the fridge, rest assured I'll be the weirdo who bolts her doors. Call me a rebel, but if I want to walk around in my own home naked I will, and I'd rather avoid getting nervous every time I hear footsteps outside.

It's different if people literally call in for 60 seconds because they were passing and wanted to return that book they'd borrowed. But in my experience, these visits rarely are "drop-ins"; they're more like "sit-ins", with you having to interrupt whatever you were doing to entertain your thoughtless friend. It's inconvenient if they turn up while you already have company – even if everyone has an attitude of "the more the merrier", your uninvited guest is still calling the shots and interfering with your existing plans. It's also irritating if they call round while you're in the middle of bathing the dog or stuffing mushrooms, but it's *unbearable* if they arrive when you're lying on a beanbag watching bad TV, because then there isn't an obvious "*this* is why I'm too busy to see you" excuse. Many people will assume that if you're doing "nothing", you'll be free to join in with whatever they've chosen for the day's entertainment – and how do you break it to them that they found you hanging out alone at home because that's exactly how you wanted to spend your day?

If you're brave, tell them you're not available right now, and "Maybe we could arrange another time to meet up?" You can remind them of your phone number, assure them you would love to see them, but "Now isn't a good time, sorry!"

If you're not quite bold enough to be that direct, you can *show* rather than tell them that drop-ins aren't a good idea. Yes, you might appear to be lazing around right now, but you definitely need the rest of the day free because you're very busy. In fact, you're on your way out right now. (Even if you actually have to get in your car and drive around the block, at least you got rid of them...) If all else fails, don't answer the door. It's simple training: arrive unannounced and you don't get to see me. Call first, and you do. It's all about boundaries, and sometimes Princesses have to be badass.

Needless to say, if you're the one thinking "Oh, we're right in Auntie Ethel's neighbourhood, she'd love it if we swung by," you need to re-acquaint yourself with a telephone, or at least keep your eyes peeled for signs of panic in your host and limit the visit to less than an hour.

General Rules about Social Events

"The test of good manners is to be patient with bad ones" Solomon ben Yehuda Ibn Gabiro

Social Excursions

When you're organising a get-together at the last minute, please don't be one of those annoying people who begins by saying: "What are you doing on Saturday / tonight / right now?" It puts people on the spot and is at best an unnecessary step in the conversation. If you ask your potential guest "What are you up to at the moment?" they have to either reply with an accurate description of what they're doing and why they're not currently available ("Um, I'm on my way to the cinema with my sister...") or they'll say, "Er, nothing. What's happening?" in which case they'll feel manipulated into agreeing to whatever plan you've cooked up.

Either way, your next sentence is going to be roughly the same: "Oh, I was wondering if you wanted to come over for dinner." In the first example, you already know they're busy because they just told you. In the second case, they could feel resentful because they've now committed to something without really being asked. It's far more polite to *start* the call with "Hey, I was wondering if you'd like to come over for dinner," so that potential guests can respond as they wish, with all the facts in.

If you have a friend who's forever saying "What are you doing / Are you free right now?" you can simply ignore the fact that she asked you a question, and reply "What's up?" thus forcing her to tell you her plans without confessing yours. (Devious, huh?) If her idea of fun is vastly different from yours, when she calls wanting to meet up and "do something" it might be a good idea to start asking "What did you have in mind?" before agreeing to join her.

Sometimes it's a mistake to let people know that you have no weekend plans beyond relaxing; you might find yourself a target for certain friends or colleagues asking you to drive them to the airport / come in to work on Saturday morning. Find out WHY they're curious about your plans before you confess that you have plenty of free time, or simply be evasively "crazy busy" whenever they ask.

If you have friends or family members who expect you to drop everything when they decide they want to see you, try to nip it in the bud by making firm plans in advance. "Hey, are we getting together around Christmas? Let's make a date now before our diaries fill up!"

Some people always feel the need to explain why they're available – "My friend cancelled, so I'm free this afternoon," or "I've got a few hours before my boyfriend finishes work, wanna hang?" They might think they're subtly drawing attention to how popular and in-demand they are, but it's more likely to make their friends feel like time-fillers.

Be sensitive in the way you invite people out; it's obvious to them if they were an afterthought. Whether it's a posh dinner party, a birthday bash, or a wedding, if it's been set in stone for ages but your distant friend gets a call at the last minute, it'll be clear that she was on your "cancellations" list. Similarly, if you organise a trip without inviting one of your friends and later ask them to join you with the words "a place has come up" it's an insulting way to let them know that someone dropped out and you still need to cover the cost of their ticket. And it should go without saying that if someone isn't invited to an event you're hosting / attending, it's horribly ill-mannered (and hurtful) to talk about it in front of them. You also (deservedly) risk them cheerfully inviting themselves; this might be gauche, but it pales in comparison to the thoughtlessness of letting them know about the shindig without including them.

Lastly, if you already have a venue in mind for dinner with your pals, be upfront about it. There's nothing more annoying than the person who says "So where do you want to go?" and then shoots down every suggestion until you hit on the one they've already picked out.

Gifts

It's a good idea to keep some non-perishable gifts such as candles or bath bombs in a drawer along with wrapping paper and a range of cards (generically pretty / jokey / cute) so you never get caught out when you've forgotten someone's birthday.

Social occasions often involve gift-giving, whether it's a festive season, an anniversary, or simply a polite gesture to the hosts. (If someone specifies "no gifts" at their birthday party, don't feel bound by convention to take one anyway – apart from anything else, you'll be showing up other guests who respected the rule.)

One vital point to remember is that once you've given someone a present, it's *theirs*. They can do whatever they like with it. You can't make them love that novelty tea cosy if their style is sleek minimalism, and you can't insist they keep it displayed prominently in their home.

Likewise if someone gives you a gift you're not keen on, don't feel obliged to keep it and bring it out every time they visit because you don't want to offend them. (If they're a regular visitor, you could show it off a couple of times before it goes AWOL forever.) If in doubt, give the unwanted item to someone who does like it, then if the original giver questions the missing frog-shaped vase or paisley lampshade, you can say "Oh, my uncle saw it and loved it so much, I gave it to him!" It might be considered rude not to keep a gift, but it's silly to keep something you don't like when some lucky person / charity shop could benefit from your re-gifting.

Lots of people have this funny little quirk where they think a gift they gave you still *sort of* belongs to them. I've heard more than one story about people "giving" friends items such as books, baby clothes or furniture and then months or years later asking for their return – too bad if the recipient had already passed them on (or worn them out). Life's too short to let your home get cluttered with other people's property and stuff you don't want, so be ruthless; you're not running a free storage facility.

Cancellations

In the 21st century, dropping out at the last minute has become commonplace; our "instant-gratification-24-hour-communication" society has turned us into a generation of flakes. Before mobile phones, if you were 30 minutes late you could easily find that your friend had gone home in disgust. These days, calling to say "I'll be there in 5!" basically traps the punctual person into waiting patiently because now *they're* the ones who would be rude to leave.

It's so easy to send a text saying "Don't think I'm gonna make it tonight, sorreeee!" We all do it; the plans we made so enthusiastically gradually turn into a dreaded chore as the date approaches. (Then there are the people who think "I'll say yes now, because I can always say no later." And the ones who just don't respond to invitations...)

So I will make this plea: if you have promised to go to something which now strikes you as a pretty poor substitute for a night in with a tub of ice cream and a Ryan Gosling movie, you have only two options:

1) Suck it up and go anyway. You might find that you get in the mood once you're there and end up having a fabulous time. If you're nervous because you're afraid nobody will talk to you at the party or you won't like the guy you've agreed to date, put your big girl panties on and do it anyway.

2) Tell the host honestly why you're not going. If it's a casual gathering, it's

totally OK to say "You know what? I've had such a tough week that all I want to do tonight is have a hot bath and be in bed by ten o'clock. Would you mind if we postponed?"

If it's a more formal arrangement which will mean severely disappointing your host (a long-awaited birthday celebration) or create a scramble to make up for your absence (a carefully-organised event with a seating plan) then you might have to refer to #1 again...

Use tact when bailing out on pre-scheduled treats; saying you can't come because you spent all your money at the shops yesterday implies that you didn't care enough about the existing invitation to keep it in mind.

You can often spot a potential cancellation far in advance, because the person will never sound THAT enthusiastic about your plans. They'll start furtively throwing hypothetical objections into the mix: "Of course I'm looking forward to seeing you, I just hope that the buses are running that day / it doesn't snow / I don't get another migraine..."

Would-be flakers are also very big on confirmations, saying "So I'll ring you next week to confirm," when you've *just* agreed on a date and time. They're the ones who say "So are you still coming over tomorrow?" because they expect everyone to be as capricious as they are when it comes to already-written-in-the-diary arrangements.

Why You Shouldn't Make Excuses

Basically, excuses always sound phony. Which is unfortunate if you really HAVE come down with a sudden stinking cold, because people will be justifiably cynical.

Examples of excuses which don't wash:

1) "I don't feel very well..."

The catch-all alibi: unfortunately, most of the time this vague, sappy excuse sounds feeble and unlikely. People don't get ill *that* often, unless they have a medical condition. Saying you're "sick" every other time your brother asks you to visit is going to sound a lot more flimsy than admitting you don't feel like driving for an hour on Friday night.

It might work if you have some audible symptoms (blocked nose / hacking cough etc) although these can also sound theatrically artificial, even when they're real. Painful periods might get you some sympathy but of course you'll need to keep track of when you last used your menstrual cycle as your reason for staying in...

2) "I didn't get the message in time..."

This also sounds fake, along with its cousins "I left my phone at home" and "I didn't hear you ringing." They're especially silly when used by people who are always surgically attached to their phones when you see them. (And "I tried calling you" or "I left a message" won't work when phones contain detailed call histories.)

If you don't want to do something, don't agree to it in the first place. The only time it really is acceptable to pull out at the last minute is when you've been bulldozed into something and you realise too late that you really shouldn't go. I'm thinking of situations like the "really cool party" in a warehouse that's been broken into by a friend of a friend, or the date with that guy who seemed quite normal online and then started texting you "Good morning darling" every day even though you've never met him. In situations like this, listening to your intuition is vital, so don't let anyone guilt you into going against your better judgement.

How to Say No

We all look forward to fun parties and events, but there will be times when you'd rather chew your own leg off than hang out with your work colleagues at the weekend or go to a sports event you couldn't care less about. Declining an invitation can open up a minefield – which is probably why so many people agree to everything and then drop out later with those feeble excuses.

Writer Jules Renard once said "The truly free man is the one who will turn down an invitation to dinner without giving an excuse." I would love to live in a utopian society where everyone was this liberated, but I can't see it happening anytime soon.

To turn someone down while still sounding airily casual, you need one simple sentence: "I already have plans." Some people might (rudely) demand to know what plans could possibly come between you and a birthday party for their cat (complete with a fish-shaped cake for Mrs Whiskers). Fob them off with a breezy "Ooh, I'd love to come if I could! I just can't squeeze it in... Sorry I can't chat for longer..."

It's fine to respond to a formal invitation with "X regrets she is unable to attend", but how to say "No, I don't fancy it, thanks," to your friend when she asks you to come shopping? As we've already seen, it may be hard to be honest but it's far better than making up an excuse, because it's unlikely that your story of urgent appointments elsewhere or sudden crippling food poisoning will be believed anyway. It's easier to be straight with good friends: "Sorry, I need some time to chill out on my own," is a perfectly acceptable response to an invitation. As long as you invest some of your valuable time with your buddies, they won't mind the odd refusal.

It's more challenging when people ask to come and see you; this is when you need to set your boundaries and make sure that you're in control of when they arrive and how long they spend with you (as I mentioned earlier, you may need some pressing errands to run if they outstay their welcome).

If you have very sociable pals but need plenty of "me time", offer them limited availability: tell them you're free after 5 pm (they don't need to know why you can't meet up *before* then).

I know someone who was put in a very tricky position when her (married) boss asked her to dinner to "talk about work" and said she could choose a date convenient for her (so no chance of wriggling out of it with "I'm busy every night... forever"). She wasn't feeling quite brave enough to point out that they could easily talk about work in his office with a coffee, so she did the next best thing: she deliberately "misunderstood". She pretended that she thought it was a group dinner for everyone in the (small) office; once the plan was made public the rather sleazy boss couldn't say "Actually, it was meant to be just the two of us" and a jolly group excursion was enjoyed by everyone!

This kind of response won't be appropriate in every situation, but it's worth remembering that playing the dumb fox can come in very useful at times...

MAKING CONVERSATION

"Silent women are seldom bores – it is the talkative ones who make one feel limp." Elinor Glyn

Conversation is an art which surprisingly few people have actually mastered. They think it means talking AT you with lots of anecdotes about that time they totally won at life, all the finer points of the argument they're having with their neighbour, or a little stand-up routine. Some dominate every social occasion until everyone in town knows the details of their colonic irrigation, and nobody else can get a word in edgeways.

At the other end of the scale we have the clams – no matter how hard you try to bring them out, they answer questions with as few words as possible and haven't quite got the hang of starting new dialogue. Shyness is usually the culprit; although there's nothing wrong with listening more than you speak, when you have confidence in your ability to make small talk over the hors d'oeuvres, socialising is less nerve-wracking and more fun.

Some people consider idle chit-chat to be far too superficial and silly for them to bother with, so they remain mute rather than engaging in pleasantries with the people on either side of them at the dinner table. It helps if you think of trivial conversation as a ramp leading to more interesting topics. Saying "Mmm, what delicious fresh peas," could open up a discussion about organic farming and the ethics of using pesticides; all you have to do is start it off.

Striking It Up

The skill of being a great conversationalist is not based on coming up with lots of great subjects in advance so you can impress your "audience" with all that knowledge and insight. It's about being able to strike up conversation anytime, anywhere, with anyone (and never boring them). After all, you never know when you're going to get stuck in a broken lift with a bunch of strangers.

To make it easier for the person you're talking to, ask open-ended questions ("What got you interested in playing the saxophone?") rather than closed questions which can be answered with one word ("How old were you when you started playing? Do you enjoy it?"). Try to avoid the phrase "So tell me..." unless you want to sound like a rookie TV presenter.

The biggest tip for sparkling repartee is the hook. Whatever your conversational partner says, there will be something you can catch hold of in your response. Suppose you're at a bar with your best friend and she's brought along a new buddy of hers. When you're left alone together because your pal is in the ladies' room, it can turn into an excruciating few minutes of silence if you're too shy to speak to each other. The obvious opening gambit would be "So how do you and (friend) know each other?" but this could easily be answered with "Dance class". Don't be put off by such a brief reply – it's enough to trigger your next response. "Do you dance a lot? It's a great way of keeping fit, isn't it? I've been going to that gym with a climbing wall..."

While it might feel more polite to focus on the other person and ask "What's your favourite kind of dance? How long have you been doing it?" this invites those dreaded one-word answers. Without blathering on about yourself too much, if there's a way to bring the conversation into an area where you can *volunteer information* (like your love of the gym) it's easier to make the conversation flow, and it feels more like give-and-take than an interrogation. Which brings me to:

Questions

"Just ask questions" is often advised for shrinking violets who worry they won't be able to think of anything to say. Appearing interested in the other person is far more ingratiating than telling them all about yourself, so concentrating on them works to some extent. Unfortunately I've come across quite a few people who must have taken this advice to heart, because they've bombarded me with a rapid-fire quiz. One guy who started casually chatting to me in a pub swiftly proceeded to ask me about my last relationship, why it ended, and how old I was, all in the first five minutes. Er – hello, boundaries?

Asking people a stream of personal questions puts them on the spot and makes them feel as if they're being interviewed. (If you're fairly belligerent in tone it makes your victim wonder if he's going to get his kneecaps shot off if he doesn't answer fast enough.) It's fine to ask something and then use it as a jumping-off point into further conversation; it's rude to simply move on to the next question on your list. Giving someone the third degree is not conversation – not least because it shows that you're more preoccupied with your own agenda than the answers they're giving.

Listening

We have two ears and only one mouth for a reason. Everyone feels validated when they're listened to, and you can become a more sensitive friend or partner by keeping tabs on what someone tells you about their likes and dislikes. Even casual acquaintances will be touched if you remember a detail about them some time later, because it shows that you cared enough to pay attention. The truth is, most people are so busy thinking up how they're going to reply, they tune out what the speaker is actually saying.

I like listening to people because I figure I can learn more that way. For instance, in a taxicab I know there's little chance of having a balanced conversation with the driver, because they like to *TALK*. So I let them – and I've heard all kinds of interesting things, like funny anecdotes about the craziest people they've driven around London.

Knowledge is power. The more you listen, the more information you'll gain and the better your judgement will be. For instance, on a date, the stories a guy tells you may give away more about his character than he thinks. For example, he might be funny and charming when he describes his dislike for his mother or the way he's been fired from every job he's ever had, but it's still a huge red flag.

Encouraging Noises

Some people listen in absolute silence, so if you're on the phone with them you keep wondering if you've been cut off. Others offer so much "encouragement" it can be quite overwhelming.

"So I got up this morning–"
"Mmm"
"And I thought I heard the postman–"
"Yeah"

"And it turned out I had a parcel–"
"Oooh"
"And it was this book I'd ordered–"
"Yep, yep..."

You really want to strike a balance between the two. If you're nodding and "yep-ing" and "mmm-ing" at the end of every sentence, it can make the speaker feel as if he's being hurried along.

Getting Everyone's Voice Heard

In a group situation, it's easy for people to get distracted and for the loudest person to get the biggest say in things. If you're interrupted, casually get back on track with "Where were we? Oh, yes, we were talking about..." If someone else gets cut off mid-sentence, I guarantee they'll appreciate it if you guide the group's attention back to them with "So, what happened after that?" Likewise, if someone starts talking and nobody is really listening, they'll love you forever if you're the one with eyes fixed on them, eager to hear the rest of what they're saying.

Generally, pathological interrupters don't actually realise they're cutting you off – as far as they're concerned, they're enthusiastically joining in the conversation. (And they not-so-secretly believe that what they have to say is more valid and important than what you have to say.) Go ahead and assert yourself: "Excuse me, I haven't finished," or "Please don't interrupt." Alternatively, allow them to speak and then when they're done, simply pick up where you left off. (A cold stare wouldn't go amiss.) If this doesn't get the hint across, the rude option would be to just carry on talking, raising your volume as necessary. The rude but silly method would be to retort "Oh, pardon me, did the middle of my sentence interrupt the beginning of yours?"

You have to see the funny side; I once went out for lunch with two loquacious ladies and if they both started a sentence at the same time, instead of saying "Oh, I'm sorry. Go on..." they would both continue to talk. The end result was that the two of them spoke simultaneously, I couldn't hear either of them, and they both heard their own thoughts spoken aloud but not the other person's. So we all might as well have stayed at home, really.

If you like being the life and soul of the party, make sure you let other people get a look-in; that way you'll be known for your social graces as well as your captivating stories.

When Someone Else is Boring

What happens when all that polite listening, gentle questioning and witty anecdote-telling is useless in the face of a monumental bore? Whether you're trapped at a party with a man who wants to impress you with his knowledge of military submarines, or your best friend hasn't quite got her ex out of her system yet, there will be times when you have no choice but to lend an ear and try not to zone out too visibly. Some people simply never stop speaking, which can bring listeners to "Kill me now!" levels of exasperation. The elderly, bless them, often fall into this category; perhaps when you're hard of hearing it's preferable to be the one talking rather than risk missing chunks of what the other person is saying. Be patient, and try not to scream.

Competitive busyness and tiredness are a modern-day addiction (I can't imagine coal miners going on and on about what a *hectic* day they'd had) and listening to your loved ones describe all the endless specifics of why they're so exhausted can be an awful bore. A simple "Why don't you go to bed then?" (in a sympathetic tone) could cut off their continuous droning.

If you're meeting a friend who always wants to fill you in on how swamped she is, you could gently redirect her to more interesting topics: "Oh, I'm sure we can take your mind off that stressful job with a few drinks. What have you been up to, aside from work?" If it gets really bad you might want to playfully ban all mention of the dreaded subject: "Oh, let's not talk about your mother-in-law, we're here to enjoy ourselves! Let's make our lunches a mother-in-law-free-zone."

Don't be too abrupt when transitioning into more intriguing matters; if your best friend has just outlined (at tedious length) the dream she had last night, she'll know you weren't really listening if you suddenly say "Ooh, did I tell you? I bought some new hair straighteners!" But if you reply with something relevant to her self-analysis, and THEN go on to mention your shopping trip, you'll bring the chat around to fun stuff without hurting her feelings. You smooth-talker, you.

You'll notice that some people expect you to listen very attentively when they go into detail about their day, but as soon as you dare to bring up your life, they suddenly get very distracted by the heat levels on the radiator, a cat passing by or the song on the radio. Don't worry, you're not boring, they're just ill-mannered.

Everyone's a Critic

Sadly, being cynical about something is seen as much cooler and more intellectual than being nakedly enthusiastic about it. Some people like to show how superior they are by criticising stuff, especially if it's popular with the masses. If you say you're going to Las Vegas, they say "Well, don't bother going to X hotel..." and if you mention that you've bought tickets for your favourite band, they throw in "Oh, they're *terrible* these days, you should have seen them ten years ago!" It's a pretty obnoxious way of telling everyone how fantastically cultured you are. If you really want to let someone know that you've already experienced something they're talking about, try to keep it positive: "Oh, I went there last year! It's amazing!"

Just as a Princess would never pour cold water on someone else's high spirits, she would never make a disparaging observation about the way they look. If somebody has a big birthmark on their face, thinning hair or raging eczema, they are well aware of this fact and drawing attention to it will be extremely unhelpful. Seriously, what's with all these people who think it's somehow socially acceptable to point out other's foibles? ("You've got a pimple on your chin / You've put on weight / you look a bit peaky, are you ill?") Even "Aw, you look tired!" is basically rudeness disguised as a thoughtful sign that you care, and it doesn't fool anybody.

Party Time

If you're in a position where you feel out of your element – say, at a big bash where you don't know many people – and you're not feeling confident enough to start chatting to strangers, you could use the trick of imagining that you're going to write the scene into a novel. That way you're paying attention to everything that's going on and people can sense you're engaged with the group rather than retreating into your own head. It also helps you to feel less shy, because you're objectively observing instead of focusing on your own nervousness.

Even the most confident people feel self-conscious when they walk into a room full of strangers. Don't wait for people to be friendly – show them how by breaking the ice yourself. Just one sentence ("Do you live locally?") will get the ball rolling.

Circulating means constantly interrupting other people's conversations. Sometimes you'll be gabbing away to someone when a friend arrives and naturally you squeal a greeting, give them a hug and start chatting. This can leave your original conversational partner out in the cold and they might timidly slink away. (If it's a creep, of course, you'll have no such luck.) To warmly include everyone, you can simply say to your freshly arrived friend "We were just talking about..." and then (bonus) you don't lose the thread of your existing interesting conversation.

Broadway actress Lisa Kirk put it succinctly: "A gossip is one who talks to you about others; a bore is one who talks to you about himself; and a brilliant conversationalist is one who talks to you about yourself." Surprisingly enough, other people might not be especially enthralled by your lengthy description of a football game or soap opera they haven't seen, or the many wonderful attributes of your new car / boyfriend / guinea pig, so be alert for signs of eyes glazing over. Without the dreaded "interview" technique, keep the spotlight on the person you're chatting with to leave them with the memory of a fantastic discussion (about themselves). You can still ask questions, but make them interested enquiries about the person's opinions rather than an interrogation about their private life: "What do you think of the latest *Star Wars* film, Dan?" rather than "So, Dan, how many girlfriends have you had?"

Final Tips

- If you're calling someone to ask a favour or give them bad news, it should be the first thing you say to them. If you go through the usual niceties of asking how they are and letting them prattle on, it makes it very awkward to break in with "So, um, I need to ask / tell you something..." (If it's somebody you don't often call, they'll already be silently wondering what you want.) Instead, START by saying "I'm calling to ask a favour / tell you I'm very sorry I can't make it to your baby's christening," and then after that, you can say "How *are* you, anyway?" That way, they know you're asking because you want to, not because you have to.

- Use people's names. If you overdo it you'll sound like a cheesy sales rep, but done right, it's very endearing. Most of us are terrible with names because we literally *don't listen* when we're being introduced – we're too concerned with the big moment when we get to say OUR name. Making an effort to listen and then using that person's name soon afterwards will cement it into your memory.

- Be clear who / what you're talking about. If you're chatting to a new person and you want to mention your boyfriend, don't just throw his name into conversation. "Billy loves the burgers at The Happy Grill." How are they supposed to know who Billy is? He could be your dog, your brother or your son! You only need to say "My boyfriend Billy..." once and then you can refer to him by name to your heart's content.

- For an introvert, bumping into a colleague on your daily commute is a nightmare – knowing that you're stuck for the next half hour can dry up even the smallest of small talk. If you're shy (or you know *they* are) you could graciously extricate yourself with something like "Well, I'll let you get on with your book / leave you in peace with your music," and then sit elsewhere.

- Focus your attention on the person you're speaking with. No matter how subtle you think you're being, they WILL notice if you start making furtive glances around the room to see who else is worth talking to.

- Avoid asking questions if the answers could backfire on you. For instance, everyone knows that you don't ask a woman "When are you due?" unless you know for a fact that she is indeed pregnant. Similarly, "Is this your mum?" could be embarrassing if the older-looking lady is actually your friend's sister, and an excited "Did you get the job?" answers itself when you realise that in some cases, no news is bad news.

TEACHING PEOPLE HOW TO TREAT YOU

"What do we live for, if it is not to make life less difficult for each other?"
George Eliot

If everybody in the world were selfless, kind-hearted and considerate, we could relax and assume that other people would always look out for our best interests. Unfortunately reality isn't that simple, and some people should really come with an instruction manual on how to deal with them. Well, here it is! Feel free to skip if everybody you know is angelic.

Most people are basically decent human beings. Your bossy officemate probably cries for joy when his team wins, and that bitchy girl who makes fun of you for knitting on your lunch break no doubt enjoys watching YouTube videos of cheeping ducklings just like you do. When someone treats you badly, it's not because they're evil. They just don't have the tools to feel good about themselves, and it has a knock-on effect on the way they relate to everyone else.

But knowing *why* someone is being a pain in the bum doesn't solve the problem of how to deal with them. They're still acting like naughty children: only seeing things from their own point of view and pushing the boundaries until you firmly draw a line in the sand.

Some people are in the unfortunate position of having "toxic" families – parents or siblings who are, in a word, horrible. I wish I could say that all problems can be worked out, people change, and everyone can live happily ever after, but generally this isn't the case. If you're living independently you have some freedom in how much time (if any) you spend with them, and you've probably devised coping strategies over the years to deal with their "funny little ways". Friends are slightly easier to handle because you're under no obligation to spend Christmas with them, but it can still be hard to separate yourself from demanding people and friendship groups. Part of growing up is learning to interpret people's behaviour and make wise judgements about whether someone is going through a bit of a difficult phase, or if they're forever doomed to be a waste of your time.

I'm Not Interested In Why You Don't Like Me

Expecting everyone you meet to treat you well because you're a nice person is like expecting a bull not to charge because you're vegetarian. There will always be people who don't like you, but when you love yourself and you're confident about your life choices, you worry far less about how others see you. Aristotle is often credited with the saying "There is only one way to avoid criticism: do nothing, say nothing, and be nothing." It actually comes from 19th century writer Elbert Hubbard, but it's such timeless wisdom, is sounds like something that could have been written by a chap born in 384 BC. Nobody who does anything interesting with their lives will be immune to criticism from wannabes – imagine if Taylor Swift or Kristen Stewart stopped working because of all the hate projected towards them.

When you're a Princess, you *lose interest* in people who treat you badly. This is a much more effective (and enjoyable) way to deal with them than the standard "get angry / confront them / try to force a change in their attitude" method. You're gone from their lives like a wisp of smoke, never to be seen again. Why would you hang out where you're not appreciated? The fact somebody doesn't utterly adore you says nothing about you and everything about their poor taste. (Unless you've been un-Princessy of course...)

If a friend tries to manipulate her, a guy stands her up, or a family member constantly insults her, the Princess will be nowhere to be found when they want to get together – she has no time for that kind of nonsense. (She doesn't even have time to *tell* them she has no time for it.) Instead, she gravitates towards people and activities that make her feel good.

Rather than going to the mall with your frenemies (the theory being that if you're there, they can't talk about you) you could learn Spanish in preparation for your next trip abroad, or bake some cookies you won't have to share with people unworthy of their deliciousness. Instead of spending hours puzzling over why that guy still hasn't called, leave your phone at home and volunteer at the dog shelter. Why wait around for someone who doesn't treat you like royalty, when you could be cuddling puppies instead? Sometimes you just have to think "Kiss my tiara, honey!" and leave the losers behind while you concentrate on the fun things in life.

What if You're the Hater?

You might find yourself struggling with envious feelings when a new girl joins your group and you feel yourself being pushed out, or paling into insignificance next to someone so good-looking, witty, and accomplished. Unfortunately no matter who you are, there will always be *someone* who's prettier / more intelligent / funnier / younger / older than you. The trick is not comparing yourself with anyone, for that way madness lies.

Do your best to avoid letting resentment cloud the way you treat people. For instance, if you're feeling mediocre and worthless, you might find yourself lashing out at someone who seems to have everything you lack. Or you could be tempted to point out someone else's faults to distract from your own, but this is destructive AND pointless. If there's something you don't like about yourself, work towards changing it. Build yourself up instead of trying to level the playing field by tearing other people down.

There's a story about a teacher who wanted to show how damaging bullying can be: she gave each child a piece of paper which they screwed up, dirtied and threw around. Afterwards they smoothed out the rumpled sheets as much as they could. The teacher then said "Now tell the paper you're sorry." Nope, not going to undo the damage.

Apart from the obvious misery it causes, bullying people has another side effect: it makes you look inferior. If you're constantly making snarky comments, it's like wearing a big neon sign saying "I don't like myself... and I'm afraid that you're better than me, so I have to try to redress the balance." Just don't do it.

Types of Toxic People

"Love your enemy. But never forget: he is not your friend." Paulo Coelho

Users

There's a nice piece of playground name-calling for you! Unfortunately, this term is painfully accurate when it comes to describing some people. You might think that you're friends, but it's amazing how often this type will disappear from your life if you stop providing them with constant favours. You'll spot them easily because they rarely call without asking for something; they're breathtakingly unaware of how transparent this looks.

I used to babysit for a friend who had a toddler, but after a while I noticed she only called when she needed a sitter; when I became less available for work, she drifted away. This made me sad because she was fun and good company, but she evidently had no time for socialising unless I could do something for her.

Users are closely related to "spongers" – they're allergic to spending their own money, but they'll happily splash out if you're picking up the bill. They're the ones who always turn up at your house around mealtimes, don't bring their own sun cream on holiday but ask to "borrow" yours, and if you invite them to stay for the weekend, they'll still be there weeks later. (Why would they go home, when they can get free food, laundry service and wi-fi at your place?) Getting something for nothing is a constant point-scoring game for them.

It's easy to get rid of "friends" like this – just stop being available for those 6 am drives to the airport, financial bailouts, and raids of your wardrobe. What's natural as part of a deeper friendship isn't healthy if it's the only contact you share.

Manipulators

These are slightly trickier customers. It won't be as simple as: "You only call me when you want something." It will probably sound more like: "When you call me, I always end up doing something I didn't really want to do, and if I try to refuse, you make me feel like a bitch."

Manipulators will pull out all the stops to wear you down – they don't care how long-drawn-out and tedious the process is as long as they get what they want in the end. They're masters of the guilt trip, can cry on cue and will always have a dying relative to hand if you attempt any independent thought. They tend to be parasitic, attaching themselves to submissive types who'll support their narcissistic view of themselves as the centre of the universe. Because you're a good person, it can be quite a shock to realise that not everybody else is as sweet. Of course, your innocent faith in humanity is the reason they've chosen you; they know very well that tactics appealing to your kind nature will be effective.

These emotional vampires would never get caught doing anything *obvious*, everything is subtle, so that if you describe their behaviour, it doesn't sound all that bad. ("She agreed to water my plants while I'm away, but then she *sighed really heavily.* So I felt I *had* to agree to walk her dog and babysit her kids as a fair exchange.") Any accusations of being devious will be met with a wounded, reproachful look that will end up making *you* feel bad for thinking such uncharitable thoughts about someone who's "done so much for you". Beware of the manipulator who insists on doing you a good turn you don't even want – accept a lift and you'll end up paying for petrol, agree to let them mow your lawn and you'll find you're now committed to storing their motorbike in your garage for the next year. Their acts of "kindness" are always motivated by pure self-interest.

Continuing to be generous with your favours in the hope you can change someone's attitude is emotionally draining for you, and you'll get nothing back but contempt; it's like feeding more and more money into a vending machine when you can see your chocolate bar is never going to drop. These people are so screwed-up, they see "being nice" as "being a doormat", and will actually respect you a little less with every helpful thing you do for them. Sad but true.

Life's too short to stick around in this kind of situation: save your good deeds and thoughtfulness for people who deserve the royal treatment.

Control Freaks

Control freaks are so desperately insecure about *themselves*, they'll try to claw back a sense of power by running other people's lives. (If you're unfortunate enough to have a control freak as a parent, this will seem so normal to you that it could be extremely hard to disentangle yourself.)

Some control freaks only emerge when it comes to food and drink – possibly because a) men want you to drink more so you'll get drunk, and b) women want you to eat more so you'll get fat. Yes, this is an outrageous and offensive generalisation, but how else can we explain this strange compulsion to decide how much somebody else consumes? People of either sex will often pressure you to have "just one more", but they can be deflected if you ask them "How does it benefit you if I have one more drink / helping?"

Control freaks pride themselves on being right about everything – even if the topic of conversation is your profession and they have zero experience or knowledge of it, they'll tell you what you've been doing wrong all these years.

Sometimes there's nothing to do but laugh (especially if you're at the point where they're telling you the correct way to peel a banana or fold your socks). They'll direct you on which outfit to wear, what you should order in the restaurant, where you should book your holiday and how you should tackle that project. Being charitable, we can assume that they truly believe their way is the only route to happiness and their advice is all "for your own good". But whether they're motivated by genuine concern or mere bossiness, they need to be ignored. It will make them panicky at first, but proving to them that you're capable of making rational decisions *might* help to shut them up in future. (No guarantees.)

Liars

They say honesty is an expensive gift, so don't expect it from cheap people. If someone is completely and utterly untrustworthy, no amount of second chances or giving them the benefit of the doubt will ever work out for you.

Why do people lie? Apart from the conman motivated by money, it's generally either to save their own skins (when telling the truth would get them into trouble) or as a way of creating the world they wished they lived in, instead of the godforsaken reality they've created. Some even do it for fun – meaningless little lies to see what they can get away with. (We call these people sociopaths.)

If you know you're talking to a liar, there's no point in believing anything they say. If they'd casually fib about where they used to go to school, why would you believe them when they say your best friend is trying to steal your boyfriend? Even when they're simply recounting facts, they'll twist the truth to suit themselves, often withholding details or adding their own – that way if they get caught out they can simply plead "Chinese whispers" and get off scot free.

If they're backed into a corner they'll brazen it out: "No, you're quite wrong, I never said that. You must be going CRAZY. You shrill, hysterical, insane person." Alternatively, they'll play dumb: "Yes, I did say that, but I didn't mean X. I meant Y. You've got me all confused now. Let's just move on."

Grumps

There are some people who seem to be in a permanently bad mood. They're always looking for the negative in any situation ("Yes, I won a trip to New York, but now I won't get to wash my car on Saturday like I planned") and it's impossible to make them happy. They're also likely to make you feel bad with their pessimistic ways: "Why are we bothering to study? It's not as if we're ever going to make anything of ourselves."

They'll dig their heels in and decide to stay miserable rather than choose to enjoy any social events or activities. There was a girl like this in a group I met for a holiday excursion; we were all meeting for the first time so there was equal opportunity for everyone to make friends. One by one we all tried to engage her in conversation, and she would be rude and sarcastic in return, so we all gave up. I have no idea what her motivation was (it didn't seem to be shyness, as you might assume if you met someone who *didn't* speak) but I felt sad that she created a lonely day for herself for absolutely no reason.

Being melancholy rather than manipulative makes people easier to deal with, but they're also frustrating because you want to get them out of their slump and make them see that life isn't all bad. If someone chooses to be grouchy 24/7, it's unlikely you'll be able to cheer them up via superficial means; if you're close you might suggest they look into solutions for depression. If it's someone you work with, you may have to smile brightly and ignore the little atmosphere of gloom they create, or try to disarm them with one of those lovely compliments we Princesses like to scatter around.

Passive Aggressives

Manipulators and Passive Aggressives (PAs) are two sides of the same coin; they both have a deep-seated sense of helplessness, so they're always desperately trying to wrest control from everyone else. While manipulators actively try to shape the behaviour of those around them, PAs resort to subtle stubbornness in order to feel they have the upper hand. They'll politely agree when you ask them to take on a task at work, then do it very sloooowly so you'll never ask them again. They'll "forget" to include you in group messages, throw out that notepad they "didn't think you needed anymore" and "help" by formatting all the documents wrongly. ("But I thought you wanted them like that...")

At the least offensive end of the scale, PAs are just too timid to speak their minds; they'd rather brood silently than confront anyone head-on. It boils down to disliking conflict, which is why we all have our PA moments (like when one friend annoys us and instead of telling her, we complain about her to our other friends).

There's an ancient Chinese proverb which sums up passive aggressive people well: "Behind the smile, a hidden knife!" PAs will *act* as if they're friendly, helpful folk, then quietly sabotage you. When all that hostility is masked by a friendly veneer, it's hard to pin anything on them; you may even wonder if you're going nuts. (The term "gaslighting" comes from the stageplay / movie *Gaslight*, about a man who tries to manipulate his wife into thinking she's insane, and it's an accurate description of some of the crazy mind games people play.)

A passive aggressive friend will never admit to having negative feelings towards you. Yet she's master of the backhanded compliment ("I wish I had the guts to wear a hat like that! You're so brave...") and when she agrees to go somewhere with you, she'll be so late you miss half the show, or she'll give away spoilers during the movie.

Once you know what passive aggressiveness is, it's actually kind of fun to spot it. If you live with a PA, they'll leave you sarcastic post-it notes "thanking" you for leaving a mess in the kitchen. Confide in your PA friend the name you've chosen for your first-born and she'll mysteriously acquire a pet with the same name, and feign forgetfulness that you'd ever mentioned it. A startlingly frequent ploy involves gift-giving; someone asks what you're going to buy your partner for Christmas, then buys the same thing and presents it to him first. (Of course, the obvious solution to this would be to lie and tell them what "he" desperately wants is the complete box set of *Desperate Housewives*.)

PA people always aim to steamroller through the boundaries you set and will take great delight in disobeying your "rules". For instance, arriving late every time they pick up their child from a playdate with yours, taking fruit from your bowl without asking, or encouraging your dog to jump up at people when you're trying to train him not to. It's as if they want to yell "I can do what I like, and you can't stop me!" Kids are often used as pawns in the game, with PAs creating numerous scenarios where they can say "Let's keep this secret from your mummy!" (ENORMOUS red flag.) It's common for them to serve beefburgers to children being raised vegetarian, or sweets to kids with health freak parents. I've also noticed that taking someone else's child for a haircut is a common issue; parents who object can be dismissed as "making a big deal about nothing" but they still feel violated somehow.

You can't change a PA, so avoiding contact with them as much as possible is your best plan of action. Being confrontational can backfire; you can't force them to stop lighting smoky bonfires just as you hang your washing out, and letting them know it irritates you will only fuel their enthusiasm for burning stinky rubbish. If you have to deal with them, play them at their own game: react *ecstatically* to all their antics. "Lovely day for a bonfire, mind if I throw on some stuff?" "Oh good, you've eaten up my cookies. I was worried they were going to sit there for months, nobody else liked them." It's a little passive aggressive in itself, but it's more fun than getting frustrated.

Why Are They So Mean?

When it comes to female friendships, you can learn pretty much everything you need to know by watching little girls playing. They create a delicate hierarchy with an honoured leader, her faithful second-in-command, and the others, whose job it is to grovel and fawn over the queen bee. One or two will always be left on the outside; it prevents them from threatening the ringleader and it keeps everyone else on their toes, as they could be next to fall out of favour if they don't play their cards right. There's a definite pecking order as girls attempt to befriend anyone they consider cooler than themselves, and treat their inferiors with contempt.

Sadly, some women carry these rules into their adult friendship groups. They'll be possessive over their own friends and try to keep you away, or they'll jealously guard the "rank" they've reached. If you have the misfortune to be more charismatic and stylish than an insecure woman, you're going to get some nasty reactions from her. (And saying "Ha, you're just annoyed that you're not me," is unlikely to help matters.)

As we've learned, picking on people is a dead giveaway that you're feeling inadequate. Confident people don't walk into a room and start finding fault with everything and everyone. There's no need for them to point out all the ways they're superior and you're inferior – they don't bother to compare themselves with anyone at all. The way people treat others is a direct reflection of the way they feel about themselves; this is why Princesses are so utterly charming and delightful.

Meanwhile, non-Princesses love to make other people feel rubbish. They'll stare at you open-mouthed if you mention that you "didn't know" something they consider obvious, and announce gleefully "You're going bright red!" when something embarrasses you. If people are eager to pick apart your appearance, your voice, accent, dress sense or whatever, rest assured that they're overcompensating for their own shortcomings. Nobody who feels great about themselves is ever going to deliberately make someone else feel uncomfortable.

Sometimes dealing with antagonistic people can actually be beneficial. A bully who makes your school years a misery could motivate you to become inwardly strong and independent (you learn to rely on yourself when there's nobody around to help you). Encountering users and manipulators teaches you to stand up for yourself and how to read between the lines of someone's guilt trips and emotional blackmail. Above all, you learn how NOT to live your life. People who scream at the supermarket cashier for being slow remind you how stupid it looks to go berserk for some silly, irrelevant reason.

Have you ever noticed how *suddenly* people can explode with rage? It must be simmering close to the surface all the time if it only takes a late bus or a missed TV show for them to erupt like a volcano. But if I'm having a particularly stressful day, I'm disturbed at how tempting it is to snap at the person standing in my way instead of politely saying "Excuse me". I've realised that the people who always get enraged so easily must be incredibly unhappy. Buddhist monk Thich Naht Hanh said: "When another person makes you suffer, it is because he suffers deeply within himself, and his suffering is spilling over. He does not need punishment; he needs help." If your officemate is always being inexplicably nasty, it gives you a glimpse into what it must be like to live in the cage of her mind, day after day. Does she have your pity yet?

I also suspect that people get addicted to the adrenaline rush of jumping from "normal" to "blind fury" in a single nanosecond. If your life is completely boring, maybe getting irate over the mistake on your hotel bill is the only thrill you're likely to get. If you encounter someone who's spoiling for a fight, walk away. They don't need to fight with you – anyone will do. If you stay blandly cheerful, they'll find someone else who'll rise to the bait and *you* won't have your day ruined.

You also have the opportunity to help people by being the calm in the storm they're trying to create. Instead of snarling back at them, you have the class to reply with serenity, refusing to be sucked into their aggression. You might find that by not responding the way most people would, you can get through a chink in the armour of a belligerent person. If it came to a confrontation, being gentle and calm might open up a civilised dialogue rather than a fight. Sometimes friendships have been formed between ex-bullies and their former victims, so here's hoping for that best-case scenario.

When nothing works, all you can do is realise that the person is an idiot. Bottom line: haters gonna hate. Allowing people to stress you out is like getting on a treadmill every morning: all those swirly thoughts about what so-and-so thinks of you and what they might say or do next. It's *exhausting*. Gandhi, famous for his non-violent leadership style, put it: "I will not allow anyone to walk through my mind with their dirty feet." When you're focused on how angry someone makes you feel, they're living in your head (rent-free) and controlling you. Let it go and take back control of your own peace.

Ways People Get Away with Behaving Badly

"No one can take advantage of you without your permission." Ann Landers

"I'll Be Offended If You Don't..."

For some reason, manipulators consider this their trump card. Sounds to me like the perfect time to point out that everyone is responsible for their own happiness. In other words, I don't care whether you're offended or not, I'm still not going to eat food I can't stand just because you cooked it / stay with your brother when I visit X town instead of going to a hotel / let you take my child on holiday with you. If someone chooses to be offended, it's their problem, not yours.

Life becomes deeply tedious when you spend it with people who use their own hypersensitivity to control others; they need to learn that everything you do isn't a personal attack on them. Why should you be the one to tiptoe around on eggshells when faced with someone who thinks nothing of trampling all over your feelings?

The Rabbit Hole of Confusion

The Rabbit Hole of Confusion is the strategy used by someone who knows they don't have a leg to stand on, so they focus on getting their opponent to go chasing after something totally irrelevant. It goes something like this:

You: "So, can we go and get dinner when this DVD finishes? I'm starving."
Whiny boyfriend: "But I wanted to watch that game show at seven! Can't you wait a bit?"
You: "But I'm really hungry – why don't you record it, and watch it when we get back from the restaurant?"
Whiny boyfriend: "Hmph! You're so selfish – you always get your own way!"

This is where the argument could easily diverge into your defence – you're not being selfish at all, and what about that time last week when you did what your boyfriend wanted? While you jump down the Rabbit Hole, the fact that your boyfriend has NO VALID ARGUMENT is swept aside, and you still haven't had your dinner yet.

Another example of the Rabbit Hole of Confusion is when people deliberately goad you in the hope of provoking a reaction. So when some guy starts talking about how women should stay in the kitchen, he knows it's a ludicrous claim. He's not hoping for a logical argument – he wants you to get angry so he can use the classic "Where's your sense of humour?" line (commonly used to defend the indefensible – see below). If you fall for it you'll be giving him exactly what he wants.

Unfortunately, if he's aiming his comments at more than one person, somebody will always get sucked in. If you deflect his arguments and refuse to get involved, there'll probably be another female who'll either attempt to prove that she DOES have a sense of humour (by listing all the comedies she's laughed at?) or she'll get angry. Either way, he's got the reaction he wanted.

"It Was Just a Joke"

Whenever I hear someone saying "I was only having a laugh / I don't know why you have to take it so seriously / you have no sense of humour!" I know immediately that this person is a loser who has absolutely no justification for whatever s/he has done. Bullies of all shapes and sizes – the nasty kid in class, the abusive spouse and the tyrannical boss – all use this line. Somehow they're convinced it's acceptable to say anything – literally the most offensive sentence they can think of – as long as they tack on "Joking!" at the end of it. That way, the fault is with you if you don't like it – you're "too sensitive" and "can't take a joke". In other words, it's YOUR issue, not theirs. Most people will be so mortified at the idea they're coming across as a humourless bore that they'll immediately back off.

When it comes to quips about violence, they're only funny if we know they wouldn't happen. Telling your best friend "I'll beat you up if you won't lend me your shoes!" is a joke, because you don't beat up your friends. (Do you...?) Rape jokes aren't funny because sexual assault is a possibility for every woman – something we're acutely aware of every time we leave the house alone. If it were a constant threat for men, I doubt they'd be so keen to make wisecracks about it.

The flaw in the "It's just a bit of fun" argument is that when something is fun, everyone enjoys themselves. If it were witty repartee, you'd laugh. The fact that you're not rolling around clutching your sides when your friend calls you a stupid bitch doesn't mean you don't have a sense of humour, it means the comment wasn't funny. Even if something IS meant as a jolly jape (and 99% of the time I'm betting it's passive aggression rather than rib-tickling humour) then the fact that it's also hurtful means it loses its "joke" status and an apology is in order. If someone tells you that you're not allowed to be offended by what they said because it was a gag, you can simply say "It still hurt." Let's see them come back from that! Ha!

"You're Too Sensitive..."

Just like "I was only joking" and "Where's your sense of humour?" this is another attempt to lay the blame at your door.

The best-case scenario here is if someone makes a joke without realising that you're touchy about that particular subject; they might blurt out "You're too sensitive!" because they're embarrassed that they upset you (and they'll later try to make amends). Unfortunately it's more often a way for bullies to justify saying whatever they like.

Sometimes adults will use this line when they tease children to the point of tears – perhaps in a misguided attempt to "toughen them up". Needless to say, it doesn't work. Instead, it leaves scars on the child who may not be emotionally mature enough to figure out "I'm not too sensitive – you're a moron!" It's said that "labelling is disabling"; some people grow up with the idea they're "oversensitive" purely because it's what they were told over and over again. Tormenting a kid under the pretext of "preparing" them for the big bad world is like throwing hot coffee in someone's face to prepare them for the possibility that it could happen to them in a café some time. (By the way, I don't recommend this as a lesson for the meanies in your life, tempting as it is.)

To deal with this without making the culprit feel like an insect pinned under the microscope of judgement, make your response about you, not them. Rather than saying "You suck for belittling me in public" try a sentence like: "I feel humiliated when you bring up my bad exam results in front of other people. Please stop talking about my failures with your friends."

"I'm Sorry You're Offended..."

Ah, the non-apology. The only way it could be worse is if they say: "I'm sorry you're so easily offended" – that would be the real kicker. This *almost* sarcastic "sorry-not-sorry" is frequently used by advertisers after they've put out some hideously distasteful commercial and can't understand what all the fuss is about. Genuine apologies start with "I'm sorry I..." Fake ones begin with "I'm sorry *you*..." or "I'm sorry *if*..."

Read the comments on any online article or video, and you'll notice that some people LOVE finding non-existent reasons to be scandalised. Being prickly and eager to find fault with everything isn't the Princess way, but we are entitled to feel our emotions. Suppose your boyfriend has been teasing you about something, and he's just taken it too far. You end up in tears, and he doesn't understand why. You normally laugh along with things, so he assumes maybe you have PMT or something. He doesn't think he's done anything wrong, because in his mind, he really was "only joking," and it's not his fault you're upset. So when you suggest he could apologise, he can only manage "I'm sorry you cried."

You can't make someone *feel* sorry if they're not, but you can explain that apologising is merely the polite, reasonable thing to do. If you spilled a drink on a stranger, you'd make amends – you wouldn't say "Sorry you got in my way" (unless you're a jerk) so why qualify the apologies you give to your closest loved ones?

"I'm Sorry!"

What's that? I'm complaining about people who DO apologise now? Yep, there's no pleasing me, is there? Like the "Only joking!" crowd, this breed think they can do whatever they want as long as they squeeze in an apology afterwards.

Sometimes you have to suck it up; if your mother tends to be volatile, blowing her top for no reason and then apologising later, learn not to take it personally, and have a quiet chuckle at her histrionics. When she's in a better mood, you could give her something to think about by saying with good humour, "Don't apologise, just don't yell at me for no reason next time!"

You don't need to start holding grudges against any friend who's forgotten your birthday / been late / got ketchup on the t-shirt she borrowed; we're all human, we all make mistakes. But apologies are *not* enough to cover physical violence (EVER, EVER, EVER!) and they start to turn stale if they're used over and over again for anything else. "I'm sorry" is not a licence to walk over someone, and it's meaningless if you know they'd do the same thing again given half a chance.

"It's Just The Way I Am..."

Along with "You know what I'm like", this is an ingeniously limitless excuse. ("Yeah, I smashed up the house, you know what a temper I've got...") Some people are habitually so rude and offensive that they've had to develop a characteristic defence which they can use on a regular basis. They normally say it with some measure of smugness; "I'm the kind of person who says what they think" (even when it hurts people's feelings). Well, guess what – that's NOT "just the way they are". It's the way they're *choosing to be*.

We all make conscious decisions every day about how to treat people. You *choose* whether to let that hurtful comment slip out or to bite your tongue. Pretending it happens randomly and we have no control over it is total crap. You could respond with "You mean, that's the way you're choosing to be," and watch them struggle for an answer, or turn it around and say "Yes, and I don't tolerate people being rude to me. I can't help it... that's just the way I am."

"You've Changed!"

Isn't that what the caterpillar said to the butterfly? If someone is used to you living life the way they want you to, you're bound to hear the tearful recrimination "You've changed!" when you stop existing purely to please them. Whether they're family or friends, manipulators are difficult to escape from. Give in to their demands and they'll be happy enough, but if you develop a spine and start saying no, it will inevitably bring a fresh round of head games and emotional blackmail. You'll notice that breaking free from someone else's dominance will often result in them accusing you of being selfish. Yes, *you're* selfish, because you've stopped doing what they want you to do for them. Wow. Can these people hear themselves?!

"Hmph!"

Giving people the silent treatment, sulking, and answering only in grunts is one method of getting your own way, for those who want to be childish about it. Passive aggressive types will use tactics such as withholding affection and attention until you give in – plenty of victims of this strategy will back down simply to get the reward of a happy response after days of the silent treatment. This is definitely the moment to become blithely unaware of atmospheres; they'll snap out of it eventually.

"I Can't Believe You Won't..."

Guilt is the manipulator's masterstroke – they know nobody wants to be thought of as a cold-hearted person who won't help out a loved one. They'll use anything as ammunition: "I thought we were *friends*! And friends lend friends money when they need it, right?"

Playing the victim pays off; they'll appeal to your sympathetic side (sometimes with tall stories of medical conditions or tragic circumstances) and hope this is enough to nab them a slave for life. Once they've got you feeling terrible for being more fortunate than they are (or claim to be) or for doubting the truth of what they say, they've got it made.

They can rationalise anything, so don't get sucked into a logical debate about whether or not it's fair for you to take on the large hairy dog they can't afford to keep (even if your living space is slightly snugger than a shoebox and they live in a mansion). It won't matter what troubles you can cite when explaining why you can't help, you'll still be roundly upstaged by the drama queen with a victim complex. You can't win against someone who considers controlling other people to be a game, so why play?

"If You Don't, I'll…"

Blackmail: the last resort of the uncivilised. If someone threatens you, the only response is to call their bluff. (You don't *have* to say "Go ahead, punk. Make my day…" but it does help.)

School bullies tend to rely on warnings like this, saying "Don't tell anyone, or else!" (Or else you'll bully me? Like you're doing now?) Suppose you tell on them, and as promised, they carry on terrorising you. Well, you tell on them again. They get into trouble again. After a few rounds of this, surely everyone will be heartily sick of the cycle?

Being slightly melodramatic for a moment; if someone has some dirt on you and they want you to pay them (in money or by some other means) to keep quiet, you have to face the music and confess all publicly. It takes away their power instantly. (Because seriously, once they know you'll pay up, they're never going to stop. It would be terrible business sense.)

In more ordinary circumstances, emotional blackmail might consist of someone using the phrase "If you really loved me…" as well as being "so upset" or hinting that they'll leave you if you refuse to do what they're asking. They might even threaten to hurt themselves if you defy them: claims like this should always be taken seriously, but they're not for you to deal with. Get the person's parents involved, or the police / hospital / local church if necessary. Nobody will keep threatening suicide if a prayer group turns up every time they try it.

And One Way YOU Allow Them to Behave Badly

"Anything for a Quiet Life…"

175

I cringe whenever I hear people use this phrase to explain why they're not going to take action against somebody's naughtiness. It's commonly trotted out in families where one person rules the roost and everyone else lets them get away with it because they don't want to rock the boat. It's the people who give in to unreasonable demands who allow the manipulator to grow into a monster. It's far better to nip funny business in the bud ("No, I don't think I will be changing my existing plans just so you can visit me on the dates *you* prefer") before it spirals out of control as the manipulator tests the boundaries and finds more and more of them go unchecked. ("Oh, all right. I'll let the entire family stay in my beach house all summer rent-free, yes, you can take my bed and I'll do all the babysitting.") Toxic people will always hold you responsible for their emotions, so you'll be told "Don't spoil the lovely day we're having" (by disagreeing with me and forcing me to sulk).

It's easy to convince yourself that avoiding confrontation with someone means that you're "keeping the peace" and thus being the spiritually enlightened one with upright morals. But this is a cop-out – it's simply teaching the person that their tactics are acceptable, their methods "work", and nobody is going to stand in their way. What's more, they'll go on doing it to others (who may have even fewer defences than you) – and it will be partly your fault for not speaking out.

Essentially, you're going to feel uncomfortable whatever you do. It will either be because you resent being put upon and kind of hate yourself for not standing up to the bully, or it will be because you've found the courage to defy them and consequently they're calling you self-centred, malicious etc. Neither option is much fun, but at least the latter means that you'll retain your self-respect and you might even spark off a change in that person. If everybody challenges them, they'll have no choice but to improve the way they act. Abusers can't exist without enablers.

So when your graduation's coming up and you're feeling torn in two because your parents haven't spoken since their divorce, don't take responsibility for pleasing everyone. If your mum is refusing to go as long as your dad's new girlfriend is invited, you might be tempted to say "anything for a quiet life" and rip up your would-be step-mother's invite. But it's not your issue, so you don't have to deal with it. Tell mum you're inviting everyone, and it's up to individual guests how they respond. If she decides not to come, that's her decision.

Meanwhile, when your sister is making a fuss because she wants to borrow your car (and she scratched it last time) don't think that giving in is the best option. It might stop the annoying whining for now, but it will open the door for more requests next time.

You're not the Peace Ambassador for the world – and if you were, the job wouldn't involve encouraging bratty troublemakers. In reality, allowing people to behave badly isn't being kind to them – you're not doing them any favours. You're actually *helping* them to be manipulative, which keeps them feeling powerless; people only try to control others when they lack real autonomy in their own lives. (If you've ever been tempted to slyly push someone into doing what you want them to – like when you NEED a night out and you're trying to convince your reluctant, broke friend to come to the pub with you – you'll know that it's when you feel desperate that you're most likely to resort to sneakiness.) Do your adversary a favour and help them out of this vicious circle and into a healthier way of relating to people, ie seeing them as fellow human beings instead of machines who provide stuff they want.

Manipulators rely on the fact that people don't want to "make a fuss" and will chicken out of confrontations to keep things civil. Nobody likes to make a scene, and people will put up with a lot to avoid them. (Which might be why kids screaming for treats in the supermarket will so often get them...)

You'll even find you have to *convince* other people to stand up to bullies like this; there are some wimpy bosses who would happily give in to the stroppiest employee rather than the one who's in the right. They'll say "You know what she's like..." if you attempt to make a complaint about the screwy conduct of your colleague – and you'll be encouraged to roll over and take it rather than kicking up a stink. People don't like having to deal with issues: if they think it will be easier to get YOU to pipe down, they'll do that rather than risk inviting the wrath of your devious workmate. This human tendency to go for the option that will be less hassle *in the short-term* means that some households allow one domineering parent (or child!) to bully everyone and control the entire family dynamic – creating harmful patterns which continue into adulthood (and take years of therapy to fix). After all, it's easier to tell squabbling kids to "play nicely" than to actually address the root of the conflict.

The way to defend yourself against a manipulator is to simply put your foot down and refuse to give in. It will be hard at first, but once they've seen that you're immune to their whinging, they'll move on – to easier prey. If you often find yourself targeted by people who need endless favours, loans and car rides, it's a fair bet they think you're a sucker. When your needy friend wants a weekend of debauchery without her kids and she asks YOU to babysit (instead of asking her assertive sister) it's a clear indication that she sees you as a soft touch who isn't likely to say no. If manipulators were as clueless as they pretend to be, they'd be trying their outrageous requests on everyone instead of carefully selecting the victims they can successfully play.

As a side note, I wonder if certain people kind of like being manipulated. They get to be a martyr and complain, while blaming the other person for being awful; maybe it creates a co-dependent relationship of sorts. I once spoke to a lady who told me horrific stories about the verbal, mental and physical abuse she'd suffered at the hands of her ex-husband. She was a seemingly feisty and independent lady, but she told me: "He got away with it for years, because he was in the police force and they look after their own." Obviously I don't know the whole story, but um... he got away with it because *she let* him! She could have put a stop to it by leaving and getting a divorce, surely? (I know, I know, it's "not that simple". Except sometimes, it is.)

On a smaller scale, I know someone who complains about her passive aggressive friend who always calls her on a Tuesday: "She knows that's when my daughter visits, and I always have to spend the time talking to her while my daughter's sitting there." Well, there is always the option of not picking up, isn't there? Oh no, apparently that wouldn't work. Because her friend would then carry on ringing for ages... So freaking unplug your phone! Come on, people!

According to Alcoholics Anonymous, insanity is defined as: "Continuing the same behaviour and expecting a different result." You can't keep caving in to a schemer and expect them to somehow magically learn that manipulating people is wrong and they shouldn't do it. They need you to *help* them learn. So instead of asking yourself why you're so unfortunate as to have all these terrible people zeroing in on you, ask yourself what you're doing that attracts them – and how you're enabling them to carry out their mischief. When you allow people to treat you like this, you're telling them it's OK.

Tactics for Dealing With Troublesome People

"When you fight with a pig, you both get dirty. But the pig likes it." John Patrick Dolan

Ignore or Confront?

Bullies want:

- To get attention
- To make themselves feel better (ie by putting you down in order to feel superior).
- To hurt you
- To know they can control your reaction to them

So the question is, what will cut them off from their aims?

As we've already seen, trying to avoid quarrels by giving in to every unreasonable request is a lose-lose situation. Forget "keeping the peace"; gird your loins and be vocal about how unreasonable (or loopy) the other person is being, even if it does make them cross with you.

Challenging a passive aggressive person is often futile; they'll just smile and pretend they don't know what you're talking about. But you might make them stop and think by commenting in a neutral or jokey way, as if you're well aware of their silly games and find them funny. For instance: "Jane, I've noticed whenever I ask you to do the laundry, you manage to shrink something of mine, is that your SUBTLE way of telling me you don't want to do it anymore? Ha ha!" Once you've called her on it, it would be quite hard for Jane to repeat the behaviour and still pretend it's totally unconscious.

However, when someone is goading you because they WANT you to speak up, it's much more effective to ignore them. "Don't engage" is often the best advice when dealing with a rude, argumentative person: the less you respond, the more peaceful your life will be. Another saying which is useful to remember is that you should never argue with an idiot because they'll drag you down to their level and then beat you with experience. When you know that troublemakers thrive on getting attention, you can spoil all their fun by ignoring them so hard they begin to doubt their own existence.

Rather than feeling unsettled when women sneeringly look you up and down, why not assume they're thinking about how much they'd like to be friends with you? Don't react to the dirty looks; be chirpily oblivious to whispered conversations or strange atmospheres. Have a vague yet friendly look on your face. (If nothing else, it will be entertaining to see them wondering why you don't appear to be intimidated.) Make-believe that the office bitch likes you; act as if you think she's a perfectly nice person and give her a friendly smile and "Good morning!" even though she never responds. Just don't go out of your way to chat to her – being rebuffed would shatter the illusion.

If you pride yourself on being a tough and assertive woman, you may balk at the thought of ignoring obnoxious behaviour when your instinct is to confront. You might see "ignoring" as a passive way of dealing with issues, while challenging your opponent to a showdown is how a strong, confident person would react. But isn't it more "passive" to get sucked into a fight that you're not interested in? And more "active" to *choose* how you're going to react? I like knowing that nobody can get me rattled unless I *let them*. A passive aggressive person might pretend there's no problem but then do everything in their limited power to hurt or exasperate the offending individual and "get back" at them. True power is deciding you're not going to let someone get under your skin, no matter what they do.

I realised how effective the "ignore" method was when somebody did the opposite to me. A girl I vaguely knew (a friend of a friend) sent me a message accusing me of playing pranks on her (ordering pizzas to her house, that sort of thing) and she was furious about it and I had to stop. I hadn't been pranking her (I'm not nine years old) but I thought: "Wow, if I had been trying to annoy her, this let me know it was mission accomplished!" I considered writing back and explaining that she was mistaken ("I barely know who you are...?") but I realised this would simply be joining in with the crazy. She's probably still wondering if I even received that email.

And while being assertive sometimes makes you feel that you're a dynamic diva, it can backfire. A friend of mine decided that ignoring wolf whistles was not enough, and any man foolish enough to disrespect her in this way needed a good telling-off. All was fine and dandy until the day she noticed two men sitting in a car apparently leering in her direction, and she yelled "What the hell are you looking at?" The answer came... "Um, we were looking for a street sign... we're trying to find the theatre." Oops!

The golden rule is: if someone has annoyed you *by mistake*, you should speak to them about it – otherwise your resentment at the way your sister lost your necklace could fester forever and ruin every family brunch. If they've annoyed you *on purpose*, ignore it: nothing will be more infuriating for them.

Play the Game By Your Own Rules

One of my favourite (true) stories about animals is the tale of a polar bear in Canada who came across a pet husky in the snow and began to stalk him; he was starving and a dog would make a tasty meal. But the husky didn't run away or try to fight or react in any way like potential prey. He jiggled his rear end, wagged his tail, and approached the bear as if they were playing a game – and they soon were.

Despite an empty belly, the bear's love of play overcame his hunger and the two animals were able to have a relationship instead of seeing each other as killer / meat. It's a cool animal anecdote, but it's also a great reminder of the way we can actually change other people's attitudes, mid-sentence. You don't have to accept someone's bad mood. You can snap them out of it (sometimes) with a more playful demeanour. If they're expecting to meet with animosity, your light-hearted approach could throw them off – and that moment of surprise might be enough time to flip the script around to a happier ending.

So when your co-worker grumpily demands that you do something, you don't have to respond in kind with a frown and a resentful attitude. Why should you match your mood to theirs? Start calling the shots and decide for yourself how the conversation will pan out. Sometimes a smile or joke can lighten the mood considerably. Have you ever seen a shop assistant going from expressionless to bright when a customer says something to make them smile? Most of the time, someone you think is unfriendly might just be preoccupied, or maybe they just haven't realised there's potential in every interaction for a bit of Princessy goodwill.

Humour

I find the "switch to playfulness" strategy is also great to use in arguments. Debates can get intense, and for most of us, "winning" seems more important in the heat of the moment than expanding our perspectives. By keeping things light and humorous, it's a) more fun, and b) easier for people to take on board the other person's point of view without losing face. You don't need to inject zippy one-liners into the conversation, but you can avoid being sucked into "ultra-serious" mode with a friendly face and light tone of voice. In debates generally, it's useful to stay a little detached – this way you can avoid getting sucked down that Rabbit Hole of Confusion, and calmly address the things YOU want to talk about.

Another useful strategy when someone is being offensive is to simply react as if they ARE joking. Laugh in their face for being so ludicrous. This is the best strategy to use when someone is trying to provoke you with outrageous statements – you can't reason with people like this, so ridicule them instead. Show them they don't have the ability to make you upset or angry.

It also works when someone makes an unrealistic request or asks you a rude question. Treat it with the mockery it deserves. "Oh, you're so funny! Pretending you're going to tell me which brand of washing powder to buy!" "Ha ha, yeah, sure I'll rearrange my entire day so I can take you to the train station, even though a cab would cost you about £5... shall I peel you a grape and wash your feet while I'm at it?" "Wow, you want to know how much I weigh? Which finishing school did *you* go to?"

Playing the Dumb Fox

One of the most useful methods of dealing with someone devious is to be even sneakier than they are. A manipulator doesn't care that much if you don't like them (as long as they get what they want out of your interaction) so getting angry with them doesn't do any good. Trying to pin them down to a straight answer by being aggressive won't work. So your secret weapon is being really *stupid*. You say in a confused way "But I don't get it. Why would I be the best person to do all the grocery shopping? I thought you worked near the supermarket?" Framing your argument as a question makes it completely non-confrontational, and the manipulator can't pull the usual "Oh, you're getting so emotional you're not thinking straight, I can't talk to you while you're like this." In fact, they're stuck because you're not saying no, you're not getting angry, you're just... puzzled. Being totally confused is a killer move.

As I mentioned earlier with regard to those hosts who pointedly bemoan the cost of the meal they provided, playing dumb also means that you take everything people say at face value. So when your housemate says "Sheesh, money's so low this month. I don't know how I'm going to make rent..." you can cheerfully reply "Yeah, I was strapped for cash a while back. I ended up selling some clothes on Ebay and rode my bike to work for a bit. Maybe you could ask for more overtime?" The fact they never actually get to the point of putting their request for financial assistance into words means you never have to turn them down and feel bad about it. If you can live with them telling people you're utterly insensitive, you're sorted.

Silence

You know when you say something a bit dumb and that annoying person exclaims your name as if they're shocked? Look them right in the eye with a deadpan expression and say "Yes?" – it leaves them with nowhere to go. The same poker-faced reaction works when someone is forcing a laugh (because what you said was so *hilariously* wrong). Forget the accepted response of laughing along with them; stare at them as if you think they're insane, and they'll be the one who looks silly. And if someone has said something bizarre to you and you have no idea how to respond, sometimes silence is the best option; at least that way only one person ends up looking crazy and inappropriate, and it isn't you.

If you're feeling the need to match someone's intimidating presence, a blank stare is surprisingly effective. When you simply look at the person with no expression, they imagine all sorts of things, because they're projecting their own thoughts onto you. It's scarier than someone *trying* to be menacing, which is why actors often do it when they're playing psychopaths.

Disabling the Button They Love to Press

The way you respond to antagonists is entirely in your control, so ask yourself this: how are they pushing your buttons? Do they have extreme views on politics or religion, which they bring up every time you're together? Do they always make precisely the same criticism of your choice of career / the books you read / your boyfriend's tattoo? Some people enjoy getting a reaction, so they'll stick to the method that's got them results in the past. If they know they only have to say "Those crazy environmentalists are wasting everyone's time with their protests again," to trigger an angry response from you, they can dominate every situation. They can *make you* react in a predictable way, any time they like. It's up to you to take this power back. What's the point in arguing anyway? It's unlikely they're going to say "Wow, your reasoning is so flawless that I'm changing my entire life perspective on this issue."

Decide what can aggravate you and what can't. I'm amazed at the amount of grumbling you hear during airport delays – who has the energy to get outraged about something so uncontrollable and insignificant? We read horrendous news stories in the paper every day and it doesn't so much as cast a shadow over our morning coffee. I'm not saying we should be depressed all the time – but I think we need to keep life in perspective and save our bad moods for events that actually deserve them. There's a wonderful saying "Make your anger so expensive that nobody can afford it, and your happiness so cheap, everyone can get it for free". You don't HAVE to get peeved when Uncle Larry airs his controversial views on civil rights. In fact, if you've always answered him a particular way, it can be hysterical to see his disappointed reaction when you smile and say "Gosh, that's an interesting point of view. Could you please pass the gravy?"

Answering Insults

Occasionally someone will come out with an unbelievably rude statement, whether it's directed at you, someone you love, or humanity in general. This is when a silent, raised eyebrow could be the best response. If that's too subtle, "What a strange thing to say" or a dry "Do you realise you said that out loud?" might work. At this point the person should have grasped that their remark wasn't appropriate.

When someone is aiming personal insults at you, it's always funny to agree with them. They'll get no pleasure out of making disparaging comments about your driving skills if you respond with "Thanks! I thought you might say that!" in a delighted manner. If anyone wants to be rude to you, they'll have to actually tell you "No, I wasn't trying to be nice," at which point you may be overcome with giggles as you feign disbelief that they could have been trying to be unpleasant rather than charming.

If all else fails (and it's someone you can't avoid seeing) make it into a silly game for yourself. Every time they send a burn your way, you get to pay yourself £1. I wonder what you'll end up buying as a treat? You could also make a bingo chart and write down every phrase you expect to hear – if you're feeling cheeky you can say "Bingo!" when they insult you, and explain the game. It's a way of pointing out that a) you're onto their spiteful comments, and b) they amuse rather than annoy you. It's the opposite of the reaction the rude person is expecting – instead of haughtily declaring "I don't take any sh*t from anyone", and starting a fight, you're simply asserting your inner toughness: "I can take any amount of sh*t you care to send my way, and still come out smiling. So bring it, bitch."

If this kind of flippant defiance isn't an option, simply keep your face impassive and say "OK" – not the long drawn out, sarcastic "Okaaaaayyyy" which is normally accompanied by an eye roll to your buddy, but the kind of brief non-answer which doesn't invite further conversation.

Creating Boundaries and Respecting Your Time

Your time is precious and none of us know how much we have left, so don't squander it on boring get-togethers where everybody gets wasted, or anyone who isn't worth the hassle.

If someone considers their own time to be far more important than yours, they're likely to treat your schedule casually. This is why your friend who works a 10-hour day might figure that she should get to choose when the two of you meet next, because if you're a student, you can "study any time". There's no need to be TOO much of a prima donna about this, but do make sure that the decision is made fairly rather than always favouring the person who makes the biggest fuss.

And whether you're an extrovert or introvert, you need to set boundaries around your time, otherwise you'll always end up fitting into someone else's timetable. Whether it's opting out of a destination wedding or breaking it to your kid's teacher that you don't want to spend your weekend decorating cakes for the bake sale, you're entitled to assert yourself and say no. "I'm afraid that won't be possible," is a great, catch-all reply to any request. Use the broken record technique if you're pushed: no matter what's thrown at you – logical arguments or wheedling – "I'm afraid that won't be possible" is your repeated reply. You don't need to explain your decisions or justify not jumping to attention when someone calls.

If you've ever been part of a committee or any other kind of voluntary group, you'll know there's often a lot of pressure to create activity, and the people who propose "what should happen" aren't the ones who expect to carry out the work. They think dreaming up the genius idea of organising a 5-day-a-week kids' after-school club is the end of their duties; someone else can sort out all the *tiny* details of actually co-ordinating and running it...

If you've been stung by this in the past, it's a good idea to take control at the next meeting by choosing your words carefully: "Why don't we all make a suggestion of what we'd like to get involved with this week?" If somebody mentions making bunting (and you're known as the sewing champ) reply "So, will you be responsible for that?" and when they splutter their negative response you can say casually "Well, I don't have time this week for a big project like that, does anyone else want to volunteer? No? Oh well, it looks like a no-go. Never mind." Alternatively, when someone comes up with a bright idea for a new way of making the schedules (and you're the person who normally sends them out) cheerfully say "Great, let me know when that's been done so I can distribute the finished copies to everyone!" If in doubt, the line "I can't commit to that," sounds as if you have a suitably heavy burden, without actually explaining your circumstances.

The worst thing you can do is to give a specific reason for why you can't help someone out, because then they can counter-argue. For instance, if your friend asks you to pick up her kids from school and you say "Oh, my car's going to be out of service next week" you'll get the response "That doesn't matter, you can borrow mine." If you say "I'd love to, but I need to do a big supermarket shop that day," she'll brightly suggest "You can just make an order online – I'll help you!" Don't get peeved with people for not picking up on your hints – if you don't want to do something, be honest about it.

Equally, respect other people's boundaries. Bear in mind that when people give you excuses, it implies they don't actually want to do whatever it is you're asking them to do. I once asked a pal of mine to help me fix my bike (she had previously told me that she loved anything to do with cycling and could give me a hand ("anytime!") with my puncture repair kit. Weeks went by, and over and over again, we made arrangements which she'd then flake out on. Slowly it dawned on me that it was never going to happen; I got my bicycle fixed elsewhere, never mentioned it again and normal social meetings were resumed. This was another lesson: people say stuff they don't mean all the time. No matter how enthusiastic someone seems, it's only when they show up that you know they were being genuine.

We live in a dual culture of "Askers vs Hinters". Some people take the attitude "If you don't ask, you don't get." They'll happily request an invitation to dinner at your house, or suggest that you could give them a lift to their doctor's appointment on the other side of town. The good news is, they're also fine with people saying no to them, because most of the time they're just asking on the off chance you'll say yes. On the other hand, you get the people who try to avoid making other people feel uncomfortable, by dancing around a subject rather than being explicit. They wouldn't dream of making a request which might appear unreasonable, because they think it's rude. If they're asked directly for a favour, they feel put on the spot and worry needlessly about how to politely refuse. These self-consciously non-grabby hinters often end up disappointed when someone of a blunter nature doesn't pick up on what they're trying to say.

If you find it hard to say no, remember that every time you say yes, you're actually saying no to yourself; with every unwanted task you take on, you're missing out on something you would have chosen to do otherwise.

Cut Off Links (That Could Come Back To Haunt You)

My friend lives with her husband in the house he grew up in – the only way his mother would agree to selling up and moving into a retirement village was to know that the house would remain "in the family". Well, you can guess what happened. New wallpaper was deemed offensive ("What was wrong with the colour I chose?") the locks weren't changed ("I popped a few things in your larder for you while you were out") and Mum never seemed to recognise that it wasn't her home any more.

This kind of set-up is surprisingly common, so look out for clues that you're marrying into a particularly "close-knit" family. Your man might think it's completely normal for his parents to let themselves in and start sorting your mail if that's what he grew up with. If you'd prefer more privacy, it's up to you to set the boundaries from the start. To do this you need to get your partner on board, otherwise you'll have to listen to him saying "Aw, I think it's nice when they do a spot of cleaning for us when we're out."

Don't Get Mad, Get Over It

Some people are hell-bent on getting revenge against those who have hurt them. The Princess knows the only people she should be "getting even" with are the ones who've *helped* her.

As we've seen, not everyone you meet in your life is going to be a sweetheart who loves you unconditionally and lives to make your life a wonderland. You might waste years believing someone is going to change into an idealised version of themselves, then finally end up rueing the day you ever met. It's tempting to get angry with yourself for putting up with shoddy treatment, as well as aiming that bitterness towards the person who's done the damage. This is only ever going to hurt *you.*

It's said that people enter our lives for a reason, a season, or a lifetime. The chances are that some of your friendships will fade away and some relationships will fall apart. The important thing is to learn whatever lesson is being presented to you – and hope that if you're someone else's lesson, you're a lovely one, like "Human beings are trustworthy and generous."

Dealing With Gossip

Suppose somebody you know is spreading gossip about you. It's not true, it's insulting, and you're worried it's going to damage your reputation. Although your friends assure you that nobody worth their salt would believe such silly rumours and that lies always unravel under pressure, you're getting anxious to set the record straight.

You have two options: ignore the nonsense and hope it blows over, or chase down the person who's telling malicious lies. Just as before, the key question is: what would the culprit prefer? Do the opposite.

If you know exactly where the gossip originated, you could approach the person in a cool, measured way. Remember the dumb fox act – you have *no idea* that she's evil personified. But you heard a vague hint that it *might* have been her words that started the nutty story, and is there any chance something she said could have been misconstrued? This gives her a little wiggle room to admit that she may have possibly given someone the wrong impression. She then knows you're onto her and will be confronted every time she tries the same trick... therefore putting her off from a repeat performance.

Another method is to ignore. The above advice works if everyone is capable of behaving like adults; unfortunately if someone is trying to poison everyone against you, this is unlikely to be the case. Confrontation could make the problem worse, as she'll deny everything to your face then run to update the gossipmongers as soon as you've gone, making up details for extra relish. Getting attention is crucial to people like this, so acknowledging their actions is the worst thing you can do. If they were hoping to get you all riled up, they'll be disappointed that you're so indifferent to their little schemes. Think about how many crazy lies are told about celebrities. If they took the time to officially deny each one, all those internet stalkers would start rumours just to get recognition from their heroes. A-listers don't dignify total rubbish with a response.

If head-on collisions or ignoring entirely aren't ideal, the third option is the sneakiest (and therefore my favourite). You make fun of the rumour right in front of the spreader-of-lies and anyone you'd like to set straight. So for instance if you know that Natalie has been whispering to Alice that you've been chasing after Rob and he's totally not interested, bring it up when everyone's there. "Ha ha, have you heard the latest on what I've been up to? Apparently I call Rob at all hours of the day and night and beg him to date me.... Lord knows where people get these things. How stupid would you have to be to believe that?" If Alice is thinking "But Natalie told me that.. yet she's not contradicting it," you've just sunk Natalie's story into oblivion. Natalie won't know that you were onto *her*, so your dumb fox cover won't get blown, and she won't be on her guard in future. You've also let her know it doesn't bother you, which cuts off her oxygen. And if Rob himself is there – so much the better. "Hey Rob, what time shall I be outside your bathroom window tonight? I've got my binoculars!"

Alternatively, there is the childish, possibly-causing-more-drama-than-a-Princess-needs method. If you don't have any direct contact with the person telling the lies, you could still mock them; they're bound to hear about it. "Have you heard what Tanya's saying about me? Ha ha, she actually said I'd slept with the entire football team! I *wish*... I suppose she's doing it for attention, poor thing."

Oscar Wilde said: "There is only one thing in life worse than being talked about, and that is not being talked about." Take comfort in the fact that people have nothing more exciting to do but spend their time and energy making up stories about you.

Safety

It might seem odd to throw in personal safety when we're talking about awkward conversations, but it does fit together. You see, predatory men (sorry to be sexist, but it's statistically the norm) will often use manipulation to get you where they want you. While there are tons of men who are exemplary human beings, you still have to keep your eyes open to spot the rotters.

When it's a guy you already know, he might weasel his way into your house uninvited, or outstay his welcome when you thought he was just popping in. ("Can I use your bathroom? Could I get a drink of water before I go? I've drunk too much wine, is it OK if I sleep on your sofa?") Needless to say, men like this know exactly what they're doing. Before you know it, you'll be having "a little bit" of sex with him because he "just" wanted to lie down in your bed because it's "comfier than the sofa" and he took all his clothes off because it was "too hot".

You might feel unbearably rude if you refuse him entry to your home, and you can bet your sweet butt he'll use this to his advantage: "What, don't you trust me? You know I'm not going to do anything." A decent man will know why you're being cautious, and accept it. THE ONLY MAN WHO'LL PUSH TO GET HIS OWN WAY IS ONE YOU CAN'T TRUST.

If the guys you're already acquainted with are a problem, what of "strange" men? I've heard numerous accounts of creepy "good Samaritans" in cars who try to flag down a woman driving at night, acting as if they can see a problem with her vehicle. When the woman drives on to a safe public place like a petrol station, she finds nothing wrong – and the man who was so eager to "help" has zoomed onwards. Another common horror story / urban legend is men who park on quiet roads and pretend they've broken down and need help – or even lie in the road as if they've been hit.

If you're driving somewhere remote and see what looks like a breakdown or accident, DON'T STOP – make a note of the location and call the police when you're some way up the road. It gives me a chill to realise how easily someone could be convinced to get out of their car because they're afraid it will look "rude" if they're openly distrustful. Safety beats etiquette, every time. There are some screwed-up people out there who know how to exploit our instincts to help others; 1970s serial killer Ted Bundy famously lured his murder victims with a cast on his arm and a request for help, knowing how hard it would be for anyone to refuse.

Every animal is born with a sense of what's dangerous; imagine if baby zebras were told to be friendly to the lion, because he's "probably a perfectly nice guy". They don't worry about how it looks or tell themselves it's ridiculous to be so skittish – they run! Don't worry that it seems offensive to cross the street when the man behind you is walking too close, or if you don't give a date your home address before meeting him, or refuse the offer of a lift home. Your safety comes first, and you're better off "rude" than dead.

Other people might tell you that you're "being silly" because you don't want to drive to a distant and as yet unknown address for a party with lots of men you don't know. They might accuse you of being "suspicious" when you insist on locking your car doors while you're driving, or deadbolting your house throughout the day. It doesn't matter. You have to use your common sense, trust your gut instincts and put yourself first.

Reassuringly, I've heard lots of real-life stories from women who found some guy oddly creepy, even though there was nothing obviously wrong with him – and their feelings were later justified when he was arrested for being a pervert of some kind. Human beings have been reading each other for millennia, and it seems we're actually well-equipped to make judgement calls. All too often we ignore the little voice in our heads or the anxious feelings flitting around in our stomachs, because we tell ourselves oh-so-logically that nothing's wrong.

I know a man who's fairly popular, although he's a bit too touchy-feely with the ladies, and likes to start fights with total strangers. He hangs out at friends' houses even after they've left for work, oblivious to hints from other housemates that it might be time to go home. Everyone keeps telling me "He's lovely really" but I never invite him to my place. Getting aggressive out of nowhere? Having no concept of boundaries? Um, no. Considering most rapes are committed by someone the victim knows, I'd rather not end up as a statistic. And I would never say that to my friends, because it sounds insane (and would be very wrong) to pre-emptively accuse someone of being a potential rapist, but I have a strong feeling that I need to never be alone with this dude, so I'm going to respect that. Life isn't like the movies, where psychos are conspicuously evil-looking and live in dingy basements. Just because someone has a steady job or is the friend of a friend, it doesn't mean they're going to be trustworthy.

With people you don't know well, don't be too much of a blabbermouth about your personal circumstances. Do you want that stranger at the bar to know that you live alone, where you work, or which car parked outside is yours? We all have the right to live the way we want to – and you might want to wander around on your own outside some bars at 2 am, or leave your doors unlocked, or walk through the roughest part of town with all your jewellery on. That's your choice – but you do have to take responsibility for your decisions, because we can't rely on other people to be honourable and respect our right to live as we please.

And if you're ever physically hurt or threatened by anyone, your first stop is always the police. Even if it takes place at school or work, it's not up to your teacher or boss to decide how to deal with it; it's a criminal offence and needs to be dealt with as such.

On the Street

Ever had the Smile Command? It seems that women's facial expressions are considered public property, and if you're not walking around looking thrilled that your appearance earned whistles from a bunch of workmen, you can expect calls of "Cheer up love", "Give us a smile!" and "It might never happen..."

I generally default to ignoring people who shout at me on the street. If they're far away and I'm wearing headphones, they can't be sure that I heard them – in which case their shouting into thin air in a public place is amusingly embarrassing for them. If they're close enough to be obviously within earshot, I still ignore them. I *could* tell them to speak to me with more respect, but why should I reward rude hollering with adult conversation?

But I'm starting to wonder if, rather than ignoring catcallers, there might be times when *addressing* lecherous behaviour could be more effective. For instance, those guys who wait until you've walked past before muttering quietly about what they'd like to do to you – I doubt they'd have the nerve to repeat themselves if you spun around and said "Excuse me, did you say something?" in your most ladylike manner. If you're feeling cheeky you could reply to "Smile!" with "Bark like a dog!" or "Hop on one leg!" – after all, if it's National "Yell Random Orders At Strangers" Day, who are you to argue?

We ladies often have to deal with men's attention on the street as part of our everyday lives, and it's not particularly helpful when you're told you should take their harassment as a compliment. Here's a handy guide to show to anyone who suggests that it's "flattering" when men make inappropriate advances towards you:

Compliment: An intelligent man engaging you in conversation and telling you something nice about yourself.

Not a Compliment: A slack-jawed, knuckle-dragging Neanderthal yelling unintelligible or obscene comments about how attractive you are / actually attempting physical contact with you.

Why would you take anything as a compliment if it came from such a risible source? Tell grandma to shut her trap – she may have liked it when men drove past and shouted "Nice tits!" but that doesn't mean you have to.

Judging from anecdotal evidence, public transport is a particular hot spot for slimy men to chat up women, possibly because it's the only place we can't escape. No matter what your travelling mode involves (the "don't talk to me" face, headphones and book etc) it won't put them off. If they're not really bothering me (eg staring rather than talking) I stubbornly refuse to make eye contact – if it's attention they want, that's the last thing I'm going to give them, no matter how many times they sigh loudly or stretch across the seat or gawk at my face. If, however, they want to talk and monosyllabic answers aren't working, then why not just turn the tables on them? There's no reason why *they* should get to be the one asking the questions. Quiz them on how much money they make, or what job prospects they have. My personal favourite is to ask them if they've heard the Good News about Jesus – they either leave me alone or I get an interesting conversation out of it.

Final Tips

- When you're not sure whether or not the way someone's treating you is "OK", you might ask yourself "Would this person treat her supervisor at work the same way? Or her bank manager, or the local vicar?" If not, you have to accept that she's not "naturally brusque" – she's saving it up especially for people she thinks will accept it. Don't be one of them!
- Another sanity-saving question when faced with neurotic over-reactions: "If I'd said or done exactly the same thing to someone else, would they have blown up at me like this?" If the answer is no, other people wouldn't be quite so upset if you made them the wrong kind of tea, then the problem is your angry friend, not you.
- If you often find yourself saying to people "I knew you wouldn't mind!" it might be a sign that *you're* the pest, and your friends are too meek to be honest with you. (Lend them this book.)
- Some experiences are horrendous at the time but you learn from them, move on and never repeat that same mistake again. Onwards and upwards is the Princess way. And when you can finally say "Thank God I had that lesson" you know you're free from the past and ready for anything.
- If someone is yelling at you from another room and it's not your boss, you don't need to run to them like a puppy. If they want you, they can come and find you.
- Some parents believe they should get a say in how you live your life even when you're a fully-fledged adult. Should you dare to pick the "wrong" partner / college / career path / location, you'll get merry hell for it. Remember: IT'S NOT YOUR JOB TO MAKE EVERYONE ELSE HAPPY. You get to live your life the way you want, just as they choose how to live theirs. *Nobody* has permission to dictate how someone else handles their own business.
- If someone likes twisting your words, make sure you only speak to them when others are present. Likewise if you have a work colleague who likes to claim credit for stuff you've come up with, only make suggestions in writing, or at the very least, in big meetings where you

can clearly flag them up with "I have an idea..." Witnesses all the way!

- It's tough when you're the target for someone's hostility and you still have to see them every day. When avoidance isn't an option, treat that person with respect and a pleasant attitude. Not because they're nice, but because *you are*.

- If you're having a dispute with someone, don't use phrases like "I'm not offended..." because people will immediately hear "I AM offended". Sometimes untruthful words carry the ghost of their real meaning, which is why it's important to pay attention to what people tell you in a "jokey" way. So when someone says "I'm not trying to take advantage of you" – know that taking advantage of you has, at the very least, crossed their minds.

- In a similar vein, if you're happy to do a favour for someone, don't say it's "no problem"; it suggests that there is a problem but you're oh-so-graciously agreeing to do it anyway...

- Occasionally you'll come across men who think it's funny to patronise you. (Seriously, what are they thinking? Is that moment of feeling superior really worth a lifetime of having absolutely no chance of dating you?) One used to tell me "Ooh, that's a big word for such a little girl!" whenever I said anything consisting of more than two syllables. One day when I threw "cerebral" into the mix, he used his favourite line again. I turned to him with a big smile and said "Aw, do you think 'cerebral' is a BIG word? That's so cute!" He NEVER tried to patronise me again, and it still makes me giggle every time I think of the expression on his face.

- If you're having an argument with someone and they come up with a zinger you know you can't answer, the only comeback is to laugh and say "Touché!"

Finally, we can all take some comfort in the words of Winston Churchill: "I get into bed, turn out the light, say 'bugger the lot of them' and go to sleep."

Part Four

Your Independence

"*Women who pay their own rent don't have to be nice.*"
Katherine Dunn

YOUR CAREER

"Deprived of meaningful work, men and women lose their reason for existence; they go stark, raving mad." Fyodor Dostoyevsky

Lovely as it would be to live off a trust fund and have nothing more taxing to think about than where your next hot stone massage was coming from, it's essential for all human beings to have a purpose. There's no honour in boasting "I don't work, dahling..." If you're not stretching yourself, discovering where your gifts lie, expressing your creativity, or enriching the lives of others, what are you *for*? (I think money's rather wasted on the rich, anyway. They seem to have nothing better to spend it on than bottles of champagne, diamond-encrusted telephones, and drugs. If I were a billionaire, I'd buy a little island to live on and fill it with puppies and baby goats.)

Your occupation doesn't define who you are, but it does play a big part in shaping your life. It's how you spend most of your waking hours and will be your means of meeting friends, learning life lessons and making cash, so choosing a direction requires serious thought. These days very few people stick to one path from school to retirement – it's possible to have three or four careers, sometimes running alongside each other simultaneously. The internet has made it possible for anyone to start their own business, work from home, or chase fame without even leaving the house.

What Should I Do?

When it comes to choosing your profession, nobody can make the decision for you. Your parents / tutors / boss may have an idea of the way they'd like you to proceed, but the choice is yours alone.

The ideal situation is getting paid for something you enjoy doing. Rather than agonising over which degree subject will lead to the best career, study what you're passionate about and you'll usually find that the right job will show up at the right time. (Unless, of course, you're only interested in philosophy, or the changing styles of Katy Perry.) Forget the idea of doing a degree in a subject you're not interested in as "insurance" in case all your other ventures fail. That has to be the most depressing approach ever, and can only lead to disaster; if you know you have something to fall back on, you probably will. But if there are two areas you find *equally* interesting, by all means do some groundwork in both of them; learning a useful trade like plumbing may see you through the lean times in your interior design business, and vice versa.

It's important to know yourself: a) what you're capable of, and b) what you can put up with. Do you thrive on interacting with people, or would you rather be left to your own devices? Some people can't stand being chained to a desk all day, others love the cosiness of a cubicle. Some would rather have the security of a steady paycheck than the thrill of flying by the seat of their pants as a freelancer. It's pointless stressing yourself out by trying to fit into a mould that doesn't suit you just because it sounds good on paper.

If you have fire in your belly for a particular vocation, don't let the prospect of a long training process put you off. The next five years are going to pass anyway, do you want to be fully qualified at the end of that time or not?

Focusing on Your Goals

These days there's a lot of emphasis on finding a fabulous calling that will enhance your life and satisfy your artistic temperament, rather than "settling" for something quiet and ordinary. Much as I believe in aiming for the stars, I have to be absolutely truthful and point out that some passions are best left as hobbies (unless you have some independent source of wealth). You might have mad skills at creating art from chewed-up bits of toffee, but can you make a living from it? As Vivienne Westwood said: "Work out what you're good at and stick to it. Fashion wouldn't have been my first choice of job. I did it because I could, and you have to earn your living." In short, pursue what you love, but be prepared to spend a *long* time getting good at it before anyone will pay you for your efforts. Lots of people work in nine-to-five jobs which they don't consider their big passion in order to fund their "real" pursuits. You might run a small business from home for years before it takes off to the extent that you can live on the proceeds, or spend a decade playing pub gigs before anyone signs your band. (Or it might never happen – but you would have had fun playing the music, anyway.)

Some jobs have only one route towards them (if you want to be a doctor,

199

you can't get around the long stint at medical school) but most are more flexible (not every entrepreneur has a degree in business studies). I left school with the ambition to work in TV and film, and eventually managed to claw my way into costume styling, which I love. Along the way I've taken some detours into childcare, photography, bartending and various office environments. There's a Russian proverb which says "If you chase two rabbits, you will not catch either one", and part of me wishes I'd chosen one course of action and stuck to it. (I could have been Queen of the world by now!) However, I value every different job I've had, because I've always left with new knowledge, new friends, or at the very least, funny stories to tell about the nightmare boss.

Dealing with Discouragers

If you have big dreams, it's inevitable that some people will try to talk you out of them. You might live in a small town that nobody ever leaves. Maybe you're expected to take over the family business, or stay at home and have babies straight out of school. If you start talking about your crazy plans to make it in the big city, it's going to ruffle some feathers.

Often the prophets of doom really do have your best interests at heart; they can't imagine how anyone could make a living from designing jewellery / inventing a new kind of printer / playing sport. (The fact that other people have managed it means nothing to them.) They're afraid you'll waste time and end up disappointed, and they want to save you the hassle.

The dark side of the naysayers is selfishness; they don't want you to follow your desires, because they've been too scared to follow theirs. If they're not enjoying the money, kudos, or satisfaction of an exciting career, why should you get to have it? They'll constantly nitpick at your ideas, disparage your chances of fulfilling your ambitions and try to convince you that it's not worth trying. (This doesn't just apply to jobs; it will encompass everything from travelling ("Haven't you heard stories about what happens to women in those foreign countries?") to living by yourself ("You're bound to get lonely...") They're just expressing their own anxieties and projecting them onto you. Have you ever heard of "crab mentality"? When you have a bunch of crabs in a bucket, it would be quite easy for one individual to climb up and escape – but the others will always grab hold of him and pull him back. Maybe humans aren't the only ones who don't relish watching someone else succeed.

There's a fine line between being cheerfully optimistic and totally deluded. Without visionaries, we'd never have achieved all of the impossible magic we now accept as everyday convenience. As Will Smith pointed out, "It's unrealistic to walk into a room, flip a switch, and have a light come on, but fortunately Edison didn't think so." On the other hand, singing contests on TV are full of auditionees convinced they're destined for stardom, when it's obvious that no amount of auto-tuning could ever help.

Learn to be objective about your own level of skill and seek out unbiased feedback. (The fact that your mum thinks you should be a movie star is of no consequence unless she's a producer.) You might fantasise about holding a courtroom enthralled, but if you don't have much of an eye for detail, you're probably not cut out to be a lawyer. You have to go with the talents you have, not the ones you *wish* you had.

Luck and timing also play a part, so even if you do have the necessary ability, you still might end up in a different field from the one you'd planned. But if you don't try, you're 100% guaranteed to fail, and if you never ask, the answer will always be no. So give everything your best shot and don't be held back by fear – your own or anyone else's. Instead of worrying about what other people think of your ideas, or imagining how they'll react if you fail, concentrate on working steadily towards your goals, and spend time with people who are inspirational and encouraging.

Getting to Where you Want to Go

No matter what fancy qualifications you get, you generally have to start from the bottom. Being on the lowest rung of the ladder isn't much fun (especially if you're first in, last out, and do all the most tedious jobs), but it can also be really beneficial. My early days of working in film involved low pay and long days, and I never had a moment to sit down. But I found that being a "runner" on the set allowed me to see a little bit of everything that was going on; taking coffee orders and helping out in a general way meant I was able to chat to everyone. Once I'd progressed into styling the clothes, I had far less time to see what other departments were doing, so I was glad I'd had the opportunity earlier. (Also, when you're the person handing out donuts, everyone loves you.)

Once you have a job, don't stagnate. If you're after promotion, going above and beyond the call of duty in your present role is a fast track to being given more responsibility. Sometimes you need to prove yourself by taking on the workload of the job you want long before it's officially yours.

I know that applying for jobs is a tough and boring process, but unless you're actively searching for a new position, you're effectively re-choosing your situation every day. If you weren't in your current job, and someone offered it to you, would you take it? Or would you veer off in a wildly different direction? If you're looking to get into a new area, ask around; you never know who might have some unexpected insight or useful contacts. Make a website if that would help. Take advantage of social networking sites which let you connect with people in the industry you work in or would like to break into.

Word of warning: you'll come across many, MANY guys who'll say "Oh, you want to get into X? I have a friend who works at Y, I could get you an interview." I've heard this so many times and it has NEVER EVER happened. (Except for the time the guy himself was in a position of power, and he took me out to lunch and spent the whole time staring at my chest and telling me his wife was "very open-minded" – but I don't think I'll count that as a triumph.)

It's tempting to pursue someone who makes big promises, but do take their words with a massive pinch of salt; it's usually an attempt to impress you with their status and supercool contacts, or a dastardly trick to get your phone number.

Finding Work: The Bad Advice

When magazines give advice on job hunting, they often mention three things which make me cringe. Having been involved in office recruitment, I know exactly how they come across in real life.

Bad Advice #1: "Be persistent."

Good persistence is about knocking on every door available: when I was first looking for jobs in TV, I had to send out *hundreds* of CVs in order to get maybe five interviews, resulting in *one* trainee position. Bad persistence is focusing 100% on one workplace: ringing up every day to see if any vacancies have opened up, popping in to check they got your application, following up with a phone call after having an interview.

The theory is they'll be dazzled by your enthusiasm. They won't. They'll think you're a stalker and quite possibly give you an unflattering nickname to that effect and giggle every time you call in. Having worked on reception, I know that telling the boss "X called about the job again" is far more likely to irritate than impress. And I was a *nice* receptionist – half won't bother passing on the message anyway. Why would they, when your constant calls make more work for them?

Bad Advice #2: "Oh, I'm such a perfectionist..."

When an interviewer asks the dreaded "What's your greatest weakness?" question, apparently we're all supposed to claim to be workaholic perfectionists. Do we really think employers are that gullible? Apart from the fact that I've read this in a million "helpful" articles (so they'll all be wise to it by now) it sounds so phony. If you do get asked about weakness, you can be honest and say "I used to have a problem with (innocuous generic imperfection) but I've been working on it and I think I've improved a lot." (It helps if you pick something lots of people can relate to, like getting nervous if you're expected to do any public speaking.)

Also, saying you're a perfectionist isn't the entirely positive problem people seem to think it is. Many bosses would prefer an employee who understands that "a good plan today beats a perfect plan tomorrow" over someone who'll nitpick at unimportant details and never actually finish anything.

Bad Advice #3: "Not yet, but I can learn..."

Often successful people have stories about how they started out as a scrappy youngster, bombarding a potential boss with daily phone calls and bluffing their way into employment by saying "Yep, lots of experience!" then quickly learning on the job. We're repeatedly told we should sneak our way into vacancies by assuring the interviewer we know what we're doing, chutzpah making up for lack of expertise. The advice goes on to suggest that if bare-faced lying isn't your thing, an enthusiastic reply of "No, I haven't done that yet, but I'm very quick to learn," is the next best thing, showing flexibility and dedication. Great, huh? Except it tells your potential employer that the first week of your new post will be wasted time.

So what's the solution? *Make the necessary preparations.* It's not hard to predict job requirements; if you want to be an accountant, you'll need to know your way around a spreadsheet. Misleading your employers doesn't exactly sparkle with integrity and isn't Princess-worthy; it's selfish to think "I want this job and I'll say anything to get it, even if it means screwing over the company."

In The Workplace

Generally, the biggest factor in your happiness will be how well you get on with your colleagues. Even the most stressful workload feels lighter if you have camaraderie, but the easiest of roles can be torture if there's a heavy atmosphere. (Although you can always be a little ray of sunshine and hope it spreads...)

The hardest part of any job is being nice to stupid people. There is a positive side – you'll develop masterful self-control and the ability to remain serene no matter what impossible problems people hurl at you.

Don't automatically expect your boss to notice how beautifully you're managing your department; if you want to rise through the ranks, speak up. Your progress will stall if you choose the easy route of suffering in silence and issuing mental ultimatums. ("If she doesn't give me a promotion / appreciate the extra effort I've put into this project / notice the hours of overtime I've done, I'm leaving.") Work is all about communication. Your boss won't know what you deserve unless you point it out. This is because – biggest tip of all – your boss might be one of those stupid people. Believe it or not, I've come across a frighteningly high proportion of top dogs who can barely tie their own shoelaces. If you're blessed with a boss who's smart and innovative, watch and learn everything you can from them.

Creating Boundaries

Your boss is like a man you're dating: you need to create the limits, because otherwise s/he will push you as far as they can. Some jobs have strict hours, others rule that you can go home "when you're done". When I was an office temp, I often had to stay late even when I had no specific tasks to do, just in case someone needed me. (Unfortunately my superiors had never got the hang of time-management; they would shriek "I'm too busy to think about what jobs to give you," instead of delegating sensibly. Occasionally they'd come to life at 5 pm with a lengthy list of orders to complete before I was allowed to leave. Passive aggressive, much?) If I queried this set-up, they would react as if I was totally weird for not relishing those hours of pointless and *unpaid* overtime... yes, they lived in a somewhat warped reality.

Finally I figured out a winning strategy: if the notoriously late-finishing department called me, I would always make up a reason why I *had* to leave at 6:30 pm on the dot before saying yes to the day's work. (They would grudgingly agree, and then refer to my leaving at the official end time as "finishing early".)

Unfortunately, most jobs don't give you the power to re-negotiate the terms of your contract on a daily basis, so read all the small print before you sign anything, and make sure you and your employer are clear on the boundaries of your role. This counts for volunteer positions too – a friend of mine had a working holiday on a farm and ended up minding the owner's kids on her "day off" – she didn't feel she could say no when she was a guest in the house. Next time, she had a clear conversation with her hosts *before she arrived* about the number of hours she'd be expected to work each day and whether her time off was really her own.

Many careers (especially those in competitive fields) require some unpaid interning, also known as being an overworked dogsbody. Internships are notorious for taking advantage of young people desperate to break into the industry while dangling the hope of a future paid job in front of them. On the plus side, they can be a great way to get your foot in the door, meet people and get a feel for what the work is really like.

There's nobody quite as obnoxious as the junior who arrogantly assumes they shouldn't have to earn their stripes like everyone else, but there's a line between the necessary paying of dues, and being too meek to demand the salary you deserve. Once you've got substantial expertise and you know you're doing a good job, people who ask you to work for nothing are being ridiculous. The trouble is, there's always someone who's so keen for the experience that they'll take the unpaid job – and so the cycle continues. If everyone refused, these cheapskates would HAVE to do things by the book.

Finally, don't put yourself in danger. Don't let anyone pressure you into doing manual work you're not capable of (are they going to pay your chiropractor bills?) or anything illegal (like moving your boss's car when the insurance doesn't cover you). The same goes for spraying chemicals without the proper protection, working so late that you don't feel safe when you're travelling home, or being left alone with creepy men you don't trust. And yes, all of the above are examples from my own adventures in employment. Wow, I've had some horrible jobs.

Cold Hard Cash

We go to work to make money. Somehow people forget this, and find it excruciatingly embarrassing to admit they'd quite like to get paid enough to live on. Bosses rely on our cash-related squeamishness to get away with paying us as little as possible. I've even had employers try to short-change me by a few pounds here and there, obviously hoping I'd be too shy to ask for the rest of my money. I can only assume they sneakily make a profit by shaving a little bit off everyone's pay.

When you're negotiating a salary (whether at an initial interview or in a staff review) always let the other person be the first to name a figure. A deathly fear of looking "greedy" often leads to us aiming low, and they know this. If it's impossible to avoid answering first, go for a high figure (and don't let your voice go up as if you're asking a question). They can then say "We were actually thinking of X amount," or "We can offer between X and Y," and you can graciously agree (to the larger amount, naturally). If it helps you to conquer your natural modesty, imagine you're an agent asking on behalf of someone else – without getting carried away and referring to yourself in the third person...

Stress

Some jobs are undeniably stressful, whether it's because you're dealing in matters of life and death, or that's just what it feels like. It's become fashionable in some circles to boast about having less sleep or working longer hours than your colleagues. (Which is silly when you realise that staying late at the office simply shows that you're not very good at finishing your work in the eight hours allotted to you.) I used to temp in an advertising company where one of the producers had a poster next to her desk that said: "Breathe". If you're at the point where you need signs to remind you of this, something is *definitely* wrong. (Maybe her motto should have been "We make commercials. When they start, people mute the sound and go to get snacks. It's not a big deal.")

Of course, the trouble is that some people *love* stress. They thrive on it, they create it when it isn't there and they consider it a badge of honour. I once had a boss who seemed to me the picture of a softly spoken gentleman. He had great ideas, put in long hours rather than delegating them, and offered mentoring schemes to youngsters starting out. Yet staff would often say in hushed tones "Chris won't like that! Change it, quick!" or describe the way he'd "gone crazy" earlier – when actually he'd been speaking in a perfectly pleasant tone. (I was a witness!) I realised that pretending their boss was an ogre made life more exciting for them.

And what about those people who bring a whirlwind of panic with them wherever they go? They're the ones who call you in a flap about something and won't calm down long enough for you to explain. There's nothing you can do but humour them and keep steadfastly calm when they "need those figures RIGHT NOW". ("They're on your desk, I put them there yesterday.") I'm guessing they enjoy feeling that they alone understand the gravity of the situation; they like to think of YOU as being the incompetent one, no matter how many times you disprove this theory. Just inwardly repeat "A lack of proper planning on your part does not constitute an emergency on my part." (If all else fails, get it printed on a t-shirt and wear it to work every day.)

Nobody is paying you enough to make anxiety part of your regular routine. When you find yourself skipping meals, cancelling holidays and lying awake at night worrying about your workload, it might be time to rethink your occupation.

Princess Cool aka Keeping Your Composure

My worst ever boss was a woman with serious anger management issues; she would work herself into a steaming rage (complete with swearing at the top of her voice) over nothing at all. Then she'd abruptly switch gears and attempt to be nice by buying us lunch, taking it as a personal insult if you'd already eaten. She once threw away someone's glass of wine at a supposedly relaxing Friday night drinks party because she didn't approve of that particular vintage. Yep, she was quite the loon.

I didn't want to get fired or encourage her wrath, so I resisted the temptation to shriek, cry or yell back at her. After that, when I worked with other rude or incompetent bosses, it became a point of pride for me: "If SHE didn't get me to lose my cool, YOU'RE not going to!"

If you have the kind of job that provides you with a pack of minions, use your power wisely. On one film set I worked with a young woman who would flap about when she was feeling pressured, shouting at everyone and creating a panicky atmosphere. She was a nice person, so she would always apologise later for "being a screamer" but it did make me think less of her. I thought "We're all on the same deadline, so if I can keep it together, why can't she?"

Having an urgent manner makes people feel as if they're really in the thick of things, and it sends a message to onlookers: if you were visiting a workplace and didn't know the hierarchy, you'd probably assume that the person crossly stomping about with a clipboard and a headset was somebody important. But being this kind of drama queen is not the Princess strategy for trying to appear high-powered, not least because you can't present yourself as stressed AND coolly unflappable at the same time.

The only problem with having an unruffled exterior is that people who prefer a more volatile mode of communication don't understand it; if you're calm when everyone else is running around like headless chickens, they might assume you're not taking the work seriously or that you don't understand how important it is. Look them in the eye and assure them you do appreciate the urgency of the task; *don't* say "Hey, let's get some perspective here..."

When You're the Boss

As the boss, you set the tone of the workplace, whether your only employee is a cleaner for your house, or you're the president of a huge enterprise. If someone isn't performing as they should, they may come to you with sob stories or excuses, but you *don't need to know* about their personal issues. Ultimately it's none of your business why they're not doing the job properly; your only concern is if and when they'll be able to improve their track record (or whether they need to be replaced). It sounds harsh, but people will take advantage of a boss who's *too* nice. Your employees might like you or they might not – it doesn't matter, as long as they respect you.

It's said that if you don't build your own dreams, someone will hire you to help build theirs. Some people can't wait to be the boss because they figure it will mean the end of answering to authority figures. The truth is that no matter what you're doing, you're answering to someone – whoever pays your wages calls the shots. If you open a boutique, it's your customers. If you run a nail salon, it's your clients. If you're an athlete, it's your sponsors, and if you're a film director, it's your audience. If they're not happy with the way you're doing things, they'll let you know. Rather than rebelling against any kind of instruction or feedback, a Princess accepts it as part of life and learns from it.

Being Self-Employed

When you run a little empire of your very own, everything from accounts to marketing is down to you (and there are no paid sick days or holidays). Part of selling yourself and retaining your prestige depends on using the proper language: you're not a dog walker, you're the owner of a small pet care business. You don't "babysit" your neighbour's kids – your neighbour is a client of your childminding business. It sounds cheesy if you overdo it (even if you are a full-time mother, you can't *really* describe yourself as a professional chauffeur, night nurse and chef) but don't sell yourself short. Your time is valuable: bill people for every minute of it. If you work for three extra hours and don't charge them for overtime, they won't think "Aw, she's so sweet" – they'll think you're DUMB. If you want to be treated with respect, you have to behave like a boss.

When you first start your trade, whether it's computer repair, personal training, or whatever, it's tempting to lower your prices in order to build up your clientele. If you do this, make it clear that you're offering an "introductory rate" – once you've built up a circle of regulars, you won't want to be stuck with those low prices forever. Factor in the cost of materials and pay yourself a decent hourly wage – if it takes an entire day to decorate that cake to the client's specifications, charge them appropriately. (If they don't like it, they can do it themselves and see how long it takes them...) They might whine "I can't afford that much!" but that's not your problem – if they want the service, they have to pay for it. The supermarket doesn't cut prices for the people who want quality goods but don't want to cough up the cash; why should you?

To keep your relationships with clients on a professional footing, avoid blurring the lines into friendship. It's lovely to get on well with the people you're working for, but if you always chat for ages when your job's finished, it makes you look as if you have nothing else to do all day. Ideally, your clients will believe that you're much sought-after and they're lucky to get you – NOT that you're short of work and will be willing to take any scraps they offer you. It's exactly the same principle as dating – people value what they perceive to be in demand. If they're picturing you as a loser who's sitting home alone waiting for the phone to ring, it's less enticing than the idea of you in a busy whirl of jobs / dates, juggling eager prospective clients / boyfriends. The only people who say yes to everything, no matter how rubbishy, are the ones who are afraid they won't get another offer. Always tell people you need to "check your diary" before you commit to a job, even if you know the only prospect you have for the next six weeks is lying around watching movies with your cat.

If someone offers you a low rate of pay or asks for a freebie, promising future work on the basis of "just this one time", it's tempting to go for it. I was pondering whether or not to take a job at a big fashion show – it was no pay, but I figured it might look good on my styling CV. My wise mother pointed out: "If they're prestigious enough to look good on your CV, they can afford to pay you." Also, they always promise "it will lead to paid work in the future" but it never does. Why would it? They already know you'll work for nothing.

Working with Friends

These days, everyone has a friend who's a hairdresser / wedding photographer / handyman, and it's natural to want to help out a budding business and maybe get "mate's rates" too. (It's always nice to get a bargain, but remember that really good friends support their pals by paying full price.) Unfortunately, mixing friendships and work can be problematic. I experienced this when I was trying to build a website and an acquaintance offered her services; I paid the price she quoted (the going rate for a basic job) but then she acted as if she were doing me a favour, saying she'd been "too busy" to do the work by the deadline we'd agreed on. I could see that her attitude was going to waste my time, so I made alternative plans (resulting in a frosty reception when I told her I was "letting her go"). Of course, I still had to pay her. Ouch! (Famous firefighter Red Adair once said: "If you think it's expensive to hire a professional to do the job, wait until you hire an amateur." Yep, horribly true.) The flipside is when *you're* the one working for friends and they assume you'll forgo your usual fees and will be happy to get paid in drinks at the bar. If your forte is something useful (medical knowledge, the ability to fill in tax forms) or something other people might do as a hobby (storyteller at the children's library, designing birthday cards), be prepared for family and friends to bug you for complimentary services. It probably won't occur to any of them that other people might also be hitting you up for favours, so you'll have to politely but firmly deflect all those zillions of requests in order to avoid spending all your free time working for needy loved ones.

Working with pals can be brilliant fun, but think carefully before you involve a friend or family member in your place of employment; they'll reflect on you, for better or worse. I once said "Hey, I know someone!" when my department needed an extra assistant, and I regretted it forever afterwards. My friend wasn't lazy exactly, but he was slow. Instead of going out at lunchtime, he would eat in the office and then spend the rest of his lunch hour reading. This would have been fine, but the boss walking past couldn't be expected to know he was on a break, and she was most perturbed by his apparent disinterest in working. I was technically his supervisor, which caused problems because a) he didn't like this fact and would avoid obeying my (gentle, politely worded) "orders", and b) I got blamed for everything he did wrong. Finally, he would ask for a lift every morning, which meant my peaceful commute was shattered.

Rich people often employ their friends as personal assistants – sounds like a great way to hang out with your buddies and do them a financial favour, right? Wrong. I've noticed from watching reality shows (don't let anyone tell you trash TV can't be educational) that friends on your payroll will nearly always do a shoddy job until you're forced to fire them. Maybe this is proof that nobody really wants a career they didn't earn on their own merit. And on that note, no good ever comes of employing people as a favour to their family members. Your friend might claim her little brother is dying to work as a waiter in your restaurant, but if he wanted the job that badly, he'd be asking for himself.

Balancing Career with Life

Two iconic blondes, two opposite views:

"A career is wonderful, but you can't curl up with a career on a cold night." Marilyn Monroe

versus

"Some women choose to follow men, and some women choose to follow their dreams. If you're wondering which way to go, remember that your career will never wake up and tell you that it doesn't love you anymore." Lady Gaga

So who's right? Both make compelling points. If you cry yourself to sleep every night because you're so lonely since your boyfriend left, knowing that you're working on a project that's important to you will provide some consolation. Equally, you could spend decades building up an impressive livelihood to the detriment of your personal life, but then find old age leaves you unable to pursue it any more. If your business relies on public support as Lady G's does, she could very easily find that her career "doesn't love" her any more.

One thing's for sure – if you allow a man to derail you from your aspirations, there's a high chance you'll end up resenting him for it.

Success Takes Time

If you're feeling down about how long it's taking for you to reach your goals, consider George Clooney. He made his first appearance as a TV extra in 1978 and spent the next *sixteen years* taking bit parts, working on his craft and gathering experience before he hit the big time with *ER*. It would have been so easy to give up at any point; imagine hoping for a break all that time. Picture the humiliation of talking to friends back home – "Nope, no film offers yet..."

But gorgeous George persevered and has become one of the most powerful movie moguls in the business.

Fellow Oscar winner Dustin Hoffman describes how his acting coach Barney Brown told him "Go to New York and understand one thing – nothing is going to happen to you for ten years."

What I find really interesting about George and Dustin is that they were clearly in it for the long haul because they loved *acting*, not because they craved fame. If you want to hone your skills to perfection, you'll do that job even when it's not comfortable or gratifying or making you tons of cash. As George puts it, "If the movie makes money, I make money. If I don't, I've still made the movie I wanted to make."

Nobody starts out at the top of their field; it's a long, slow process and you'll only make it if you have a strong belief in yourself *and* the determination to keep going. Remember the proverb "After a full day in the mines, you may not have found any diamonds, but you will have strengthened your back." Work even when it doesn't feel as if you're getting anywhere, and you'll be prepared when opportunity comes knocking at your door. And if you don't hit the big time, you'll still have worked at the job you find most satisfying.

Your Contribution aka What is Success, Anyway?

"Making your mark on the world is hard. If it were easy, everybody would do it. But it's not. It takes patience, it takes commitment, and it comes with plenty of failure along the way. The real test is not whether you avoid this failure, because you won't. It's whether you let it harden or shame you into inaction, or whether you learn from it; whether you choose to persevere." Barack Obama

When your career is turning out just the way you dreamed it would, it gives you a real purpose in life. You won't even notice the long hours you're toiling away, because you're having so much FUN. As the saying goes, "Choose a job you love, and you will never have to work a day in your life." I'd add that you can *choose* to love any job! Making a living isn't all sunshine and roses, but with the right attitude you'll be able to find an enjoyable *aspect* to whatever you do, whether it's having a friendly chat with customers, bonding with your colleagues over your shared hatred of deadlines, or even being on your feet all day (tiring, but you get lots of exercise). And if you can't find anything likeable about your workplace, why are you still there?

All work is a contribution of some kind; whether you're sorting post, grooming horses, taking care of children or cooking meals, you're providing a service and giving back to your community. Of course, your mission in life doesn't have to revolve around your money-making endeavours; some of the most fabulous people I know don't have lucrative or high-profile careers, but spend their days making the world a better place via their gifts of hospitality, generosity, or empathy.

Lots of taxpayers get angry with the people who deliberately choose to live on benefits. When you're getting up at 5 am every day and enduring a long, grim commute to start your 12-hour shift, it sucks to think about all those people getting money for rolling out of bed at noon and watching TV all day. But do you really envy people who take pride in doing nothing? Most of us have had periods of unemployment and there's no shame in that, but opting out of life so that you can spend all day hanging around the house and living on handouts – that's not *winning.*

We all have the odd day of blissfully doing nothing, but we have to weigh up what we say is important to us, versus how we actually spend our time. (I don't know what your life's purpose is, but I'm pretty sure it's not fiddling around on Twitter while half-watching TV.) If you can give your time to worthwhile projects and people without worrying about getting the credit or making a profit, you'll be a real mover and a shaker, unlike someone who boasts about loafing around all day.

As writer Erma Bombeck said, "Don't confuse fame with success. One is Madonna, the other is Helen Keller." Our society puts enormous emphasis on the outer trappings of "success" – having the money to buy a big house or a flashy car, being seen in all the right places or getting your face in the paper. Yet money and fame are not an indication that you're great at what you do, any more than a lack of those things means you're untalented. There are drivers, teachers, shop assistants and care workers all doing their bit for society without ever being interviewed on TV or bringing out their own perfume. You have to work for your own satisfaction, rather than because your goal is to have a fawning assistant to pick up your dry cleaning.

A huge income doesn't automatically lead to a satisfying life. You could be a prosperous business tycoon, but when you can never turn your phone off or relax completely, and you spend every holiday checking your emails, you're basically company property, not a human being. Drug dealers and criminals might be able to live the high life, but they have a negative impact on everyone else, and while some ladies claim they love working in the sex industry, it's a path rarely taken by financially secure women with happy childhoods. The point is, it's relatively easy to make money, but you can't buy self-respect.

Suppose your dream is to be a pop star: even if you were to become an overnight "success", you might find that the real work is just beginning. When you're micromanaged by a record label, you become something of a geisha: all your appointments made for you, all your opinions neatly tapered to fit the non-offensive personality you've been told to project, and instructions to smile and keep your mouth shut if you can't conform. Is this success?

In any kind of business, you'll find a battle of the egos: squabbles over who gets the biggest office with the nicest view, conflict when your peer gets a promotion or raise before you do, back-biting, idea-stealing, gossiping and bullying. Is this success?

No matter what your job or status in life, you can make a difference. How? Live with integrity. Inspire someone else to try new things and never give up. Be a force of positivity, wherever you go. Promote fairness. Be the best you can be, and listen to your calling.

I'm pretty sure that actually would be "success".

Final Tips (that might come in handy no matter what your job – some of them are sneaky!)

- Never hand in a project more than 24 hours early – they'll pile more work on you. Projects always take as long as you have; if you give an underling ages to finish a task, they'll stretch it out to last the entire time. Give them a few hours less and they'll speed up and become more efficient. Likewise, if you're given a budget, try to use as much of it as you can (within reason). If you're good with money and skimp, they'll give you less next time.
- If there's a spelling mistake on your job application, it will probably go straight into the bin, even if everything else is fantastic. Check everything: details DO matter.

- No matter how excited you are to see the clock ticking towards 6 pm, don't be too loud in your joyful shouts of "Thank God it's Friday!" Apart from the obvious negative implications if overheard by your boss (who might guess that you've spent the last few hours browsing shoe websites and shuffling papers until home time), it also suggests that you hate your job. And who wants to admit they're the kind of non-starter who spends forty hours a week doing something they can't stand?

- People tell you who they are in your first meeting. For instance, if you're interviewing someone and they show up late, chances are they'll always be late for everything. If someone contradicts you over some insignificant detail in your first conversation, they'll have no qualms about being antagonistic once they start working for you. As a production assistant, I once watched actors audition for a role in a commercial; one guy constantly made up his own version of the lines, but he still got the job. The trouble was that the advert required him to stick to a very specific script and it turned out his quick-witted improvisational skills were due to his total inability to remember lines as they were written. The shoot day involved many, many re-takes.

- Remember what Henry Ford said: "Nothing is particularly hard if you divide it into small jobs." Take that first little step, and then the next.

- If you have an appointment coming up with a potential client, don't call "to make sure the meeting is still on". This makes you look as insecure as you would if you called a boy with the same question. You *assume* the meeting will go ahead as planned, but if you scheduled it ages ago and you're worried they'll somehow forget, you can contact them on a pretext – "Where's the best place to park when I come for my meeting with you on Tuesday?" and then you've subtly reminded them, without looking as if that's what you were doing. If you do ever come across someone who "forgets" the meeting they planned with you, be aware that this is a well-known corporate move to put you off. They didn't forget; they wanted to stand you up. (The same goes for men.) Proceed carefully.

- Give your work everything you've got. Slacking off and doing just enough to get by means you're doing a number on your employer AND yourself. There's a memorable saying about this: "If you succeed in cheating someone, don't think that the person is a fool. Realise that the person trusted you much more than you deserved." Princesses are honourable enough to do the right thing even when nobody's watching.

- Listen to your gut. How often have you thought "I *knew* that would happen!" when it's too late to change the situation? Pay attention to this feeling BEFORE everything falls apart – don't dismiss it with "I'm sure everything is fine... they know what they're doing."

- If something is impossible, don't just agree to it and hope for the best. Your boss might be slightly annoyed if you say "Sorry, I won't be able to finish a project that size in just two days," but s/he'll be far more annoyed if you blithely say yes, then end up failing. You'll score more brownie points if you under-promise and over-deliver.

- Always get everything in writing, just in case. Note down the name of the person you spoke to, the date and the time. When things go wrong, a paper trail can back you up. (If nothing else, saying "I've been speaking with Mr Jones" gives you more credibility than: "So, this guy told me...") I love emails even more than letters, because nobody can deny receiving them or fudge the dates.

- Don't point out all the weaknesses in a project you're handing in to your manager. I used to do this as a way of protecting myself from criticism; it was my way of saying: "Look, I'm so alert I can spot all the potential problems." By the third time I'd had the response "You don't sound very sure of yourself", I realised it was just making me look incompetent.

- There's a proverb "If you correct a wise person, they will become wiser; if you correct a fool, you will get abused for it." Take on board other people's suggestions – even if they wound your pride because you thought what you were doing was pretty awesome already.

- The art of appearing authoritative is down to your manner, not your job title. When I work on commercial shoots, often the entire crew will be meeting for the first time. It's normally easy to tell who's who in the hierarchy from body language, but I was once surprised to find that the man I assumed was the producer was actually a runner (the most junior role there is). He walked and talked with such confidence that I have no doubt he probably is a producer by now. This isn't about acting above your station: it just means making firm eye contact, speaking clearly rather than mumbling, and saying things like "Yes, I can take care of that," instead of "Hmm, well, I'm not sure..."

- Don't be afraid to admit to your mistakes. (If it was a real doozy, it'll probably be obvious to your colleagues whose fault it was, anyway.) People will have far more respect for you if you own up and apologise than if you try to wriggle out of it or pin the blame on someone else.
- Finally: rather than worrying about the petty side of work (out-performing a rival, making sure nobody pinches your ideas, making more money than your peers), be competitive with yourself instead. Someone else might come up with the same brilliant idea you've just had, but nobody will develop it in quite the same way you can.

YOUR FINANCES

"Discipline is choosing between what you want now and what you want most."
Augusta F. Kantra

So, the cash is rolling (or trickling) in, and you're a woman of independent means – what a great feeling. Unfortunately, many of us have trouble handling our money.

"Budget" is sometimes considered a dirty word, bringing to mind grotty bargain basements, the cheapest own-brand groceries, and staying in watching repeats on TV instead of having glamorous nights out. Yet keeping your accounts tight is the key to freedom; when you take control and plan the use of your capital in advance instead of letting it slip unnoticed through your fingers, you'll feel as if you have more, not less.

What's Important to You?

Ultimately, finances are all about priorities. I spent £750 on a great stereo system, which is admittedly expensive (my friends thought I was crazy). However, I expect it to last for years, I use it for hours every day and whenever I listen to music I appreciate the fantastic sound. What's not to like? For me, it was a great investment, and it's true what they say: if you'll never remember what you spent on it, only the joy you got from it, it's worth the money.

To put it in perspective, I only spent £800 on my car, which I've had for ten years. I bought it second-hand, it looks somewhat ancient now (people tell me it has "character") and I've spent a fair amount on repairs over the years. But it gets me from A to B, it's cheap to run, and I was able to buy it outright. (Luckily, "Use my car to impress people" has never been on my list of priorities.)

Meanwhile, one of my "You're crazy to spend that much on a stereo!" friends bought a car on finance, which meant paying extra interest on top of the thousands it costs to get a brand new model. He then ended up defaulting on the loan, which meant he gave the car back to the shop, having paid off around half its value with nothing to show for it. This doesn't bother him, because money is just something he uses up until it's gone: he earns almost twice what I do, but has no savings because he fritters it away on designer trainers, booze, and late-night kebabs. He's the kind of person who'll buy his favourite DVD again because he left the first copy at his mate's house and he wants to watch that film today, not tomorrow.

The point is, we're free to do whatever we like with our own dough, even if other people don't agree with our choices. If you show off your fancy new camera, it might upset those friends whose invitations you turned down when you were pleading poverty. They won't realise you've been saving up for months, and the only reason you had the money for such a nice gadget is BECAUSE you missed lots of awesome events. Likewise, you might feel annoyed when you see a friend apparently throwing cash around like a drunken sailor after telling you she "can't afford" to go somewhere with you. But it's none of your business if she wants to blow her wages on clothes rather than drinks, or her own holiday instead of the one you chose. We all have the right to invest in what we personally value the most.

Unforgettable experiences are generally worth splurging on; unlike *stuff*, memories don't wear out (or take up space, get dusty, break, or get stolen). If you really want to go and work at an orangutan orphanage in Borneo, it will be worth the cash. The same goes for seeing your absolute favourite singer or sports team, the experience day at the Formula One racing track, and travelling to get together with family, even if you have to stay in and clip coupons for the rest of that month.

And remember – if you've got enough, you're a millionaire!

Your Budget

Put simply, you need to spend less than you earn. Start by writing everything down: how much money you bring in every month, how much gets taken up with "unavoidable" bills (more on those in a moment), and how much goes out on non-essentials. Lots of us make the mistake of listing all our regular expenditures without allowing for any extras; we write off dentist fees or birthday presents as being outside of the normal budget. But the sad truth is, there will be "added" costs every month – it's just the way life goes.

It's incredibly useful to keep a money diary to see how much you REALLY get through; most people massively underestimate their outgoings and genuinely have no idea why they're always broke. It's also a good way to spot your greatest weaknesses – is it the daily pack of cigarettes you "need"? Do you comfort shop for little luxuries because you feel you've "earned" them for your hard work? For a lot of people, the biggest killer is the everyday stuff: buying sandwiches instead of making lunch at home, grabbing a sugary soft drink because water's "boring", or popping into a favourite "cheap" shop and accidentally coming home with three new pairs of earrings and a neon pleather belt.

We often justify lavishing our cash on others, because it's so unselfish. I recently calculated the amount I'd shelled out on a close friend's engagement (the gift, the celebratory meal, the hen night...) and it was terrifying. Birthdays, graduations, weddings, anniversaries, christenings... if you have a big family and a wide circle of friends, spending on celebrations is virtually unavoidable. Even though it's going to a worthy cause, your generosity still adds up and depletes your bank balance. If you're close enough to buy someone a present, you're close enough to be honest about what you can afford.

One way to make budgeting more fun is to shift your mindset so things you used to buy without a second thought become a "treat". Dropping cash on a new outfit feels more special when it's something you do once in a blue moon rather than every weekend. I love going out for coffee with friends because it's so needlessly *extravagant*; I have coffee at home, yet I'm paying £3 for a shot of hazelnut syrup and a seat on a particularly squidgy sofa. Changing a mundane routine into a rare indulgence makes life feel more festive, and it's amazing how much you can save by skipping the *daily* lattes. You'll be loaded in no time...

Saving Money

Start with the basics: go through all your bank accounts (current, savings etc) and make sure every penny in your name is getting the best interest rate it possibly can. Interest is FREE MONEY and it's so satisfying to watch it mount up. Banks often use special rates or cash incentives to entice people into switching to them, so look out for rewards that could give your savings a boost.

When you're planning a budget it's easy to overlook those "unavoidable" bills because you pay them automatically and consider them non-negotiable. Most people stay forever with the same providers for their electricity, gas, insurance, telephone and internet in order to avoid hassle. Take half an hour to check competitor's rates and ensure you're getting the best deal; it could save you a bundle in the long run.

Sometimes we see shopping as a hobby or a means of entertainment; simply avoiding trips to the mall could help you to save. (Or you could try tricking yourself: "I'll get that *next time* I'm here.") Some people find it helpful to calculate how many hours they'd have to work in order to buy the goodies they're after. Unfortunately, it has the opposite effect on me; I think "What, I only have to work for ONE whole day to buy that incredible furry coat I can keep forever? Brilliant!"

What are the biggest drains on your finances? Little fripperies you don't really need? Alcohol? (Who's keeping an eye on the cost after the third shot?) Or maybe subscriptions you never use (why, hello there gym) or have forgotten about – film streaming websites must make millions from people who forget to cancel after that first free month. Assuming you're not on the breadline, you can still spoil yourself with treats now and then. An effective way to do this is to keep a piggybank and pop in the appropriate amount of money every time you DON'T spend it. Walk everywhere for a week and set aside whatever you'd normally blow on petrol. Add what you've saved by making dinner from scratch instead of getting a takeaway. Invite the girls round for homemade cocktails and tot up how much more it would have cost if you'd gone to a bar. At the end of the month, you can use the money you "saved" to buy yourself a reward. This way, you might still be spending the same amount in the end but at least you're really reaping the benefits instead of squandering your hard-earned cash on things you barely notice. (Unfortunately, cheating doesn't count – it only works if you use legitimate means to get there. For instance, "I didn't buy that glossy magazine I wanted, because I know I would only read it once and it's mostly adverts anyway" = good. "I didn't buy a £400 pair of sunglasses, and I wanted to! Can I use the money for a designer handbag instead?" = bad.)

And as a side note, you can save a hell of a lot of money if you don't care *when* you get something. Only a total fashion victim would join the rest of the (sheep) herd and queue up in the early hours for the latest phone, when they already have a perfectly good one at home (and the extortionate new release will drop in price in a month or so anyway).

If you're saving up for something big – a holiday, a car, or even a house – focus on delayed gratification. You might love renting a spacious flat, but would you be better off in more modest accommodation *now* so you can afford to buy a bigger place later? What will ultimately make you happier? Travelling business class rather than economy, or knowing you have security set aside for emergencies? We all need to make our everyday lives enjoyable, but if you *always* choose the instant gratification, you'll never get to the long-term goal.

Saving When You Shop aka Living the Princess Lifestyle on Pauper Wages

In case you hadn't heard, couponing is big business. With minimal time and effort, you can find great deals on your basic groceries. The danger is that you'll be tempted to buy things you don't really want just to make a saving; you'll need nerves of steel to resist the lure of dirt-cheap goods which will only go to waste. Buying in bulk works for toilet paper, not so well for fresh peaches or milk. (Although you could get away with buying a glut of spoilable food if you have enough freezer space.)

If you're open to change, picking whatever's on special is more savvy than sticking to your usual brand of olive oil / chocolate cake / shampoo. When it comes to food, see what's on offer and then get creative; it's easy to search for recipes online and then base a meal around your bargains.

You can also find internet vouchers to save on everything from restaurant meals to days out and spa treatments; when I bought a juicer I idly googled "discount voucher" for the brand I was getting and found a "10% off" code. Other tricks include cashback websites (great for big purchases like your car insurance or trips abroad) and supermarket reward cards. (It's a little bit creepy the first time they send you money-off vouchers for all your favourite things, but if you don't mind the stalker aspect, it's a great way to save.)

If you get tempted by sales, don't look at the reduction, look at the price. Is it worth that much? And do you really need it? Buying that slinky cocktail dress might save you 20%, but not buying it will save you 100%. I'm not generally a big fan of sales because it means buying what the store considers "crap that didn't sell because nobody wanted it and now we have to discount it heavily to convince people to take it off our hands."

If you're feeling cheeky you could try a bit of bartering at the shops; some of them will look at you as if you've got two heads, but you should certainly get a discount if, for instance, you're buying a fridge that's been used as the display model in the store.

Don't be snobby about buying own-brand merchandise; often food in deluxe packaging has been produced in the same factory with the cheapo stuff. Buying second-hand used to be looked down on until it started being trendy to scour thrift stores for hidden treasure – you can find everything from clothes and jewellery to furniture in charity shops and online. There are also websites like Freecycle and Gumtree where people advertise "free to collector" items; this is invaluable for anyone who's setting up home and doesn't mind having a sofa that other people have sat on.

Sharing Your Money

It's *crucial* to choose carefully when it comes to sharing your money with anyone. A joint bank account with your love is very romantic, but you could lose your savings or even damage your credit rating if the person you're sharing with is a bad risk. (And nobody ever *thinks* their partner is going to be untrustworthy, but it does happen.) Listen to your bank when they say you should never tell ANYONE your pin code.

Many happily married couples use three accounts. The first is for household expenses, and you both donate a share (either equal amounts or based on a percentage of income, so whoever makes more, pays more). Ideally, you also both contribute to a second account for savings.

Thirdly, you each have a separate account for your own indulgences. It doesn't matter if he thinks scented hair gloss is a waste of cash or you think his comic books are a ludicrous obsession – you both get to dig into your own stash without any judgement or criticism from your partner.

Lending or borrowing moolah can ruin a friendship, so proceed with caution. I've given loans to extremely close friends because I trusted them to pay me back (and they did) but I've also lent a fiver here and there to scatty or flaky friends, and ended up out of pocket or feeling awkward around that person. (It's amazing how *rude* it feels to ask for money back!)

If you're going to share your riches with anyone, make it a charity and sponsor someone who really needs it. Look out for the companies that tell you specifically what's being done with your cash (I like micro-lending sites such as Kiva.org, zidisha.org and shared-interest.com). Sending support directly to small businesses will be far more beneficial than donating to huge organisations who pay their management generous salaries and create a cycle of helplessness. Real change happens when people are enabled to empower themselves instead of being kept dependent on handouts, and it starts with a philanthropist Princess like you...

Social Spending

It's frustrating when you don't have total control over your outgoings. We've all had the awkward group meal where ordering soup and tap water all night is to no avail because the people who've been quaffing wine and stuffing themselves with starters and desserts want to split the bill equally because it's "easier". Sometimes it's virtually impossible to say no; when I went to a party (consisting of about twenty people) in a restaurant, the organiser came round after the meal to inform us: "It's £25 each." How could anyone tactfully say "Actually, mine only came to £15"? I loved the way my best friend answered (after carefully choosing a low-cost meal): "I'm a bit short on cash at the moment, so I can only afford to pay for myself, sorry!" It was polite, truthful, and brought attention to the fact that an extra charge would mean paying for someone else's more decadent food choices.

It's vital to stand up for yourself and say no to stealthy debt-dodgers. The people who are so keen to "keep things simple" know exactly what they're doing – why do you think they're so eager to control the division of the bill? It's not because they're going to be paying MORE than their fair share.

If you know someone who habitually does this you might notice them dropping hints before the meal starts as a way of preparing you: they'll say "They do the best lobster here", or "Don't you think it's totally worth spending a bit extra to get a good bottle of wine? We should make tonight really special." You can always drop some hints of your own: "Gosh, I don't think I'm up for anything too outrageous, my bank manager would never forgive me! *You should get what you want, though.*"

It's not your job to subsidise other people's meals. Keep a mental note of what you ordered and have a wad of cash ready so you can say "Here's my share" the minute the check comes, before anyone tries to introduce the usual shenanigans. Moochers rely on everyone being unwilling to look "tight" by making a fuss, and they can get away with it indefinitely if nobody challenges them.

Another difficulty is when you're invited to events which will inevitably cost more than you want to spend. Sometimes just transport and entry fees will wipe you out before you've had a single drink. If you've been asked to a bash that you simply can't afford, it's a mistake to go anyway and resent every minute. Gracefully decline (you don't have to say why) and arrange to meet up with that friend for a cheaper alternative date.

Some people get you to fit in with their plans using a "bait and switch"; they'll ask if you're free on Saturday because they'd like to "take you" to a Broadway show, then after they've booked the tickets they'll casually drop into conversation that you owe them £50. Either they're socially clueless, or they knew you wouldn't normally spend this kind of money on a show, but they wanted someone to go with. Then there's the kind of person who says "Oh, you can have it!" when you admire one of their paintings or hand-woven baskets, but presents you with a bill on your way out. To clarify the situation before you end up feeling obliged to pay, ask "Do you mean you're treating me to a ticket / I can have that nice picture of a donkey as a gift?"

Spending Money Wisely

Oscar Wilde once said that "People who can live within their means suffer from a lack of imagination." Much as I love the chap, I have to point out that Oscar died penniless. Clergyman Charles Simmons took the opposite view: "Live only for today, and you ruin tomorrow."

Although loans are an accepted part of life when it comes to mortgages and university fees, generally it's preferable to save up your pennies *before* spending them. Debt will always involve interest charges, which means you end up paying back more than you were loaned. (Which sucks, obviously.)

When your outgoings are more than your income, you create a never-ending cycle of borrowing and playing catch-up. Credit cards charge you interest unless you pay them off immediately, and the dreaded "payday loans" are even worse, with extortionate fees building up every day. If you don't have the cash to pay your current bills, then by next month you certainly won't be able to pay your bills AND a hefty interest charge on top. Being flat broke can seem like an impossible situation, but living on noodles and using all your teabags twice to keep costs down is still a better option than borrowing with no means to repay.

Store cards also tend to be a nightmare – while you might balk at paying £200 for a buttery-soft leather jacket, the idea of paying just £15 a month makes the offer more attractive. The shop is hoping to lure in people who can't do maths – you'd end up paying far more than £200 in the end.

Credit of any kind is a slippery slope and once you're in a little debt, the downward spiral will get worse until you feel as if there's no point even *trying* to improve the situation. It's almost always best to pay off any debts before you attempt to accumulate a nest egg, because the interest you earn as a saver is so much lower than the interest you *pay* as a borrower. Thankfully it's possible to get free advice from experts who can help you to divide and conquer the debts. (www.moneysavingexpert.com is a great place to start.)

Having said all that, credit cards are not evil incarnate. If you set up your account to pay off the balance IN FULL every month and don't spend more than you have, they can be awesome. Some offer cashback (I earn a penny for every pound I spend) and you get the benefit of a month's buffer before you pay for big purchases (while your money earns interest in your bank account in the meantime). If you don't think you can be disciplined about staying within your budget, cut up your cards. Some people advise putting them in a block of ice in the freezer so you're forced to have a literal "cooling off" period before you run to buy that thing you desperately want. (Personally, I don't understand how this helps when we have access to hot water.) Some people are more frugal when they use cash because seeing the physical notes and coins in front of them helps them to realise how much they're coughing up. On the other hand, when you use a card you'll have a clear record of where your money went.

Sometimes we just have to be firm with ourselves and *go without* something we want when we can't afford it. If you don't physically have the money in your bank account to spend on a new laptop, you can't have it. If you really need a break but paying for a holiday in Spain would deplete next month's rent, you can't go. Being brutal is wiser than kidding ourselves that borrowing cash for a luxury is a good idea.

Conscientious Shopping

We've already touched on buying clothes which haven't been made by tiny children in sweatshops; the other obvious area for making principled choices is your everyday grocery list. If you buy animal products, please do your bit to encourage responsible standards by sticking to the ethical options. Buying fish from a sustainable source – for example, products certified by the Marine Stewardship Council (www.msc.org) – means less money going to the unscrupulous fishermen who always take fish from one area, damaging the marine eco-system. Buying RSPCA-approved meat (labelled "Freedom food") means the animals you're eating lived and died under humane circumstances. Meanwhile, choosing the cheapest pack of eggs instead of the slightly pricier free-range ones means you're supporting the system of keeping chickens in tiny battery cages. You can find out more about products and companies that implement higher levels of animal welfare from Compassion In World Farming (www.ciwf.org.uk).

Likewise, where there are options to buy "Fairtrade" and you decide that the extra few pence for a bunch of bananas isn't worth it, you're essentially saying "I don't care if the farmers get a fair deal. I'll just keep giving my money to the people who treat them like slaves."

Even if you're watching every penny, knowing that you're making the right moral decision makes up for the fact that it sometimes costs a teeny bit more.

False Economies

When you have very little money, it's costly in the long term. I realised this when my third pair of winter boots crumbled after only one season's use; much as I love inexpensive fashion, it's worth forking out for the items that need to last. In the end it was far more economical to spring for a high-quality (frighteningly expensive) pair of leather boots rather than carry on buying cheap plasticky ones which regularly fell apart. When you don't have the funds to invest in high-calibre goods, you're forced to buy the bargain option, which could potentially be less hard-wearing. Do your research and read reviews to check on reliability when you're choosing your kitchen gadgets / sports equipment / car, so you'll only have to buy them once. The best choice won't necessarily be the one that makes the biggest dent in your wallet, but being prepared to spend a bit more gives you some leeway when making a selection.

Likewise, investing in a sturdy bike might be a shock to your bank balance, but it'll cost less than bus fares over the year. Purchasing a sailboat sounds extravagant, but if going out on the water every weekend provides you with better entertainment than boozy nights on the town, it could be a good investment.

Some of us get so concerned with scrimping to save our salaries that we end up falsely economising. I quite often see a low-priced CD or book that I *kind of* want, and I convince myself that such a thrifty treat won't have a big impact on my budget. But then if I spot a couple of bargains every week, it all adds up, and I'd have been better off setting aside that money for one of the more expensive things I REALLY wanted, but had put off buying because of the price.

What value do you put on your time? For instance, you can often get the do-it-yourself version of anything for less than the ready-made edition, but is it worth the cost when you factor in a day of struggling with work you don't enjoy? Sometimes the cut-rate buy takes so much extra effort that it would be more prudent to share some of your hard-earned wealth on some professional expertise. Of course, if you enjoy making clothes, building furniture and cleaning your own bathroom, you get the privilege of saving bucks while enjoying yourself. Bonus!

You Can Always Make More Money

From paupers to millionaires, everyone has a story about the time they got a parking ticket / missed the half-price deal they wanted / never got back the cash they loaned to a pal. Stuff like this can be incredibly annoying, but it does happen to everyone, and ultimately, it doesn't matter. You can't control everything, and letting it go rather than dwelling on it will make you far happier in the end.

I know someone who was offered a short-term, very lucrative contract when

229

her baby was a couple of weeks old. Everyone was advising her to take it, even though it would mean travelling without her child: "Think of all the dosh you'll make, and it's only for a few weeks of your life." The problem was that it was three weeks out of her daughter's life that she would never get back. The lure of the big paycheck was tempting, but she didn't take the job.

Likewise, some couples move in together as soon as possible because they see it as wasteful to continue paying rent on two separate places – it's hardly the most romantic reason to progress your relationship. Why let your heart be swayed by your financial situation when *you can always make more money?* It's a simple philosophy, but it's also a really empowering way to see things; it allows your decision-making to be free from the murkiness that's introduced when we get greedy.

And Finally...

I hate to say it, but some of you may be thinking "This budget crap doesn't apply to me. I'm gonna find me a rich husband." Ladies... it's the 21st century. Let's rethink this.

First of all, you don't know what the future holds. You might not meet any wealthy men you find attractive, or you might marry one who loses everything in a poker game. I know a woman who goes out with men she's not remotely interested in, but she claims "Money makes up for a lot." Except it doesn't, which is why she always manages to find guys who treat her like crap (probably because they secretly resent her for seeing them as a meal ticket). She always ends up miserable but tries to convince herself that having designer shoes makes life really satisfying.

Obviously, I'm not saying any man who's rolling in it must be unpleasant – if you happen to fall in love with a smart, kind and funny billionaire with a yacht, good for you. (Send me a postcard!) But the old folk wisdom is true: those who marry for money end up earning every penny. As well as the downside for you, targeting men purely because you want someone to pay for all your stuff is a lousy way to approach life. Fooling a man into marrying you so you won't have to get a job is an egocentric, un-Princessy move. If you make wise decisions about your finances, you'll be a lady of independent means – and you can marry whoever you like.

Part Five

Your Media

"It takes tremendous discipline to control the influence, the power you have over other people's lives." Clint Eastwood

CREATING A SOUNDTRACK TO YOUR LIFE

"We should consider every day lost on which we have not danced at least once." Friedrich Nietzsche

The soundtrack to your life has a big impact on your frame of mind and the memories you form. Building up a collection of your own personal theme tunes, using pop as a motivator while you're working hard, or capturing the mood with some romantic or peaceful albums: music is an incredibly powerful tool which shapes our lives.

I'm fairly easygoing with my musical tastes (I'm one of those annoying people who says "Oh, a little bit of everything" when asked what my favourite genre is). I think people who truly love music as an art form will probably enjoy all kinds of different sounds, not just one small slice of the action (eg the top 40). But there is some really bad music out there, and it's played over and over again until it starts sounding normal to us. I'm talking about songs that debase women, lyrics which call us hoes and suggest we're good for nothing but sexual favours, and those accompanying videos featuring oiled-up, half-naked teenage girls writhing around while some guy wearing a fur coat talks about how much money he makes.

I can't be the only one who finds this screamingly irritating.

There are many defences for objectionable music like this. Saying it's "just a song" is overly simplistic and misses the point: the reason we learn the alphabet and nursery rhymes by singing is because tunes stick in your head more effectively than ordinary prose. Another excuse is that anyone who doesn't like it doesn't "get" it. Yep, your problem is that you're not *cool* enough to understand why those lyrics about beating up women are actually hilarious and ironic. Hmm...

When we're out dancing, it's more about the bassline than the words, and we might consider music background noise when we're chatting with friends, doing the washing-up or trying on shoes. But the fact is, those messages seep into your brain whether you like it or not. Why not fill your mind with uplifting, empowering lyrics instead? Let the guys with mother issues work it out on their own time; they have no right to pollute our ears with their misogynistic ranting. Equally, the female artists whose lyrics describe their highest ambition as finding a rich guy to pay for all their designer swag deserve to topple from the charts, too. As far as I'm concerned, valuing men only for what they can pay for is just as abhorrent as basing a woman's worth on her twerking ability.

You don't HAVE to listen to music that makes you feel like taking a shower with a pumice stone; try limiting your aural intake for a week or so and listen exclusively to lyrics which reflect the sexy, graceful, lovable woman that you are. It's empowering to listen to music which makes you feel good and songwriters who've deliberately chosen to uplift rather than insult you.

I highly recommend making soundtracks of your own for every mood; here are mine to get you started. (They're unashamedly heavy on Christina Aguilera, Kelly Clarkson, P!nk and Katy Perry, because they've got this positivity thing *down.*)

You can listen to them here: https://play.spotify.com/user/princessguidetolife

Soundtrack #1: When You Need a Carefree Blast of Optimism

Because stuff happens and we all have bad days when we need some help to get back on our feet. If life is hard and you need perking up, listen to these tracks and remember that everything is going to be OK.

• Sugarland: It Happens • The Hollies: I'm Alive • Wallis Bird: The Sunshine Song • Jordin Sparks: One Step at a Time • Nina Simone: Ain't Got No / I Got Life • Kelly Clarkson: People Like Us • Fleetwood Mac: Don't Stop • Stacie Orrico: Bounce Back • John Mayer: Bigger Than My Body • The Source, Candi Staton: You Got The Love • Ingrid Michaelson: Keep Breathing • Ana Popovic: Fearless • Linda Lewis: We Can Win • Melissa Etheridge: You Will • Sara Evans: Born to Fly • Ledisi: Raise Up • Barbra Streisand: Don't Rain On My Parade • Kelis, CeeLo Green: Lil Star • Leona Lewis: Happy • Ernestine Anderson: Wrap Your Troubles in Dreams • Beth Hart: Life is Calling • Tom Petty and The Heartbreakers: Learning to Fly

• Maria Mena: All This Time (Pick-Me-Up Song) • Pistol Annies: Lemon Drop • The Real Tuesday Weld: The Show Must Go On • Lauryn Hill: I Gotta Find Peace of Mind

Soundtrack #2: When Other People are Giving You Attitude

Where would artists and writers be without a touch of angst for inspiration? It turns out even the biggest stars have to put up with crap from people, hence the songs below. Don't let the haters get to you.

• Mousse T, Emma Lanford: Is it Cos I'm Cool • Destiny's Child: Dot • Christina Aguilera: Shut Up • Miranda Lambert: Only Prettier • Kanye West: Stronger • Bonnie Raitt: I Will Not Be Broken • Gwen Stefani: Hollaback girl • Christina Aguilera: Beautiful • Keri Hilson: Pretty Girl Rock • Alicia Keys: Brand New Me • Sugababes: Ugly • Demi Lovato: Skyscraper • Nicki Minaj, Rihanna: Fly • Jamie Liddell: What is it This Time? • Taylor Swift: Shake It Off • Destiny's Child: Survivor • Janelle Monáe ft. Erykah Badu: Q.U.E.E.N • Katy Perry: Roar • Jill Scott: Hate On Me • Christina Aguilera: Fighter • Tanya Lacey: Born to Fly • Kelly Clarkson: Whyyawannabring-medown • Romi Mayes: Don't Mess with Me • Jessie J: It's My Party • Taylor Swift: Mean • The Staves: F**k The Cool Kids • Christina Aguilera: Keep On Singin' My Song

Soundtrack #3: When You Need Inspiration

Ready to transform the world? Bucking the system and breaking new ground isn't easy, but you can start by getting the soundtrack right. The rest will follow...

• Christina Aguilera ft. CeeLo Green: Make the World Move • Bill Conti: Gonna Fly Now (Rocky theme) • Mariah Carey: Make It Happen • Joss Stone, Buick Audra: This Little Light of Mine • Michael Jackson: Man in the Mirror • Amerie : Gotta Work • Gavin DeGraw: Change is Gonna Come • Kelly Clarkson: Impossible • Mama Cass: Make Your Own Kind of Music • Beyoncé: I Was Here • Melissa Etheridge: Change the World • Dolly Parton:

9 to 5 • Saint Lu: Don't Miss Your Own Life • Mariah Carey: Hero • New Radicals: You Get What You Give

Soundtrack #4: When You Need Reminding of How Awesome You Are

Because you are. You can do anything and be anything you like, and nobody can stop you. Even when you can see nothing but faults, know that you are perfect in your imperfection.

• Alicia Keys: The Element of Freedom (Intro) • Katy Perry: Firework • Christina Aguilera: Keeps Gettin' Better • India.Arie: Strength, Courage & Wisdom • Noisettes: Winner • P!nk: F**kin' Perfect • Alicia Keys: Girl on Fire • Christina Aguilera: Army of Me • Jerry Fish & the Mudbug Club: Be Yourself • Colbie Caillat: Try • Lady Gaga: Born This Way • Selena Gomez & The Scene: Who Says • Christina Aguilera: Soar • Jessie J: Who You Are • Rihanna: Diamonds • Carrie Underwood: Nobody Ever Told You • Fiona Apple: Extraordinary Machine • Alicia Keys: Superwoman • Meghan Trainor: Close Your Eyes • Christina Aguilera: The Voice Within

Soundtrack #5: When You're Going Through a Break-Up (And Feeling Bitter)

When you're over a bad relationship, you'll discover there is *no joy on earth* like the joy of knowing you're not with that loser anymore: he was totally wrong for you, you deserve much better and quite frankly, you dodged a bullet. Unfortunately, getting to this moment might take some time (plus some sessions of photograph-burning, vodka, junk food and movies). These songs help.

• VV Brown: Leave! • Kelly Clarkson: Since U Been Gone • Gloria Gaynor: I Will Survive • Beyoncé: Me, Myself and I • Allison Iraheta: Friday I'll Be Over U • John Mayer: I'm Gonna Find Another You • Basement Jaxx ft. Lisa Kekaula: Good Luck • Christina Aguilera: You Lost Me • Miranda Lambert: Mama's Broken Heart • Summer Camp: Better Off Without You •

Alicia Keys: Karma • Taylor Swift: We Are Never Ever Getting Back Together • Skunk Anansie: Weak • Rihanna: Take A Bow • Kelly Clarkson: Stronger (What Doesn't Kill You) • CeeLo Green: Forget You • Miranda Lambert: Crazy Ex-Girlfriend • Beyoncé: Single Ladies (Put a Ring On It) • Imelda May: Watcha Gonna Do • Fried: Things Change • Jo Dee Messina: My Give A Damn's Busted • Anjulie: Brand New Bitch • Carly Rae Jepsen: Tonight I'm Getting Over You • Skeeter Davis: Gonna Get Along Without You Now • Beyoncé: Irreplacable • Carrie Underwood: Before He Cheats • Kelly Clarkson: Never Again • Aly & AJ: Potential Breakup Song • Katzenjammer: I Will Dance (When I Walk Away)

Soundtrack #6: And When You're Feeling Less Bitter...

Whether it's an amicable break-up, you're feeling Zen-like acceptance over the whole thing, or you're cool with it because it was your idea, you still need an anthem so you can smile and shed a bittersweet tear when you hear it on the radio.

• Aretha Franklin: I Say a Little Prayer • Rachael Yamagata: I Wish You Love • Katy Perry: The One That Got Away • Lily Allen: Smile • Whitney Houston: I Will Always Love You • Fried: Sorry I Ruined Your Life • Carole King: It's Too Late • Miranda Lambert: Same Old You • Jamelia: Thank You

Soundtrack #7: When Some Guy isn't Paying You Sufficient Attention

He has a girlfriend already? He's single but blind to your charms? Listen to these and feel smug in the knowledge that he doesn't know what he's missing.

• Kelly Clarkson: Dirty Little Secret • Joss Stone: Don't Cha Wanna Ride • Etta James: Tell Mama • Destiny's Child: She Can't Love You • Beverley Knight: Gold • Fried: You're With the Wrong One Baby • Pussycat Dolls: Don't Cha • Sugababes: Red Dress • The Dixie Chicks: I Can Love You Better

Soundtrack #8: To Remind Yourself that Men Cannot Mess With You

He thinks he can get away with treating you like *just some chick*? I don't think so. You're a PRINCESS, dammit! You demand respect at all times, and if he doesn't like it he can get lost.

• Aretha Franklin: RESPECT • Kelly Clarkson: I Do Not Hook Up • Destiny's Child: Bills Bills Bills • Jill Scott: Making You Wait • Imelda May: Smoker's Song • En Vogue: My Lovin' (You're Never Gonna Get It) • Anna Nalick: Consider This • TLC: No Scrubs • Katy Perry: If You Can Afford Me • Alicia Keys: Slow Down • Destiny's Child: Independent Women • Kelly Clarkson: Don't Let Me Stop You • The Wreckers: One More Girl • P!nk: Just U + Ur Hand • Aretha Franklin: Think • Leona Lewis: The Best You Never Had • Alicia Keys: A Woman's Worth • Etta James: Pushover • Destiny's Child: Bug A Boo • Madonna: Express Yourself • Pistol Annies: Hell on Heels

Soundtrack #9: When You Need an Energy Boost

Music to keep you going on the treadmill or to get you into the mood for partying. Crank it up – it's better for you than drugs. Cheaper too!

• Christina Aguilera: Let There be Love • Grace Potter & The Nocturnals: Paris (Ooh La La) • Katzenjammer: Demon Kitty Rag • Wagner: Ride of the Valkyries • Lady Gaga: The Edge of Glory • Elvis Presley: Blue Suede Shoes • Armand Van Helden: MyMyMy • Sha Na Na: Born to Hand Jive • P!nk: God is a DJ • Queen: Don't Stop Me Now • Madonna: Vogue • Jerry Lee Lewis: Whole Lotta Shakin' Going On • The Noisettes: Don't Upset the Rhythm (Go Baby Go) • Kenny Loggins: Footloose • Survivor: Eye of the Tiger • Rossini: William Tell Overture • Junior Senior: Move Your Feet • David Guetta ft. Sia: Titanium • Lil' Chris: Checkin' it out • Hayley Reinhart, BoB: Oh My! • Kool & The Gang: Jungle Boogie • Gossip: Standing in the Way of Control • Freestylers: Push Up • Lady Gaga ft Colby O'Donis: Just Dance • A-ha: Take On Me • LMFAO ft. Lauren Bennett and

GoonRock: Party Rock Anthem • Jackson 5: ABC • Christina Aguilera: Bionic • Bill Haley & His Comets: Rock Around The Clock • Madonna: Into The Groove

Soundtrack #10: When You Need to Chill Out

Kick back, unwind and let the music wash over you for a calming session of relaxation.

• The Acorn: Lullaby (Mountain) • Trespassers William: Lie in the Sound • The Staves: Wisely and Slow • Brightblack Morning Light: Star Blanket River Child • Sia: I Go to Sleep • Debussy: Clair de Lune • Keren Ann: Lay your Head Down • Grizzly Bear ft. Victoria Legrand: Slow Life • Fila Brazillia: Soft Music Under the Stars • Laura Marling: Tap at My Window • Aqualung: Strange and Beautiful (I'll Put a Spell On you) • O + S: Lonely Ghosts • Mazzy Star: Fade Into You • Gabrielle Aplin: Salvation • Shuggie Otis: Aht Uh Mi Head • Zero 7: Warm Sound • Beach House: Silver Soul • Hawksley Workman: Oh You Delicate Heart • Robotanists: Exiled State of Mind • Priscilla Ahn: Lullaby • Hope Sandoval and the Warm Inventions : Feeling of Gaze • Bon Iver: Wisconsin • Liszt: Liebesträume No. 3 • Sigur Rós: Stormur • Eels: Theme for a Pretty Girl That Makes You Believe God Exists

Soundtrack #11: When Your Inner Feminist is Feeling Feisty

Sick of being followed around or yelled at by creepy men when you just want a nice stroll around town? Tired of men assuming you know nothing because you're "just a girl"? Annoyed that you have to spend all your money on "essential" beauty products men have never even heard of? Let's overthrow the patriarchy.

• India.Arie: Video • P!nk: Stupid Girls • Shania Twain: She's Not Just a Pretty Face • Eurythmics, Aretha Franklin: Sisters Are Doin' it for Themselves • Mary J. Blige: Good Woman Down • TLC: Unpretty • Beyoncé: Run the World (Girls) • Nancy Harrow: Wild Women Don't Have the Blues • Robyn: Who's That Girl? • Gaye Adegbalola: Big Ovaries, Baby

• Christina Aguilera ft. Lil' Kim: Can't Hold Us Down • No Doubt: Just a Girl • Pistol Annies: Being Pretty Ain't Pretty • Queen Latifah: U.N.I.T.Y. • Vanessa Hudgens: Never Underestimate a Girl • P!nk, Scratch: Respect • Billy Bragg: The Busy Girl Buys Beauty • Madonna: What It Feels Like for a Girl • Emilie Autumn: Thank God I'm Pretty • Little Mix: Salute • Helen Reddy / Betty Wright / Martha Wainwright: I am Woman • Ani Difranco: Not a Pretty Girl • James Brown: It's a Man's Man's Man's World

Soundtrack #12: When You Need Cheering Up

Blasting out songs guaranteed to make you smile is the cheapest and fastest antidepressant I know. Create your own playlist entitled "I'm going to be happy if it kills me" then fill it with your personal selection of sure-fire winners.

• Beach Boys: Surfin' USA • Joan Jett: I Love Rock 'n' Roll • Sonny J: Can't Stop Moving • Christina Aguilera: Vanity • Simon & Garfunkel: Baby Driver • Wham!: Club Tropicana • Oli Brown: On Top of the World • Katy Perry: Last Friday Night (T.G.I.F.) • Marvin Gaye, Tammi Terrell: Ain't No Mountain High Enough • Blondie: Atomic • A.R. Rahman, Pussycat Dolls ft. Nicole Scherzinger: Jai Ho! (You Are My Destiny) • Lou Bega: Mambo No. 5 (A Little Bit Of...) • Aretha Franklin: I'm Sitting On Top of the World • U2: Beautiful Day • Rosemary Clooney: Sway • Vampire Weekend: Oxford Comma • Jess Penner: Life is Rosy • Otis Redding: (Sittin' On The) Dock of the Bay • Huey Lewis and The News: Hip to be Square • The Beatles: Here Comes the Sun • Joe Nichols: Life Don't Have to Mean Nothin' At All • Naughty Boy, Emeli Sandé: Wonder • Kim Wilde: Kids in America • Billie Holiday: The Way You Look Tonight • Daft Punk, Pharrell Williams, Nile Rodgers: Get Lucky • Moxy Fruvous: My Baby Loves a Bunch of Authors • Frankie Valli: Grease • Dixie Chicks: Some Days You Gotta Dance • Marilyn Monroe: Diamonds Are a Girl's Best Friend • Wham!: Wake Me Up Before You Go-Go • Katy Perry ft Snoop Dogg: California Gurls • Cream: I Feel Free • Madonna: Where's the Party • Chuck Berry: Roll Over Beethoven • Pharrell Williams: Happy

Soundtrack #13: When You Need to Remind Yourself that Nice Guys Do Exist

See, not all men would call you a bitch if you so much as asked them to lift their feet up while you're vacuuming around the couch. As well as having happy tunes which tell you that you can do anything, it's helpful to have a go-to list of songs which prove there are plenty of guys who sing respectfully and romantically about the women they love. Listen every day for the perfect antidote to the rubbish spewing out of the morons.

• Jimmy Clanton: Venus in Blue Jeans • Tarrus Riley: She's Royal • Mario: Let Me Love You • Diamond Rio: Unbelievable • Bruno Mars: Just the Way You Are • Sam Cooke: Lovable • Ne-Yo: Miss Independent • Scouting For Girls: She's So Lovely • The Platters: Only You • Brad Paisley: She's Her Own Woman • Justin Timberlake: Take it From Here • The Everly Brothers: Devoted To You • Stevie Wonder: Knocks Me Off My Feet • CeeLo Green: Everybody Loves You (Baby) • Billy Currington: When She Gets Close to Me • Otis Redding: My Girl • The Mock Turtles: And Then She Smiles • Nat King Cole Trio: Gee Baby Ain't I Good to You • John Mayer: Your Body is a Wonderland • The Beatles: Something • Trace Adkins: Ain't No Woman Like You • Usher: There Goes My Baby • Cary Brothers: Can't Take My Eyes Off You • Jamie Foxx: Gorgeous • Robert Palmer: She Makes my Day • The Beach Boys: God Only Knows • Frank Sinatra: You Do Something To Me • 100 Proof Aged in Soul: She's Not Just Another Woman • Blake Shelton: You'll Always be Beautiful • The Flamingos: Dream Girl • Nat King Cole: The More I See You • Lee Fields and the Expressions: You're the Kind of Girl • B.o.B ft. Bruno Mars: Nothin' on You • Little Walter: My Babe • Luke Bryan: Every Time I See You • Eric Clapton: Wonderful Tonight • The Animals: The Girl Can't Help It • Mario Vazquez: One Shot • The Everly Brothers: Love of My Life • Brad Paisley: She's Everything • Art Garfunkel: I Only Have Eyes For You • Joe Matthews: She's My Beauty Queen • Craig David: Unbelievable • The Union: If I Could Make You Mine • Spin Doctors: Two Princes • Kevin Rudolf: She Can Get It • Ne-Yo, Jamie Foxx, Fabolous: She's Got Her Own • Tom Jones: She's a Lady • Jerrod Niemann: They Should Have Named You Cocaine • Jace Everett: Your

Man • Michael Bublé: Haven't Met You Yet • Andy Williams: Can't Take My Eyes Off You • One Direction: What Makes You Beautiful • Josh Turner: I Wouldn't Be a Man • Bruno Mars: Marry You • Jamie Cullum: I Get a Kick Out of You • Tavares: Heaven Must be Missing an Angel • Billy Joel: She's Always a Woman • Al Green: I'm Glad You're Mine

There. Isn't that better?

THE POWER OF MOVIES

"Usually when you see females in movies, they feel like they have these metallic structures around them, they are caged by male energy." Björk

Like the music you listen to, movies can have an uplifting or depressing effect. An adrenaline-fuelled thriller is exciting, but how many times can you watch a scantily-clad woman being hacked to death before it starts getting to you? Those images can't be un-seen, and they're not the most pleasant thoughts to have stuck in your head. (Especially just before bed. Or while you're eating.) I'm a big movie fan and regularly watch all kinds (including some of those horror flicks) but sometimes my inner Princess gets on her high horse and says "Enough". I refuse to watch another movie in which the women are brainless dead weights who only serve to slow down intrepid heroes, or rape is presented as a plot twist / routine consequence of going out after dark or stopping at a gas station.

It's not just low-budget slashers which objectify women; some of the most critically acclaimed dramas have been condemned for glamorising sexual violence. Most crime shows have a fetish for attractive female victims – when did you last see one which DIDN'T feature a nubile young lady lying naked on a slab at the morgue?

It's obvious when women are featured purely as eye candy / the provider of sexual titillation / fodder for torture porn, but there's often a more insidious anti-female bias. How many movies show a successful career girl who's gained her great job and nice apartment at the expense of her personal life? She can only be happy when she finds a man, duh.

A woman who's ambitious will normally turn out to be cold-hearted and / or psychotic as well, but the arrival of a baby makes *every* lady happy (even if she thought she didn't want kids). Then there's the kooky, unstable girl who attracts men like moths to a flame... some guys WOULD love a girl who needs to be "rescued", but what's so unattractive about ladies who are emotionally healthy, solvent and full of zip?

And let's not forget the shamelessly common twist on "playing hard to get"; according to Hollywood, if you sleep with someone but insist you don't want any commitment, you're *certain* to win the guy's heart. Now ladies, let's think for a moment: what motivation could there possibly be for male moviemakers to brainwash us into thinking that true love will come our way if we put out on a first date and then don't hassle the guy afterwards?

Actresses talking about characters they've played often use the phrase "strong woman", which kind of irks me. Firstly, the description appears to be reserved for two kinds of female: the gun-toting chick in tiny-vest-and-shorts combo, or the tough-talking businesswoman who secretly longs for a man to bring out her softer side. So obviously, our idea of strength is pretty narrow and one-dimensional. Secondly, why isn't Brad Pitt ever asked about how much he enjoys playing a "strong man"? Is it automatically assumed that men's roles will be complex and interesting?

It's fascinating to compare the representation of males versus females in media, and it's especially illuminating in those jokey gender-reversal pictures and videos. Suddenly the kind of pouting, wiggling and licking inanimate objects that's become routine for young women looks utterly ridiculous when it involves men. Magazine covers featuring male Hollywood heavyweights show them looking smart and dignified in suits. Respected, award-winning actresses are more likely to be photographed naked and snuggled up together under a sheet. (And the story inside will inevitably address rumours of their catfights, because women aren't really allowed to be friends.) Fashion shoots have become ever more fascinated with models looking like lifeless mannequins, puppets or victims of violence; in advertising, women are shown to be primarily concerned with their appearance, how to clean the house or how to feed the family (while men like drinking beer and driving cars).

So have things got better or worse for women in the movies? In black-and-white films, starlets may have answered to "dollface" and "sweet cheeks" but they tended to be smart, adventurous, and witty. These days women are usually allowed to be funny only in gross-out comedies, or by falling over a lot.

However, there are plenty of movies from every era starring female characters with real backbone; you just have to look out for them. So let's focus on the women who have positive attitudes, integrity and the moxie to become true legends... and remember them next time we see a commercial featuring a woman who's really worried because her deodorant leaves little white patches on her black dress.

Inspiring Movie Heroines

- *Erin Brokovich* (2000): Julia Roberts stars in the true story of a gutsy single mother who became a legend for taking on a gigantic corporation. When she discovered that a power company was supplying people with contaminated water which caused brain tumours, she launched a legal battle against them – even though she had no formal training or qualifications in law. Not only did she bring the company to its knees and earn payouts for the people who had suffered medical problems, but she did so by *memorising* legal details (she was dyslexic and didn't trust herself to be able to read properly under pressure). Plus she was super-feisty and talked her way past security guards with just a push-up bra and a cheeky grin.

- *Precious* (2009): This movie is not for the faint-hearted, because Precious is a teenager with a truly hellish family background. Gabourey Sidibe plays the young woman who never gives up hope of improving her circumstances, even when her life is at an all-time low. She uses her imagination to escape from reality, but when she's offered the opportunity to improve her education and forge a new path for herself, she grabs it with both hands. This film is a testament to those people who give their time to helping the helpless, as well as anyone who has the determination to overcome the past and reach out for the life of their dreams.

- *The Sound of Music* (1965): (Loosely) based on a true story, Maria is a novice nun sent to live with a widower and his children as a governess. When the couple fall in love, she has the sense to be flexible – so what if life doesn't turn out exactly how you planned it? God has a better idea. Later the family form a singing troupe and manage to upset the Nazis occupying Austria. Will they escape with a daring midnight flit into the mountains? Check out a sing-along screening for maximum fun when you watch this one.

- *The Girl with the Dragon Tattoo* (2009 / 2011): Lisbeth Salander (played by Noomi Rapace in the original Swedish film and Rooney Mara in a later remake; brilliant either way) doesn't exactly fit into what we'd expect a "Princess" to be like. She isn't interested in being pretty, or making friends, or doing anything except living with total freedom in her own little world. But she is an incredibly intelligent computer hacker who can get hold of any information she wants in a matter of moments. Woe betide anyone who dares to underestimate this scrawny, chain-smoking young woman – she may look harmless, but she's stronger and more resourceful than you could imagine.

- *Elizabeth* (1998): Cate Blanchett takes on the role of Elizabeth I – the Queen of England who was described as ruling "like a man" (because she was, er, good at it). She's thrown in at the deep end – one minute she's in prison, the next she's become the reigning monarch. She has to learn to trust her own judgement and shut out some of the "helpful" advice she's given. Much of the pressure she faced would be familiar to women today ("So when are you going to get married and have a baby already?") and she also has a rather fabulous wardrobe. While the movie has several historical inaccuracies, it's still a superb glimpse into the kind of world this lady inhabited when she began her rule.

- *Silkwood* (1983): Before Erin Brockovich came Karen Silkwood, who worked in a plutonium plant which violated worker safety rules and put everyone in danger. Meryl Streep gives a typically believable performance as the woman who vows to stop the company from doing more damage. This resulted in her bosses harassing her; blaming her for radiation contamination, stripping her entire house and destroying her belongings. After her death (in suspicious circumstances) her family sued the plant and were awarded compensation. Karen's legacy is proof that anyone can make a difference – and she'll now forever be remembered as a martyr to corruption and greed.

- *Auntie Mame* (1958): This movie is such FUN. Rosalind Russell stars as the eccentric lady of a certain age who takes on her orphaned nephew and gives him the gift of living life richly instead of simply existing. Nothing fazes Auntie Mame (at least not for long) and her manners are impeccable – unless you REALLY push her. The movie was later remade as a musical starring Lucille Ball as the woman who will never stay down, no matter what life throws at her.

- *Terminator* (1984) & *Terminator 2* (1991): Forget the cyborgs, Sarah Connor (Linda Hamilton) is the real star of these sci-fi movies. Sarah's an ordinary gal who enjoys hanging out with her friends – until she learns that she's due to give birth to the future saviour of mankind. Rather than trying to run away or reject her destiny, she meets it head-on and devotes her life to protecting her son. This results in her being sent to a mental hospital (predicting a robot apocalypse will do that for you) where she builds up her strength to prepare for the trouble ahead.

- *The Help (2011)*: A tale of civil rights in the 1960s – when slavery had been abolished but treating African-American maids without any respect was still perfectly legal. When a young writer asks them to tell their stories, the "help" express how it feels for them to raise white babies who learn to love less and hate more as they grow up. Risking their jobs and their lives (Mississippi was not a terribly safe place to be outspoken) the ladies' contributions create a book which tells the truth behind the smug facades of the middle-class white families.

- *Legally Blonde* (2001) & *Legally Blonde 2* (2003): Reese Witherspoon as the sweet but apparently silly Elle Woods is a master class in Princess style. Because she's blonde and wears pink and likes to dress up her dog in the cutest accessories, people assume she's a brainless bimbo. All the smarty-pants students ridicule her when she rocks up to law school – but she doesn't let it get to her. Instead she proves their assumptions wrong – ever so politely, of course – and uses her own unique knowledge (of hair products) to fight her case. In the sequel she proves how important it is to disregard the way people treat you and carry on acting "as if" your actions count. Don't think like them – think like *you*.

- ***Temple Grandin* (2010):** Claire Danes plays Temple Grandin, a young woman whose autism makes it difficult for her to connect with people or live in any kind of normal way. Far from letting this put her off from doing something useful with her life, Temple uses her "different" way of thinking to enlighten the people who run slaughterhouses. She has a special insight into the way animals relate to us, what scares them and what keeps them calm, and as this true story shows, her input has completely changed the way we keep livestock.

- ***Amélie* (2001):** This quirky French film stars the enchanting Audrey Tatou as good-hearted Amélie, who decides to impact the world around her in a positive way. Along with living consciously and enjoying what each day brings, she uses her imagination to find ways to help other people. It's a whimsical look at how we can all do little things to improve the lives of everyone around us in true Princess fashion.

- ***Gone with the Wind* (1939):** In many ways, Scarlett O'Hara is a terrible role model. She's selfish and conniving, shamelessly manipulative and willing to exploit anyone silly enough to let her. She's definitely more of a femme fatale than a Princess. However, when there's a crisis she's tough as old boots, refusing to give up or fail. When everyone else is at their lowest, she makes her boldest move and steals her sister's fiancé. It's not really selfish; she knows her sister would leave without looking back, whereas Scarlett is determined that marrying into money will save the family home. In the end she realises that Melanie, the woman she's always dismissed as weak and feeble, has an inner strength that Scarlett's selfishness could never hope to compete with. Melanie is the true Princess, but Scarlett is gutsy and likeable despite her faults.

- ***Soul Surfer* (2011):** What do you do when your life is right on track, your future is bright... and then disaster strikes? This movie is based on the true story of Bethany Hamilton, a teenage surfer who seemed destined for great things until she lost an arm in a shark attack. That

247

would be enough to put off some of us from ever returning to the water, but Bethany finds something good can come out of every experience – and the way she deals with her handicap becomes an inspiration to others.

- *Freedom Writers* (2007): This movie is based on a true story; Hilary Swank plays the teacher who's disappointed to find her class of high school students are more interested in fighting and racially abusing each other than learning. She teaches them about the Holocaust and the way people were set against each other on the basis of nothing but their ethnicity, and engages the kids in writing journals chronicling their lives. Like the similar true story of *Dangerous Minds* (1995), this film shows the difference that one teacher can make if they persevere in reaching out to the teenagers who really need it.

- *Cold Comfort Farm* (1995): When Florence (Kate Beckinsale) arrives at the grimmest of dark, gloomy farms to meet a plethora of odd relatives, it seems more like a gothic horror film than a sprightly comedy. However, she is the bounciest, more resilient person there and rather than allowing them to depress her and change her attitude, *she* changes *them*. She's immune to the charms of lotharios (treating them with amused disdain) and is resolutely cheerful. It turns out that when you simply ignore the grumpiness of others and carry on talking to them in a chirpy manner as if you were having a perfectly pleasant conversation, they forget to be cross. Textbook Princess behaviour.

- *Gorillas in the Mist* (1988): Dian Fossey was a shy and insecure child, and turned to animals for acceptance. She grew up to be a zoologist and devoted her life to the study of gorillas, living among them and working hard to conserve their habitats and keep them safe from poachers. Sigourney Weaver stars in this biopic of the complicated lady, who was passionately protective of "her" gorillas and butted heads with poachers and fellow anthropologists alike. The legacy she's left us is greater knowledge and respect for these incredible animals.

- *Nine to Five* (1980): Jane Fonda, Lily Tomlin and Dolly Parton are the women who join forces instead of letting bitchy office politics, jealousy and competition get between them. The result is a hilarious story about the strength women have when they band together, not to mention a revenge fantasy for anyone with a horrible boss. Dolly's rousing anthem for the working woman helped to make the movie a hit, and she proved her mettle as an actress – she memorised the entire script because she thought it would be filmed all the way through, like a stage show. Bless.

- *The Color Purple* (1985): Starring Whoopi Goldberg and Oprah Winfrey, this is an inspiring tale which reminds us we can find moments of joy even in a life which is relentlessly hard. It's about being thankful and appreciating what you have, and not giving in to the kind of subservience others expect from you. It's also a reminder that women are (and always have been) as strong as men, and that real power is not found in violence but in mastering your own mind.

- *Kill Bill Vol. 1 & 2* (2003 / 2004): Uma Thurman is the Bride who's shot and left for dead on her wedding day; when she wakes up from her coma she swears vengeance on everyone involved. And thus begins a two-part movie so violent that 450 gallons of fake blood were used. So, how is this a *Princess* story again? Well, the Bride is one determined lady. It doesn't matter to her that she's only one person, that she's coming up against trained assassins, or that her task is impossible. Even (spoiler!) being buried alive doesn't slow her down for long. She just keeps going, never to admit defeat or give up. I'd say that's pretty royal behaviour.

- *Whale Rider* (2002): Keisha Castle-Hughes stars in this stunningly beautiful film which also features some rather awesome whales. Set in modern-day New Zealand, this tale is about Pai, a young girl whose wish to become chief of her tribe is rejected by her grandfather. Why? Well, she's only a girl, and we all know girls are rubbish at that stuff, right...? Let's just say that she isn't put off easily, and when your destiny is for greatness, ain't nothin' can stop you, even sexist elders. Get over it, Grandpa!

RECOMMENDED BOOKS FOR PRINCESSES

"A well-read woman is a dangerous creature." Lisa Kleypas

Reading isn't just a pleasure; it's a way of opening your mind to a new way of thinking, soaking up knowledge, and shaping your philosophies. Books *change* us. The following titles have made a big impact on me and I highly recommend them.

- *Feel the Fear and Do It Anyway* by **Susan Jeffers:** If you only read one non-Princess-related self-help book in your life, make it this one; it transformed the way I see the world. Although the title speaks for itself, it's certainly not a one-hit wonder of a message – there are lots of practical tips on how to create the life you want. Writer Susan Jeffers is steadfastly positive, pointing out that your subconscious believes what you tell it, so make sure you're telling it good stuff about how strong and capable you are. Instead of hoping bad things won't happen, she encourages us to develop our confidence to know we can handle whatever happens, good and bad. And while sitting around and blaming other people for everything negative in your life makes you feel passive and weak, taking responsibility for your own actions is the single most empowering thing you can ever do.

- *The Beauty Myth* by **Naomi Wolf:** This is Naomi Wolf's classic diatribe about the incredible pressure for women to look a certain way. *So what* if we have wrinkles? She puts forward a convincing argument that the unattainable standard of physical beauty has become a more dominant force as women have gained more power through legal rights. It's *almost* as if men want to find a way to control us (through insecurity and fear and self-consciousness) because we seem to be catching up with them or overtaking them in other ways...

- *The Battersea Park Road to Enlightenment* by **Isabel Losada:** This has been one of my "comfort books" for a long time, so it's now rather crinkled from hours of reading in the bath. Isabel Losada tries out a number of different therapies, from re-birthing to hypnotism to awakening the inner goddess. She's brave enough to write about her vulnerabilities and funny enough to make every bit of it entertaining. What a gal! She's one of my favourite writers and I'd also recommend her other books; she's written about nuns (*New Habits*), men (*Men: Where the **** Are They?)* and politics (*For Tibet, with Love: A Beginner's Guide to Changing the World*).

- *The Handmaid's Tale* by **Margaret Atwood:** This is an absolute classic of feminism and literature, which is why it's often on school reading lists. Creepy and unforgettable, it will have you re-examining the power women have in our role as mothers, and questioning how much society as we know it could change. (I can't say any more without spoiling the story!) Margaret Atwood's writing is almost always un-put-downable, and the threatening atmosphere of this novel makes it a haunting page-turner.

- *Why Good Girls Don't Get Ahead... But Gutsy Girls Do* by **Kate White:** Another great book not only for shaping your career, but your life. While *Feel the Fear and Do it Anyway* author Susan Jeffers says you shouldn't worry about other people stealing your ideas (because who cares, you can have more of them), Kate White takes perhaps a less noble, but more relatable view. She advises the assumption that everyone is out to get you, and explains how to take defensive action. She's very funny and has some surprising tips on what makes for success: it's all about doing the unexpected rather than sticking slavishly to the set pattern everyone says you "have" to do. Forget being "good" and allowing people to push you around, forget evaluating every tiny detail before making a decision, and just go with your gut: break the rules and create your own path. Follow it up with sequel *9 Secrets of Women Who Get Everything They Want* for more life hacks.

- *How to Talk to Anyone,* by **Leil Lowndes:** This book is full of clever tricks to make conversation flow easily and have everyone eating out of the palm of your hand. It also explains the giveaways that someone is a "Big Winner" – one is that they don't "notice" anyone's faux pas. If you dropped a tray of drinks in front of a bunch of losers they'd all clap and jeer at you; classy people would pretend nothing had happened. Leil Lowndes has also used her relationship expertise to write *How to Make Anyone Like You* and *How to Make Anyone Fall in Love with You,* which are packed full of amusing anecdotes and examples to illustrate her scientifically-based rules of communication.

- *Men Are From Mars, Women Are From Venus* by **John Gray:** The original and the best. This should help you figure out some of the weird stuff men do – and why we ladies have our own special brand of irrational craziness, too. When I see couples arguing (on TV or real life) I often think: "They could easily solve their dispute if they read this book." Assuming that your boyfriend will react to events the same way you do will end in confusion, because men and women really are wired differently. This should help you to understand those all-important differences.

- *The Princessa* by **Harriet Rubin:** The female equivalent of "The Prince" by Machiavelli, this book aims for women to gain power by any means possible. It's a thought-provoking read (even if becoming "Machiavellian" wasn't exactly on your Princess to-do list). Harriet Rubin points out that our femininity is a "vast inheritance" and there are things we ladies can do that no man could get away with. I personally don't agree with weeping at work (I've seen the way criers lose people's respect) but I can't argue with the point that "Nothing changes the game faster than tears." (Just use it as a last resort, OK?) Other advice includes doing the last thing anyone expects of you: Joan of Arc showed her enemies that she wasn't afraid of them when she rode into battle wearing bright, conspicuous white instead of trying to hide away. And one last essential tip – never feel guilty for winning.

253

- *The Gift of Fear* by **Gavin de Becker:** I believe this book should be taught in schools; with chilling true-life examples it suggests that dangerous behaviour is actually not as unpredictable as we think it is. It's a great reminder that we all have a reliable self-preservation system known as intuition, which we ignore at our peril. Gavin de Becker points out that it's a huge mistake to try to convince yourself something is OK when you have a still, small voice in the back of your mind saying "No, I have a bad feeling about this." He also has a very logical, no-nonsense approach to the statistics on domestic violence: it's in the victim's power to leave, rather than waiting around for the situation to change or for someone else to save her.

- *Female Chauvinist Pigs* by **Ariel Levy:** Are we modern women really doing ourselves any favours? Ariel Levy examines the hard-drinking, porn-watching "ladette" culture and the effect it's had on society. She essentially pulverises the idea that women should be attempting to "keep up" with men as a feminist act. We've been indoctrinated with the idea that being free and easy with our sexuality is far superior to the prim ways of past generations; it's now women who pride themselves on being promiscuous, go to lap-dancing clubs, hire strippers and call you a prude if you don't like it. Is this really progress?

- *The 5 Love Languages* by **Gary Chapman:** We all want to have happy, loving relationships, but the problems start because we all have a different idea of what this actually means. Gary Chapman has helpfully categorised the different types of love and how to assess what your partner / family / friends appreciate most. There's no point showering your hubby with gifts if his love language is time and you're always too busy to see him. Meanwhile your sister might think she's doing you a favour by offering "acts of service" because that's her love language, while you'd rather she gave you some encouraging "words of affirmation". If your friend's language is touch, she'll prefer a reassuring hug to a long chat. Simple but effective, this book is a great one to keep around for every relationship in your life.

- *How to Be a Woman* by **Caitlin Moran:** This book is absolutely hilarious, but it also makes some shrewd points about the ridiculous expectations women feel they have to live up to. Touching on feminism, children, and being fat, Caitlin Moran manages to make me laugh while simultaneously making me think. "Why, yes, it IS outrageous that all the women who've had cosmetic surgery look exactly the same / it's considered a woman's job to clean and she's "selling out" if she hires a cleaner / girls think they're awesome feminists if they've made lots of money by posing in their underwear."

- *Misconceptions* by **Naomi Wolf:** PLEASE read this before you have babies. The message is disturbing but undeniable – health care professionals are more interested in their work than in you. Childbirth is a business, and you'll be a cog in the wheel unless you take evasive action. Forget all those Hollywood scenes of women on their backs in the "stranded beetle" position having "essential" interventions, forget the horror stories you've heard, and read up on how birth *should* be. Along with *The Politics of Breastfeeding* by Gabrielle Palmer (which points out that businesses make money when mothers DON'T breastfeed), this will open your eyes to the profiteering that comes from separating women from the natural instincts of motherhood.

- *The Alchemist* by **Paulo Coelho:** If you'd rather devour a novel with a compelling narrative than wade through a solemn self-help tome, Paulo Coelho's your man. *The Alchemist* is massively popular with good reason; it's a short, deceptively simple story of a shepherd boy, and the journey he embarks upon in his search for treasure. Essentially it's a fairytale for grown-ups; about listening to your heart, discovering your purpose, and understanding your place in the universe.

Part Six

Your Life

"You only live once, but
if you do it right, once is enough."
Mae West

A DAY IN THE LIFE OF A PRINCESS

"The only way to have a life is to commit to it like crazy." Angelina Jolie

Right now, I am sitting at a desk which features a tiny vase of flowers, a pot of blackberry tea and my favourite mug. A magnolia candle scents the air, I am listening to happy-making music as I type, and admiring my manicured hands, which are adorned with silver and turquoise rings. These are simple pleasures, but proof that it's possible to feel like a Princess even when you're working. (I wonder if I can get a tax break on things like incense and pretty china? I swear they help my productivity...)

So, how does a Princess spend her days?

Where it All Begins

Jumping out of your skin at the sudden buzz of your alarm clock is no way to start the day. Setting a clock radio to ease you out of dreamland with smooth jazz or the dulcet tones of a newsreader is a much gentler way to rise and shine. Another tranquil way to rouse yourself is with softly increasing light, whether from natural sunlight or one of those clever machines which gradually builds up the brightness in your room, so it feels as if you're awakening with the dawn just like a cavegirl.

Wake Up in Style

- Appreciate the fact that you're not hungover. (You're not hungover, are you?)
- Take a minute to enjoy the snuggly warmth of your bed and think happy thoughts about the day ahead of you. Yes, even if what awaits you actually fills you with dread – you can pretend, can't you? Remind yourself that you're a powerful woman who can make the best of any circumstances... and any day you wake up is a good day.
- Wrap yourself in a gorgeous silky dressing gown, get your breakfast,

and bring it back to bed with you. For some reason people see breakfast in bed as the last word in hedonistic depravity, but what's the big deal? Wherever you eat, you're going to be sitting down, so it might as well be under a cosy duvet...

I try to eat something nourishing even if I'm forced to get up horrendously early. If it's a more civilised hour, I give myself enough time for a laid-back breakfast while I read the paper. I was once chatting to a colleague about our morning routines and she was aghast that I had such a relaxing way of slipping into the day. "I can't do that, I've got kids," she ranted. Choices, Princess. We all have choices. And if you're blessed with a sweet little head on the pillow next to you, take it as a fair exchange for those long-ago days when you could sleep until noon on weekends.

So, What Makes A Delicious, Healthy And Sustaining Breakfast?

- A smoothie – blend some fresh fruit / yoghurt / oats, and top with flaxseed for an amazingly satisfying breakfast you can drink on the way to work. (Plus it will make you feel like an inhabitant of some cool suburb of Manhattan or LA.)
- If you're in no rush, why not take your fruit and yogurt un-whizzed? A bowl of sliced banana and grapes topped with yogurt is gorgeous. Add the chopped nut of your choice to keep you going for longer.
- Wheat, oat, or bran-based cereal sets you up for the day, and a sprinkle of blueberries makes it even scrummier. Make your own granola for true Stepford wife satisfaction.
- Eggs. Don't worry about cholesterol, eggs are healthier now than they ever used to be. Don't ask me how that works, but it's true.
- Salmon. Actually, the thought of this makes me want to barf, but a lot of dieticians swear by it for a protein-rich start to the day.
- Peanut butter on toast. This fills me up for HOURS. Drizzled with honey = extra tasty.

Morning

The right frame of mind can be like a spiritual Valium pill, making little everyday annoyances seem totally unimportant. What will get you raring to go and feeling great?

Ways to Get into the Groove of the Day

- Take a minute first thing in the morning to set your focus for the day. It could be reading a religious verse, saying or writing some positive affirmations, or spending a few minutes in prayer or meditation. You don't need to do anything elaborate – just a few minutes of stillness will get your mind clear. This habit makes an unbelievable difference to the quality of your life, helping you to feel grounded and serene no matter what happens.
- Alternatively, start your morning with some stretches, yoga, or heart-pumping cardio moves. Some people like to get up at 5 am and go to the gym: I say they're crazy, but I bet they feel fantastic with all those endorphins flowing.
- Have a shower with an exhilaratingly citrusy, minty or spicy scented body wash.
- Write your thoughts down in a diary – as well as using it to log events after they've happened, you can consciously shape them in a positive way. "This is how I'm feeling as I start the day and this is what I'd like to achieve" is a good place to kick off.
- Make your journey to work a pleasant routine: listening to uplifting tunes on your mp3 player as you stride along as briskly as you can, using your bus journey to read / daydream, or listening to an audiobook in your car.

No matter how much you love your job, there'll still be days when you long to burrow back under the covers. (And when it's your day off, you can – YES!) Even when you don't feel as if you're a valuable cog in the machine, pretend you are. Convince yourself that you're essential to the team and not seeing your pretty, smiling face would send the rest of the workforce into a tailspin. You owe it to them to be on time. Otherwise they'll cry and be so, so sad.

Being a Princess in your Workplace

Some jobs can make you feel distinctly unglamorous (anything which involves a net over your hair generally falls into this category). Being on your feet all day (it forces the issue of flat shoes), being outside (thermals and balaclavas or dripping sweat, depending on the weather) and being the skivvy who has to do the tea run can all feel rather un-royal. But remember all the ways you've already mastered feeling like a Princess: are you allowed to wear perfume? Sparkly little earrings? A slick of lipstick and a smile? You can make the effort to look as good as possible no matter how strict the dress code rules. And with the right attitude, even the worst days can have some redeeming features: "I looked outwardly poised when I was feeling frazzled on the inside" is a real achievement.

Ways to Make Your Workspace Fabulous

- Bring in a vase of flowers or a colourful plant. Not only will it look pretty and give you nice fresh oxygen, it might be your only source of intelligent conversation.
- Get a decent chair. Even if it means smuggling yours to the nearest dump and then "needing" to order a brand new one. If in doubt, just steal the boss's and disguise it with a cute throw. (Only kidding. Sort of.) Add a spongy seat cover or a back-massaging cushion for the ultimate in comfort.
- Display some pictures that are bound to cheer you up when you've been on hold for ten minutes. If you don't have much space, tiny ones will fit around the frame of your computer – and of course, you can personalise your desktop background. Preferably with something non-embarrassing for those times when someone needs to borrow your laptop; not everyone will appreciate your post-ironic love for the hunks of *Baywatch.*
- Store a pot of hand cream in your desk drawer, along with an emergency nail kit in case of breaks or chips. If you're likely to go out on the town straight from work, stash a small makeup bag and toothbrush as well.
- Depending on how private your work station is, you might be able to get away with kicking off your heels and going barefoot or keeping some soft slippers under your desk to make you feel at home.

Slipper boots can look cunningly similar to outdoor winter shoes.

- Keep some fruit or a bag of nuts on hand so that when you get the urge to nibble, you'll have healthy options; grapes or cherries are a juicy alternative to processed snacks.

Lunch

Time for something homemade and yummy? Personally I prefer to bring my own lunch to work, so that I know exactly what's in it and I can avoid the temptation to overspend – shopping on an empty stomach is the worst idea ever. I'm inclined to use food as a reward ("I deserve two desserts – I'm having a tough day") but it's much more sensible to plan your cuisine in advance so you can save money and avoid junk food impulse purchases.

Things to Do at Lunch to be Super-Productive

- Too many of us stuff down a sandwich without taking our eyes off the computer screen. Even if you're just checking out your dating site messages, you're not going to enjoy all the flavours of your meal or feel you've had a conscious respite from your work. Try your very best to get out of the office, even if you work in one of those weirdo places where everyone eats hunched over their desks. (Huge, creativity-killing mistake: human beings require breaks.) The trouble is, once a few people stay in, there's pressure for everyone to do the same. You can always be running "essential errands" to the bank. Or, you know, the park. A quick walk with your headphones in will make the world seem right again.
- Go window-shopping. Don't actually start shopping properly; it's all too easy to get carried away taking armfuls of clothes to the dressing room and then wonder why your phone keeps beeping madly at you two hours later.
- Squeeze in beauty treatments: getting your eyebrows threaded or topping up your spray tan is one way to liven up your look for the afternoon. Do allow for waiting time and travel to and from the salon,

and use experienced beauty therapists. I once had a haircut with a salon trainee and it took double the time I'd expected, meaning I had to make apologetic phone calls to my boss over the roar of the hairdryers, and return to the office with insufficiently styled tresses.

- Find a peaceful seat – a park bench, a quiet café, a library – and give yourself a few minutes of breathing space. You may spend much of your time fending off men, as they often think a woman sitting by herself is in need of company. This could be a good thing or a bad thing depending on the current condition of your love life, and the quality of the men approaching you.

- If you work near a place of interest, make a short visit every once in a while. I used to pop into the National Gallery occasionally when I was working in Soho; even though I only had twenty minutes or so to spare, the total change of environment made a refreshing break.

- Go for a mini workout. If there's a gym nearby you could drop in for a quick session on the rowing machine, or take a dip in the pool. Alternatively, you could run or cycle around the area and take in some fresh air as well as the sights.

- If you have a fridge in the office, get the groceries for tonight's dinner so you can go straight home after work.

- Read a book. People who say they don't have time to read are silly and deluded. You have tons of time, and you can read dozens of books throughout the year if you utilise all your spare moments.

- Get a head start on those phone calls you keep planning to make, like getting a better deal on your internet bill or a tête-à-tête with your sister. It's an especially good time to ring people who chatter endlessly; your return to work is the perfect excuse to "reluctantly" end the conversation.

- Meet a friend who works nearby, or go out for lunch with your colleagues. It's a great way to split up the monotony of the day and rejuvenate everyone for the afternoon ahead.

Afternoon

This is the time when boredom can set in, with that "can't be bothered" feeling as well as possible sleepiness. Why can't we have naps at work? It'd be so cool and European and I'm sure it would boost afternoon efficiency. It's tempting to reach for an energising sugar rush: I once worked in a tiny, windowless office in August, and the bag of sweets I consumed every afternoon was the only thing that kept me awake. (That, and the annoying people who kept calling me with asinine questions.) Have a nice big mug of zingy herbal tea to pep you up without feeding your caffeine addiction. Coffee jitters can be fun (I have economical taste in drugs; music and espressos are all I need) but unless you find it amusing to watch your typing getting ever faster and more erratic (as I do), tea might be a better choice.

Ways to Add Sparkle to Your Afternoon

- This may be the time to catch up with your colleagues – it's not gossiping, it's networking!
- Set yourself targets (ten sales calls / five emails written / one finished project) and give yourself a reward for achieving them. (Tired of the healthy stuff? Bribe yourself with chocolate.)
- Turn up the radio and invite your co-workers to a stress-busting dance-off (this works especially well around 4 pm on a Friday).
- Work standing up. Inactive desk jobs have a debilitating effect on your health, and simply jamming an hour's walk or workout into your day won't solve the problem. Office managers are beginning to catch on to the benefits of the standing work station, but it's still typical for workers to spend eight hours a day sitting down. If an under-the-desk stair-stepper is out of the question, make sure you get up a couple of times every hour. Your colleagues may think you have a weak bladder if the only place you can walk to is the ladies' room, but it's worth it to stop your limbs from atrophying.
- Alternatively, find a legitimate reason to move around a little bit – volunteer to clean up the kitchen, run an errand or visit someone on the next floor.
- When you can't get your brain into gear, try a quick puzzle, like a crossword or sudoku. (Even the most conscientious Princess needs a breather sometimes.) It will stimulate your little grey cells and you'll

probably find that the problem which previously seemed impossible suddenly looks much simpler.

- Have a look around and see if there are ways you can improve your work station. Get rid of old paperwork, get your files in order, and prune that plant you bought to brighten up your cubicle.
- Try doing something a new way – lots of us get caught up in routines which may or may not be the most efficient use of our time, when a quick rethink could revolutionise the office.

Evening

When the working day is over, you have a few hours of chill-out time before the daily grind starts again. So, what are you going to do?

- Go to the gym: pack some headphones with tunes to get you hyper and go to that boxercise class, get spinning, or keep your balance on a wobble board. You'll thank yourself later. Plus the gym is a great place to meet men – whether you're looking or not, you can practise your feminine allure (it helps if you have cute pink workout clothes and a supply of sweet-smelling shampoo in your locker).
- Alternatively, you could exercise at home. If you have a treadmill or weights, you can catch up with essential TV at the same time. Half an hour will fly by when you're paying attention to your favourite show, and you'll barely notice the fact that you're toning your arms while getting your fix of drama.
- Play a game with your housemates. A few rounds of Trivial Pursuit, Monopoly or Scrabble will be much more entertaining than you'd expect.
- Catch up with all those itty-bitty things that pile up – sorting through your post, changing the bag in your rubbish bin, de-frosting the fridge... you'll feel super-organised as you tick off everything on your to-do list.
- Spend time cooking a fantastic meal with healthy, organic ingredients – and savour every bite.

- Go to the pictures – cinemas often have a cheap night mid-week for thrifty Princesses to catch up with Hollywood's latest.
- Or kick back with a movie at home for the ultimate comfort. That way you won't pay an extortionate fee for a little plastic cup of cola, or miss anything when you go to the loo.
- Sometimes even a film seems like too much work, and vegging out with some sitcoms or some truly brain-dead reality TV is the only way to spend the evening. Don't feel guilty, just enjoy.
- Go dancing. You may not be shimmying under the stars in Buenos Aires, but tango-ing the night away in your local community hall is the next best thing.
- Meet up with friends. Whether it's a quick cocktail at happy hour, taking a class together or hanging out in your jammies, a little regroup will lift your spirits for the rest of the week.
- Any number of the *101 Ways To Feel Like A Princess...*

Bed time

Beauty sleep is crucial; it's probably the most important thing you can do for your health, both physical and mental.

Ways to Wind Down

- Take off all your makeup and use a lovely cream or oil on your face to give your skin its best chance of looking radiant in the morning.
- Have a hot bath with tons of fluffy bubbles or heavenly fragrance oil... yep, this is really obvious, magazine-level "how-to" stuff. Which brings me to the next step in a blissful soak: reading material. If you don't have a good book on the go, try working your way through a big pile of ancient teen glossies. You could also entertain yourself by doing all the beauty treatments they recommend: I'm talking cheap face masks / foot scrub, deep conditioner, and blackhead removal. I can't guarantee you'll feel like a Princess while your face is covered in clay, but your skin will reap the benefits.

- Lay out your clothes for the morning so you don't have any last-minute panics because you've run out of un-laddered tights.
- Jot down your to-do list for tomorrow. When it's on paper, it won't whizz around your brain in that horrible chaotic way it does when you're feeling overwhelmed. Keep a pad by your bed so you can add more items if they pop into your head once your light's out.
- A cup of hot milk or cocoa is ultra-cosy and soothing. (A dash of an alcoholic beverage of your choice makes the tasty adult version, for special occasions only.)
- Listen to some relaxing music while you get ready for bed.
- If you're too sleepy for an intellectual read, a funny book will send you to sleep with a smile. If you can't get into anything, sometimes a nostalgic flick through a childhood favourite is the way to go.
- A spritz of lavender on your pillow will help to calm your mind as you drift off...

Sweet dreams, Princess!

VALENTINE'S DAY

"I have an everyday religion that works for me. Love yourself first, and everything else falls into line." Lucille Ball

What does a Princess's Valentine's day look like? Well, she wakes up in a leisurely way, has a really good cup of coffee while drizzling syrup on her blueberry pancakes, admires the soft, plump roses that fill a vase next to her bed... you get the picture. The important point is that the picture is the same whether she's single or attached, because the Princess outlook is all about making the day a celebration, no matter what her marital status.

Until you try it the Princess way, it's easy to loathe February 14th. If you do have a boyfriend, you're stuck with the expectation from society (ie your friends and family) that the two of you will express your love in one of the approved ways:

- Going out for dinner (in a restaurant which jacks up the prices especially for occasions like this) to spend the evening surrounded by other couples ostentatiously trying to out-romance each other.
- Going on a weekend away (ditto).
- Being seen with armfuls of flowers and chocolates (if not a brand new flatscreen TV or adorable puppy).

This is all very well if your boyfriend goes in for competitive courting, but most guys don't. Even if he's a softy with all sorts of ideas about baking you cookies and icing personalised messages onto each one – he still may not realise that what you really want is to have flowers delivered to your office so all the other girls will see them. If he's been trained into thinking that spending pots of money will keep you happy, he won't understand why you'd rather curl up with a cosy film and a bottle of wine. Men's egos are extremely delicate and I find that making a show of being appreciative is the best response, even to inexplicable (possibly panic-bought) monstrosities. You can tactfully let him know what you'd really like when the garage-forecourt bouquet isn't such a raw memory. Men rarely live up to the unrealistic expectations we have for them, bless their hearts.

What if you're a single Princess? These days there's no stigma attached to flying solo and there are bound to be some fun singles events in your area. If you're interested in meeting someone new, you could try out whatever wacky new social trend has emerged. Speed dating is so over; it's now silent dating and dating in the dark. Wait, did I say "fun"?

So how do we make February 14th a pleasure, rather than an opportunity for the postman to smirk at our lack of cards and presents? One way is to make sure you have a lavish heap of gifts: perfume, flowers, chocolates. The first time you buy them all for yourself might seem *slightly* tragic, but I guarantee you'll get over it.

The logic behind this method is that if you were coupled up, you'd probably be squandering your cash on special kinds of beer, golf tees and DVDs of boring political dramas, while hoping for a few gift-wrapped goodies in return. So why not cut out the middle man and treat yourself? It's a foolproof way to get exactly what you want, feel cherished and have a lovely memorable day. Alternatively, you could get together with friends – one year I had dinner with some pals (we were all either single or had lost our boyfriends to their work shifts) and we had a delightful evening of sophistication and chocolate. Lots of chocolate.

The fun doesn't stop when you meet the man of your dreams; self-gifting means there's no need to drop hints and worry about what your partner is going to dredge up. Once you've bought yourself a luxurious spa day, it won't feel like the end of the world if he doesn't magically pick out the exact silver necklace you saw in the jeweller's window. Just a note for future reference: most men don't really get "subtle". If you want something specific, be blunt or forever hold your peace. It's not fair to sulk because he's not psychic.

The other plus point of a DIY approach is that you won't feel any pressure to "do something romantic" with your guy. If he has any brains, he'll know that Valentine's day is important, and will cancel the football game / fishing trip / operation on his kidneys in order to spend time with you. However, if he doesn't volunteer – whether because he's a doofus or because you only started dating him ten days before V day – you can relax and leave him to it. This has a twofold effect: firstly, you get to chill out and have a nice day of decorating cupcakes with your mum, or lolling around with Tom Hanks movies (better without sarcastic commentary, anyway). Secondly, he wonders WHY you didn't call him or pressure him. Are you seeing somebody else? His wondering will be intensified when he comes round later that week and sees the vase of pink tulips on your kitchen table...

When you've made your own Valentine's Day special, why not spread the love around? Donate some flowers to an old people's home, take your dog to visit a children's hospital, or send cards to all your best buddies. A friend of mine buys a copy of her most cherished book every February (aforementioned Princess fave *The Alchemist* by Paulo Coelho), re-reads it as a gift to herself, then passes it along to someone who'll love it just as much. Isn't that a refreshing way to make the world a sweeter place?

A YEAR IN THE LIFE OF A PRINCESS

"God has so much faith in you that you were entrusted with the gift of life and a unique mission to fulfil." Iyanla Vazant

I confess, I haven't included all of the National holidays so please don't feel left out if your country's big day isn't listed. (And as I'm all about snowy Christmases, apologies to those in the Southern hemisphere.) Father's Day and Mother's Day differ depending on where you live, so it's down to you (and those helpful TV commercials) to remember when to make your parents a lovely breakfast in bed, take them out to lunch, and buy them a set of golf balls / chintzy tea-cosies / posh bottles of wine. With your Princessy savoir-faire, I know you'll come up with the perfect celebration – and here are some suggestions for making the rest of your year special.

January

- Avoid signing any contracts or parting with any money during the surge of "New Year, New You" crap which appears without fail every January. Your burst of enthusiasm may soon wane, leaving you with a bunch of stuff you'll never use (a sushi-making kit, really?) or your credit card number in the hands of a sniggering fitness instructor. (Nobody really goes to the gym while there are still Christmas chocolates left over. I think it might be against the law.) Make small changes when YOU decide on them throughout the year and you're more likely to stick to them.
- Wildly unrealistic resolutions aside, you could use the time for some deliciously self-centred introspection instead. It's a good exercise to note down what you accomplished last year, and what you hope to do this year. I'm a total nerd – in addition to my daily journal, I make a "yearbook" and write about all the good stuff, bad stuff and most memorable moments of each month, as well as listing the books I've read and films I've watched. It's like a little time capsule of the year's

highlights – I can flick through it and remember all the cool stuff I might otherwise have forgotten.

- One secret to achieving goals is to word them very specifically. If you write down something vague like "Get fit" or "Be better at my job", how will you measure your success? It's far more effective to aim for a specific target like "Exercise three times a week" or "Complete all my projects and ask if I can take on more responsibility at work."

- Rather than boring (but necessary) targets like "Use up all the cosmetics I bought last year" be brave and push yourself. It's true what they say – if your dreams don't scare you, they're not big enough! So get dreaming, and make a list of every aspiration you have, no matter where it fits on the easy-to-impossible scale. Check the list regularly and use it to keep yourself accountable – are you moving in the right direction?

- Organise some nights in with your friends. It can be a real letdown when all the December festivities are over for another year, so arrange some events you can look forward to and brighten up the dark days. There's always a severe lack of spare cash in January, so what could be better than simple evenings of playing cards or board games and doing quizzes?

- January sales are great for picking up cheap Christmas paraphernalia, or making big purchases like furniture or electronics. For clothes... not so much. As I mentioned in my earlier anti-sale rant, you're looking at the dregs left behind (after the big party season). Unless it's a timeless classic which suits your style, don't get sucked into the "it's cheap so it must be a bargain" mentality.

- The Jewish holiday Tu B'Shevat normally falls around the end of January or beginning of February: it's the New Year and "birthday" for trees. Isn't that beautiful? It's about time they got a day of their own. Can't you just see them now, with their party hats and birthday cake? Go and give some hugs to trees and whisper to them that it's nearly time to wake up after their long winter sleep.

- We have another contender in the contest for loveliest festival EVER: a Hindu celebration known as Mattu Pongal in Southern India. Families bathe their cattle and dress them in flowered garlands to honour them for all the hard work and milk-providing they do all year. As well as enjoying their tender grooming and pretty decorations, the lucky cows get to roam around wherever they like and eat bananas, sweet rice and sugar cane as a yearly treat. Aw – every cow should get to feel like a Princess for the day!

- Throw a shrimp on the barbie to celebrate Australia day on the 26th. Or grab a tinnie and watch *Crocodile Dundee* – still a top film no matter how many times you've seen it.

February

- Congratulate yourself for all the progress you've made on your goals.
- Have a wonderful February 14th, whether you have a man in tow or not. Once you've tried it the Princess way, you might find that you actually prefer Valentine's day on your own...
- If celebrating V day doesn't appeal, you could always suggest that your local community take up the ancient celebration of Lupercalia instead. The men have to run up and down the street naked, while attempting to whip nearby women with strips of goat-hide. It's got to be more fun than paying £20 for a giant cookie cut into a heart shape.
- Invite your friends over for a craft session. Even if you're all working on different projects, you can encourage and advise each other and catch up on the gossip – they don't call it a stitch 'n' bitch for nothing. You could knit, cross-stitch, crochet, sew, quilt, scrapbook, mould some polymer clay or even experiment with resin – you can make fantastic jewellery by embedding glitter or other bright objects in it. (Check out how-to videos online.)
- Spend some time with your family and get the old photo albums out. It's cosy and comforting and your parents will love it when you show an interest in them.
- It's National bird feeding month: give the little poppets a treat and make an extra-special birdy cake for them. Mix up all your scraps, bread crusts etc, melt some bacon fat, add seeds and it's a gourmet meal for our feathered friends.
- If it's a leap year, for goodness' sake don't propose to anyone on the 29th. Princesses don't need to do any chasing; if the guy isn't smart

enough to ask for her hand in marriage, she might lose interest anyway...

- You know you're getting old when you stop feeling excited about snow and start grumbling about it instead. Forget the inconvenience and channel your carefree inner child instead: start a snowball fight, toboggan down a hill and build a snowman.
- If you have the cash and some willing pals, why not go for a snowboarding break? Stay in a log cabin, stoke up the fire, flirt with the instructors... Who knows, you might even have time to get out there on the slopes and work up an appetite for your hot chocolate with extra marshmallows.

March

- It's St David's day on the 1st, so let's get practising our Welsh accents. (In Wales, microwaves are sometimes known as "Popty-Pings", a piece of trivia I find strangely pleasing.)
- If it's freezing outside, comfort yourself with the fact that spring is on its way. You might even catch a whiff of scent from some flowers or see some little green shoots. Isn't it exciting to see nature do its thing?
- On March 8th it's National Women's day, yay! Wear your most feminine dress, purr at people and flutter your eyelashes. You're on the winning team, baby!
- Celebrate the spring equinox and the fact that mornings and evenings are now looking a bit lighter.
- Visit a farm and see the unbearably cute baby lambs, chicks, and calves. Just don't go for a roast dinner right afterwards.
- Summer will be here before you know it, so it's time to step up the beauty treatments. No doubt you've already been exfoliating, moisturising and deep-conditioning your entire body throughout the winter, because you're a bona fide Princess. Why not add a few highlights to brighten up your hair, pop on some fuchsia lipstick and use a perfume that brings to mind those budding blooms?
- Dress up in a silly green hat, drink a Guinness and celebrate St Patrick's day on the 17th.

- Take inspiration from Wordsworth and find somewhere with a huge display of daffodils "fluttering and dancing in the breeze" – it's guaranteed to lift your spirits.

April

- It's definitely springtime! Celebrate with the shedding of some layers as the first watery sunshine touches your skin.
- On the 22nd, join in the celebrations for Earth day. Until we colonise Mars (don't hold your breath on that) earth is the only planet we've got, so we need to do our bit to keep it in tip-top condition. Start recycling: silver foil and used stamps have value and are often collected by local charities, so get online to see who could benefit from what you'd otherwise throw out. To make compost for the garden, you'll need a container for your old teabags, vegetable peelings and fruit pulp. Collect it up and add to an outdoor compost bin; throw in some dead leaves, grass clippings and soil and you'll soon have a useful fertiliser – and no waste.
- It's St George's day *and* Shakespeare's birthday on the 23rd: what a great day to celebrate everything English. Let's wear our pearls and have some cucumber sandwiches and Earl Grey tea. (Even if you're already English and don't do any of these things. Make an exception.)
- Have a good old spring-clean: scrub your floors and windows, do the kind of vacuuming which involves moving furniture, and donate anything you don't need. You'll feel like Snow White in no time.
- If you have a garden (or a window box) plant some seeds and reap the benefits later in the year. Being outside and getting your hands into the earth is really therapeutic.
- Easter sometimes falls in March and sometimes April – either way, celebrate with some chocolate eggs and maybe some bunny-shaped treats. Whether you're Christian or not, we can all relate to the joy of a fresh start and the concept of grace and forgiveness.
- If you're ever going to go on Safari, make it now – South Africa celebrates its Freedom Day on the 27th and you're sure to find some happy braais (barbecues) going on.

May

- Find a friend with a convertible and drive around with the top down, just for the hell of it. Don't zoom along too fast, or you'll get chilly and it'll take weeks to untangle your hair – but a leisurely cruise around the block is perfect for feeling like a movie star.
- Go for a ramble through a forest and admire the spectacular mass of bluebells – the scent is incredible. In the words of writer Edward Abbey: "There is beauty, heartbreaking beauty, everywhere." Breathe it in and let yourself relax...
- Learn a sexy new skill like Egyptian dancing, hula-hooping, or poi. They're all fun, graceful (once you get the hang of them) and very addictive.
- Take a hike (in the nicest possible way). If your friends aren't the trekking type, it's easy to find groups who organise walks, ranging from rugged mountain slopes to leisurely strolls around the park.
- Now might be a good time to visit somewhere with a large Buddhist population: either in April or around the first full moon of May, Buddha's birthday is celebrated across the world. Beautiful bright lanterns are let loose to float into the sky and floral shrines are created to remember Buddha's birth in a garden. Some believe it rained tea on the day he was born. (How amazing would that be? Make mine an oolong!)
- Slap on your knee and elbow pads and get your rollerblades on. It's great exercise and checking out the guys in the park will make you feel fifteen again. (If you are fifteen – enjoy! Life does get better, I promise.)
- Have a picnic. It feels more special when all the food is homemade – salad, individual mini pork pies, lemonade, jam tarts. If you can get hold of one of those classic wicker baskets with little holders for the champagne glasses, you'll feel as if you've just stepped into a P.G. Wodehouse novel.
- Lie down under a fruit tree and let the blossoms drift onto you. Heaven.

June

- Put Puccini on the stereo, pound up some pesto and slurp up some spaghetti, it's Italy day on the 2nd of June. Finish off with some gelato or a creamy slice of tiramisu. Actually, can we have an Italy month?
- Ride your bike around the neighbourhood; waving to the kids playing outside, stopping for a milkshake... it's the perfect way to spend a mellow Sunday afternoon. Add some little streamers to your handle-bars for extra pizzazz, and don't forget your safety helmet.
- Play miniature golf. It's a great way to spend a warm evening – as long as nobody gets too competitive.
- Read a book that's set somewhere hot and steamy – you'll appreciate the atmosphere that little bit more.
- If you're not in the mood for sunshine, an ice bar might be the place to cool off. Sip some vodka and ask them to crank up the Tchaikovsky – it's the perfect way to celebrate Russia's National day on the 12th.
- Celebrate the summer solstice. Stonehenge will be full of hippies, so you could pop along if you fancy some interesting conversations. If the bliss of solitude is more your thing, you'll get a kick out of a quiet sunrise or sunset with no company other than a sense of wonder. (Try not to think about the fact that the nights will be drawing in from now on.)
- Bitten by the tennis bug? You don't need to go to Wimbledon to eat strawberries and cream or wear a cute, flouncy tennis skirt. There are lots of free local courts which are open to anyone, so all you have to do is turn up with a friend, a couple of racquets and a *generous* supply of balls (in case of wild serves which go into the bushes, never to be seen again).
- Cool off with a stroll along the river. Romantic walking companion optional...

July

- It's Canada day on the 1st, eh? Get out the maple syrup!
- You don't need a special machine to make your own delicious ice

cream. It's the churning action which makes it so smooth and creamy, so all you need to do is pop it in the freezer and take it out every couple of hours to give it a good mix and get rid of ice crystals. You'll find a zillion recipes online, with no end to the scrummy flavours you can create.

- If you're American, have a great time on the 4th, and congratulations on your independence. Let's face it, we were never going to agree on how to spell "aluminium".
- By now you're probably hooked on hijacking other countries' parties, so why not celebrate the Bahamas' special day on the 10th? I like to spend the day in a hammock, dipping my toes in some water (well, a paddling pool) and sipping a drink with a tiny umbrella in it. I'm sure that's not what people really do all day in the Bahamas, but I like to pretend.
- Head to the park with a frisbee and a dog for the ultimate free workout. You'll have a blast and so will your furbaby.
- Zut alors! Any more National days this month? You guessed it, we have Bastille day on July 14th, so insert your own frogs' legs / snails / garlic note here. Alternatively, stock up on tasty crêpes and croissants and perfect your Gallic shrug for anyone who asks about the calories in your breakfast.
- At the end of the Ramadan fasting (which occurs at a different time every year, calculated according to the Islamic calendar) Muslims are required to give food or money to the needy people in the community, so that even the poorest can celebrate Eid al-Fitr, their most joyous occasion. Giving to the under-privileged is something we should all remember to do, no matter what the season.
- How about a trip to the beach? Ride the waves, sunbathe all day, or splash about in the rock pools. You'll come back all sticky with salt water, you won't get the sand out of your car for a month, and you'll have the best time ever.
- Head for the garden with your buddies and lie in the grass sipping sangria while you catch up on the gossip.
- It's Belgium's National day on the 21st, so tuck into some delicious waffles – I like them with melted chocolate and strawberries.
- Book a cheap trip abroad – visit cultural landmarks, eat the local

delicacies and broaden your horizons. English is spoken as a second language in many countries but they'll still appreciate it if you make a bit of effort, so learn a few phrases and throw yourself into the experience.

August

- The 1st is Switzerland's National day, so I think it only right that we celebrate with some Swiss chocolate – once you get into the good stuff, there's no going back.
- Have a barbeque with homemade burgers, kebabs and fruit punch. Of course, you'll probably end up getting rained on and shivering towards the end of the evening, but you can always finish by heading inside for a movie.
- Go to a theme park, ride all the scariest roller coasters and SCREAM. It's great for getting rid of bottled-up tension.
- Camping is an essential summer escape; cooking over a tiny gas stove and collecting water from a pump is like recapturing your childhood dreams of living in an Enid Blyton story. And sleeping under canvas (or the stars) feels fantastic... for a night or two. After that, your own bed is bliss and showering feels amazing. So it's life-enhancing all round, really.
- Find a bunch of pals, arm everyone with water pistols, balloons or hoses and have a gigantic water fight – it's the best way to keep cool.
- Go to an open air film – even if it's a crap one or you can't hear anything, you'll still enjoy yourself. (Take a blanket with waterproof lining in case of damp grass.)
- Alternatively, try one of those open-air theatre productions. There's nothing like experiencing Shakespeare the way it was intended to be seen, and watching Midsummer Night's Dream would be a great way to spend a balmy evening.
- Road trip! You and your BFF will have a great time deciding what sights you want to see, working out an itinerary and then exploring the country you live in. Warning: you may find the planning part more

enjoyable than the spending hours sitting in a car part. But it's all good, and the memories will be priceless.

September

- Enjoy the September sunshine. As a kid, going back to school in September always felt like the beginning of the build-up to Christmas, but now we seem to get an Indian summer every year, and it's become my favourite season.
- Take a slug of tequila (if you can stand the stuff) and roll up a tortilla with some hot peppers – it's Mexico day on the 16th.
- To celebrate Rosh Hashanah, Jews eat delicious apples dipped in honey to symbolise having a sweet new year. Speaking of which...
- Go fruit picking. Apples and blackberries will be ripening, and whether you head for a fragrant orchard or the nearest wild hedgerow, you should be able to find enough for a bit of pie-making. I get obsessed with picking blackberries from my local park and freeze as many as I can to enjoy throughout the year, as well as trying my hand at making jam, wine and desserts (with varying degrees of success).
- Make a dinner table centrepiece out of pine cones; they look great au naturel or spray-painted gold and silver.
- Remember celebrating Harvest Festival at school, when you packed up a box of groceries for someone less fortunate than yourself? Well, churches are still all over that. Find out what your local congregation is collecting and lend a hand – it's really satisfying to pack all the dinky tins into a shoebox and think of the happy person who's going to get your little package of love.
- It's Brazil's National day on the 7th; I like to mark the occasion by dancing to samba music and playing football. Simultaneously, of course.
- Appreciate the fact that you don't have to go to school anymore. If you are still in school, then enjoy shopping for all that shiny new stationery and remember your resolution to be really hardworking and neat this year.

October

- Mmm... autumn's here. Take a walk and enjoy the vividly changing colours, the feel of crispy leaves underfoot, and the unmistakable moment when the season shifts and there's suddenly a chill in the air. Sweeping leaves into a big crunchy pile and then jumping on it is fun no matter what your age.
- It's Germany's National day on the 3rd, so make yourself a sophisticated plate of Bratwurst and Sauerkraut and blast out some Beethoven.
- Prepare for Halloween! I love it, although I think of it more as "The Festival of Costumes and Candy" than anything too spooky, so you can leave your rubber severed hand at the door, thanks. Get imaginative and create a whimsical, original ensemble to wear on the big night – it can be a bit of a giggle to dress slutty, but Princesses don't NEED to in order to get attention. We leave that to the amateurs.
- Carve a pumpkin: this has become a serious art form and you'll find inspiring pictures online. Use the flesh to make pumpkin pie, soup, cookies or cupcakes to get into the festive mood.
- If all that commercial stuff isn't your bag, what about the spiritual side of Samhain? Legend has it that it's the time of year when the "veil" between the living and the dead is at its thinnest. Sounds to me like a great excuse to stay up all night telling ghost stories by flickering candlelight.
- Alternatively, you could do things the Mexican way and celebrate Day of the Dead: traditionally, families gather around the graves of loved ones and create altars with sweets, flowers and candles. Call me an emo, but I think there's something rather lovely about honouring your ancestors this way.
- When the nights are drawing in and it's howling a gale outside, snuggle up with a gratifyingly scary book. I love old-fashioned Victorian horror stories because of their exaggerated language and general hysteria; they're just creepy enough to give you a gratifying shiver, but not frightening enough to make you sleep with your light on for a week. For a vintage kick, try Dracula, Frankenstein, or anything

by H.P. Lovecraft. If psychological thrillers are more up your street, I'd recommend anything by Daphne du Maurier, because she's fab.
- Hindus and Sikhs celebrate Divali, the festival of light which signifies the triumph of good over evil. They get the party started with fireworks, which illuminate the sky and remind Brits that Bonfire night is just around the corner...

November

- It's Guy Fawkes night! Stock up on fireworks for the 5th, build a bonfire and wrap up warm. Cups of hot soup are always welcome, and don't forget to write your name with a sparkler.
- It's never too early to start thinking about Christmas. I know it's annoying when the shops start blasting carols, and commercials keep trying to scare you with those "Only X number of days to go!" proclamations. In fact, I BLAME them for lulling me into a false sense of security, because when you've been hearing about Christmas since September, you get into the habit of thinking "Oh, it's ages away..." and then suddenly it's Christmas Eve and you still have to choose, buy and wrap about ten presents. If you start shopping now, it will spread the cost and you'll feel much calmer as the big day approaches. If you don't celebrate Christmas, you can take it easy...
- Enjoy all the enticing things about winter: hot-water bottles with velvety covers, warming vegetable stew by the fire, coming in from the cold and having a hot bath, and treating yourself to some new fuzzy-soft hats and gloves.
- If all that bracing weather is getting to be too much for you, maybe you can squeeze a winter break into your budget. Morocco is lovely and sunny and it's their National day on the 18th. Why not do your Christmas shopping at a Souk in Marrakesh?
- Go ice-skating with some pals – you'll heat up in no time, and gliding around is a good giggle (even though there's always someone who insists on skating backwards to show off).
- Mix up some yummy mulled wine or hot spiced cider. You'll never want to go back to cold drinks again.

- You don't have to be American to celebrate Thanksgiving – it's a great reminder for all of us to appreciate what we have. Let's try to keep hold of our attitude of gratitude rather than forgetting it the next day as we shove little old ladies aside in our eagerness to get into the shops to BUY MORE STUFF!
- It's St Andrew's day on the 30th, so why not head out for some sprightly Scottish dancing? A ceilidh is a very energetic way to spend an evening and you'll be breathless with laughter from being spun around the room – hopefully to the sounds of bagpipes and fiddles for a really authentic experience.

December

- Put up your Christmas tree and use all the decorations you made when you were little for retro charm.
- Have a deliciously cosy afternoon making all the Christmas recipes and homemade goodies you'd never feel inclined to bake at any other time of the year. I love making snickerdoodles, chocolate gingerbread, and little stained glass biscuits made with melted boiled sweets (they make great tree decorations too).
- Spending days on end cooped up with family can be tough. Make sure you get out for a quick walk when you can feel your sanity slipping away. And remember that *you're* the family someone else is stuck with – choose your battles and try to keep everything as chilled out as possible.
- Go to a carol concert or go singing around the neighbourhood. Wear your mittens, light some candles and crunch your way through the frost for that wonderful Christmassy feeling.
- When you're searching for gifts, get as much as you can online. You can buy almost anything without leaving your house (I do most of my shopping in my pyjamas) as long as you leave plenty of time for deliveries, and check the shipping rates before you buy.
- If you like to get more hands-on when you're choosing potential presents, I recommend malls, so you can leave your coat in the car (to avoid either overheating or having to carry it) and make return trips

with heavy packages throughout the day if you need to. The best times to go are very early in the morning or in the last hour before the shops shut – you'll often find they stay open later in the evenings as you get closer to Christmas. Try to plan your shopping session so you'll go on a full stomach: hunger pangs will make you irritable and the whole ordeal will become unbearable. (Talking from experience here...)

- If you're single, don't feel sad that you don't have anyone to help untangle the Christmas tree lights, just think about all the cash you're saving on presents (and spend a little bit of it on yourself).

- If you know anyone with small children, try to wangle an invite to any nativity plays / Christingle services / carol concerts they're involved in. There's nothing cuter than tiny children dressed as sheep and singing about reindeer, and their excitement is infectious.

- There's no rule that says you MUST go out on New Year's Eve – sometimes the best memories will just be you and a couple of friends having a low-key evening at home. The best part is that in the morning when everyone else is suffering from their night of excess, you'll be bright-eyed, bushy-tailed and ready for anything the new year brings.

101 WAYS TO FEEL
LIKE A PRINCESS

Being a Princess is about living consciously: not letting the days pass you by, but taking the time to build the life you want and appreciating every minute of it.

So here are 101 ways to channel your inner Princess:

1) Remember when you were a kid and you imagined that being a grown-up would mean you could have cake for breakfast? Well, it's all true. So if you fancy a slice of gateau, leftover pizza / curry, or a full English, go right ahead and do it. It's one of the perks of being an adult (and it almost makes up for the fact that your workday no longer ends at 3:20 pm).

2) Get lost in a brilliant book. With every novel you open you're entering a new world, and you can experience a million different lifetimes – all for the price of a paperback. Reading is a go-anywhere, enjoy-anytime experience: in the garden, in waiting rooms, on the bus, by the pool. It's especially delicious when you're snuggled up with a plate of snacks, a purry cat and some ambient music. BLISS. In the summer, nothing's nicer than lounging in the sun or sitting in the shade of a tree with a book. And no matter what the season, going to bed early to read is always a treat.

3) Books aren't just for heavenly wallowing and losing yourself in pure imagination; as I mentioned along with my reading recommendations, non-fiction is a valuable way to absorb new information and enhance your perspective on life. There's a quote I love from Charles "Tremendous" Jones, a writer who said: "You will be the same person in five years as you are today except for the people you meet and the books you read." Devouring all kinds of books can also give you a new kind of confidence in yourself – who cares if someone else is prettier?

I bet they haven't read *The Art of War*, Bill Bryson's entire back catalogue and Margaret Thatcher's memoirs.

4) Keep bars of soap in your underwear drawer. It will make your panties smell delectable and when you finally use the soap, it'll last longer. Weird but true.

5) Make cupcakes. Frost them with pink butter icing, and then decorate them with edible glitter / sugar paste flowers / fondant animals of your own choice and creation. Keep them in the prettiest cake tin you can find, and share them out when your friends come over. Alternatively, eat them all yourself. They make a great breakfast.

6) Travel. There are tons of ways you can do this without spending too much money – look online for sites which match up thrifty travellers with friendly hosts. I spent several happy months "couchsurfing" my way around North America, and when I returned to England I hosted travellers from all over the world as a way to give back. Your level of safety is entirely down to you – www.couchsurfing.com is an excellent resource but anyone can sign up, so it's important to take responsibility for yourself. Obviously, there is risk involved when you stay with strangers, so be careful, trust your instincts and always tell lots of people where you're going. Choose wisely and you'll have the time of your life: staying with locals is the best way to soak up the culture and find out all the secret non-touristy highlights of the area. For longer trips, there are ways to earn your keep; in addition to finding standard house / pet sitting jobs, check out volunteering companies which offer food and accommodation in exchange for work. The variety is huge – from picking fruit or helping out on a cattle ranch to working as a receptionist on a yoga retreat, there'll be something which is right up your street. The bonus is that you also meet like-minded people – I made some lasting friendships when I spent a few weeks renovating cottages in Italy. Wherever you've always wanted to visit, save up your pennies, hop on a plane and go.

7) Do the thing you "don't have time for". Seeing your parents, going horse riding, calling up that old friend, using the spa voucher you got for Christmas. If you wait for the perfect slot of time, it will never come, so seize the moment. We all get a bit shy sometimes when it

comes to friends we haven't seen for ages, and wish they'd make the first move. Be brave – you won't regret it.

8) Grab someone who's always up for a crazy plan, and go for a picnic at midnight. A starry sky, a cool breeze, and a blanket on the ground – if you have a private garden and the weather allows, why not sleep out there too? Life is all about creating fabulous memories.

9) Think about your circumstances from someone else's point of view. It's easy to get green-eyed when you look at other people's lives, but you're bound to have plenty of enviable assets. Whether it's a loving family, a quick zinging wit, lustrous hair, artistic talent or even the ability to spot a sleazeball from thirty paces, I bet somebody out there wishes they had something you have.

10) Buy some flowers. Arrange them prettily in a vase and admire them every time you go past. Displayed prominently in your window, they even let passersby see that you're the kind of girl who gets bouquets all the time.

11) Sign up for that evening class you've always secretly hankered after. Maybe you'll learn calligraphy, a new language, or how to make stained glass windows. It doesn't matter if you're terrible at it – that's the first step to getting good. Even if it turns out that you're not a natural talent when it comes to editing videos or basket-weaving, you'll meet new people and hopefully have a bit of a laugh. If that's really too scary, you could do an online course, and add to your skills without leaving the house.

12) Spend the day watching old movies – it'll make a refreshing change from the latest formulaic franchise. Whether it's an elegant film noir where straight-talking dames swig whisky and wear heels at all times, a big bright musical with lots of zany tap dancing, or a silly sex comedy from the 1960s, grab the popcorn and enjoy.

13) Go for a walk somewhere green. Preferably barefoot – it feels incredible to get the grass between your toes and touch the sun-baked earth. Walking in nature is a guaranteed mood-enhancer; I've often gone out in a grumpy state of mind, spent an hour marching through the woods and returned home feeling exhilarated.

14) Have a clear-out. Does everything in your home fulfil the criteria of being either beautiful or useful? Sometimes possessions start owning

us – if you're only keeping something because of its sentimental value, it'll end up getting passed on to your children and will be a weight around their necks too. Think of the future generations and chuck it out.

15) Read through your cookery books. I've been cutting out recipes from magazines since I was a kid, although I've only made a fraction of the mouth-watering dishes. For some reason, my inner housewife finds it very soothing to flip through the pages choosing what to make next.

16) Let go of your idea of how life is "supposed" to be. There's nothing wrong with having a vision in mind to work towards, but don't be devastated if it all turns out differently. Think about your life so far: how many times have your expectations been spot on? I bet no matter how much you tried to imagine your trip to Thailand or your first day at university, the reality was different from what you'd expected. What fate offers you might be better than anything you've dreamed of, and if you stick too doggedly to the picture in your head, you could miss what's thrilling about the alternative.

17) Get super-cute nails. You don't need to go to a manicurist when you can grab a packet of nail transfers / foils for an elaborate pattern with minimum effort and cost. Or paint your own designs – leopard print is just blobs of different colours. When you have pretty nails, no matter what you're doing – chopping vegetables, typing, making elegant gestures as you talk – your hands will look gorgeous.

18) Keep a gratitude notebook: every day, write down five things that make you feel thankful. Have a flick through when you're feeling melancholy and remind yourself of your many blessings. If your life right now is miserable (boo!) then try thinking back to the happiest times in your life and remember vividly what it feels like when you're flying high. Hopefully that positive mojo will spread into your current situation.

19) Scrap the gigantic mug with the wryly amusing caption for a dainty china cup. If you make your tea / coffee in a pot it will stay hot and you can have endless top-ups. (If your beverage of choice is coffee, it's always extra fun to pretend you're a cop when you get your refills. Just sayin'.)

20) If you're feeling grouchy, put on your favourite song (the happy, cheerful one, not the one that makes you feel righteous anger at how your ex treated you) and dance around the room. Extra points if you're naked and there's a mirror.

21) Do some research into your ancestry, or quiz your resident genealogy expert (there's one in every family). It's fascinating to see where you came from; one of my friends discovered that her interest in education wasn't as unique as she'd thought, as three previous generations of her family had also been teachers. If you find living relatives in far-flung places, it's the perfect excuse for taking a trip abroad. (Maybe start out as pen pals before showing up on their doorstep for the dreaded "pop-in"...)

22) You don't have to go out with friends to indulge in cocktail hour; there's something rather suave about having a sideboard all stocked up full of yummy liqueurs, with ice and maybe some maraschino cherries on the side. It's got to be better than hanging around outside the off-license swigging from a can of cider, or throwing back disgusting shots. If we're going to drink alcohol, let's keep it classy.

23) If boozy afternoons aren't your thing (very sensible) maybe high tea might hit the spot? It's become very fashionable to go for sandwiches and cake in top hotels, but it costs a bomb and it's just as elegant to drink tea at home. Get that china teacup we talked about, one of the cupcakes (if there are any left) or the pièce de résistance: a scone with JAM AND CLOTTED CREAM. Damn, if you've never tried this I don't know how to convey to you how amazing it tastes. Give it a whirl right now!

24) Get a jewellery box that looks like a treasure chest. That way, every day when you go to accessorise your look, you'll feel like a lady pirate pillaging the natives' treasure. Works for me.

25) Explore your spiritual side and get out of your comfort zone by going on a retreat. There are zillions of options and you can choose from spending the week in silence, to living with nuns, to meeting a guru at an Ashram. It might sound a little bit daunting, but it will be an unforgettable experience.

26) Make a reward chart for doing chores around the house (even if you live alone). Who wouldn't want to load the dishwasher if they get a

shiny gold star for it? It'll start as a joke of course, before everyone gets really competitive over who's got the most bling and starts fighting over the bathroom mop.

27) Get your body moving. I sometimes go to a dance class which is quite tough, both in the amount of sweat produced and the fast-paced choreography. Even though it's hard work, I always come out glowing. I don't know if it's the endorphins, or the fact that I've survived, but I always think "Wow, if I did this kind of exercise every day, I'd feel fantastic ALL THE TIME!" (And then I have to try really hard to convince myself to even make it there the following week...)

28) Use a lovely fabric softener when you do your laundry. Having invitingly soft and fragrant clothes turns the mundane chore of getting dressed into a sensuous experience.

29) When deciding on a course of action, ask yourself: "What would make a better story to tell my grandchildren?" – it clarifies things nicely. One choice might be a month travelling around Europe with a friend, sitting in little Parisian cafés, exploring Venice in a gondola, waking up to the scent of orange blossoms in a quaint Spanish village. Your alternative choice might be staying at home because your boyfriend hates foreign food and doesn't want you to go without him, or because doing something so drastic just seems *scary*. With the perspective of considering what kind of life you'd like to look back on, everything becomes simpler.

30) Buy some new underwear, and parade around the house wearing it. You saucepot!

31) Get some prints of your favourite pictures and spend a few happy hours arranging them into a wall collage. It'll look stunning and you'll have a comforting visual reminder of the fun times you've had with your friends and family / places you've been / kittens you've known.

32) Go offline for a day or two. I'm a huge fan of the internet (what was life like before all the information and entertainment in the world was just a click away?) but it can be horribly addictive. If you get the shakes when you can't check your messages, it's definitely time for a break.

33) Celebrate your successes. Bought the perfect pair of shoes? Did an ace job on a project at work? Someone you know (vaguely) is getting

married? Make the little things a reason to have a glass of champagne, a jig around your bedroom or a glitzy night on the town.

34) Nobody likes to think about it, but we're all going to die. Sign up for organ donation and you'll know that after you've gone, you can still make a difference to someone's life. Let's face it, the only other options are to become a pile of ashes or worm food. At least this way, part of you will live on in somebody else. If you'd like to save lives while you're still around, donate blood – hospitals depend on volunteers to keep patients alive. You can also sign up for the bone marrow / stem cell registry, which means you'll get a call if you're a match to someone on the waiting list. (Wouldn't that be a heroic way to feel like James Bond on a special assignment?)

35) Get up close and personal with some animals. Whether it's going to the coast and booking a whale-watching trip, splashing out on an experience day at a zoo where you get to feed the elephants, or crouching for hours in a hide to spot some badgers, interacting with beautiful creatures is an uplifting experience.

36) "Review" your wardrobe. Get some upbeat tunes blasting out, lay all of your clothes on your bed / floor / wherever they'll fit, and take a long hard look at what you've got. You'll find you can afford to get rid of some stuff, and (bonus) you'll also rediscover old favourites and the odd dress that used to be too big / too small but now fits perfectly. Not only that, but when everything is neater, it'll fit back into the closet more easily. You'll feel as if you have more clothes AND more space! If you have no self-discipline, get a ruthless friend to help you throw out what you're *really* not going to wear again.

37) As for those clothes you don't need any more, you have a few options: a) charity shop – to make you feel like a generous philanthropist in the style of Angelina Jolie, b) swap party or giveaway with your friends – you might find they have something you adore. And if they don't, let them have that cute skirt anyway – you'll get a kick out of it every time you see them rocking your style. Or c) sell them – nothing makes you feel like a kickass entrepreneur like making cash over the internet.

38) Listen to classical music. Some of it's pretty nifty and you'll feel all sophisticated.

39) Try a new recipe – something really special that you figured you might make one day for a swanky dinner party. Practice it now, even if you have to eat the leftovers for days; it'll be worth it. Or if you've got time to spare, make some meals you can freeze in batches and bask in the satisfaction of feeling fantastically organised next time you don't feel like cooking. The smugness is super-charged if the recipe is packed full of antioxidant-rich, healthy ingredients.

40) Wear a costume just for the hell of it. If it's a national holiday, you can go all out (I love dressing up so much that I consider Halloween attire to be appropriate for the entire last week of October). If there's no occasion but you feel like being festive anyway, you'll have to be a bit subtle. Perhaps a blue dress, Alice band and knee-high socks? Or maybe a yellow tracksuit with a black stripe (samurai sword optional). If you're the only one who knows you've dressed up, you'll giggle to yourself all day long.

41) Do something that scares you. A charity skydive, a meal by yourself in a restaurant, calling up the HR manager of your dream company to ask about job vacancies... Even if things don't go as you planned (I hope the skydiving one goes OK) you'll feel high afterwards.

42) Speaking of getting a crazy rush, you'll also have one when you tell someone "No". Is it a ripple of fear? A surge of excitement? Whatever. It reminds everybody that you're a Princess and you make your own decisions.

43) Go through your old CDs and decide which ones you can live without; there are bound to be some you never listen to anymore. If it's hard to make a decision, ask yourself who will get more enjoyment out of the album – you, or a fan of that band who'll be thrilled to find it in the charity shop?

44) Wear your favourite sparkly earrings, even if you're not going to see anyone. It will perk you up every time you check yourself out in the bathroom mirror.

45) Have a nice long talk with someone who's always on your side. Whether it's your mum, your best friend, or a supportive teacher, we all need encouragers around us – the people who say "Of course you should go for it! You'll be brilliant!" Alternatively, mentor somebody else. If you've been through something they're now

struggling with, your kind words will mean more to them than you can imagine.

46) Make something. Getting crafty is great fun and you'll end up with a lovely new and unique necklace / skirt / patchwork quilt. Being artistic is also an effective de-stresser; you'll be concentrating so hard on getting your hem right, you'll forget everything else. "Don't talk to me about exam results, I can't find any buttons to match this corsage. I have real problems now!"

47) If you're not sure of your clothes-making skills, you can still express your individuality; instead of looking like everyone else in an outfit from the most popular shop in town, buy a cheap top (or dig out one you never wear) and customise it. Glitter! Sparkles! Ribbon! BOOM!

48) Invite the funniest or most fascinating people you know to a little dinner party at your place. It doesn't need to be a formal do with lots of couples – sometimes I've done this with just two friends, and we had a hoot. You could even make it a regular event, take turns hosting and then judge each other, *Come Dine With Me* style. (Keep it kind, please.)

49) Give someone a *proper* cuddle. I'm talking belly to belly contact, not a flimsy hug where it feels as if you're holding each other away. (It may be best to try this one with a close friend, no matter how nice your boss seems.)

50) Have a "staycation" – instead of spending money and eating horrible airline food to end up lounging by the pool, skip the first and second steps. Set up a paddling pool in your back garden (nobody really *swims* on holiday, do they? We just like splashing about to cool off). Have some day trips to all those interesting places you always mean to visit but don't get round to because they're only a short train ride away and you can go any time. Eat out. Wear a sarong while buying postcards. Go out in your local town and pretend you're a tourist. You'll see everything with new eyes – the lush gorgeousness of the woods, the cosmopolitan atmosphere of the café area with al fresco dining, and the variety of stores. It'll feel like a rejuvenating mini holiday.

51) You're never too old for a slumber party! It's a blast having everyone snuggled in sleeping bags all over the living room floor,

watching movies, gossiping about boys, and doing each other's hair. Time to bond with your besties!

52) Go for a run when it's really cold. You'll come back with the same kind of all-over glow that you get by jumping into cold water. (Not recommended.)

53) Make a dramatic change. Paint your bedroom a new colour, get your hair put into cornrows, make a resolution to stop seeing that negative friend. Sometimes life's routines can feel a bit stagnant, and shaking things up helps us to avoid feeling stale. Visible transformations spur us on because when nothing seems to be shifting or progressing, we can think "Well at least X is different now..."

54) Read a magazine from cover to cover, paying special attention to the fashion rules and all the bitchy comments about how awful people look when they don't follow them, and then yell "Who gives a crap what you think? I can wear whatever I want and you can't stop me!" That'll show 'em.

55) Have a DIY session of psychoanalysis. Write down some of the negative beliefs you have about yourself: "I don't make friends easily," or "I always say the wrong thing." Then think back to when you first started feeling that way: maybe you had a moment of bashfulness at a party when you were six, and since then you've considered yourself "shy". How many images of yourself that you're carrying around are actually years out of date and totally irrelevant to the person you are today?

56) Buy a plant. I have two orchids in my bedroom, and I love seeing them go through their growth cycle, with flowers starting as a bud and then suddenly blossoming into a glorious display. It's only slightly embarrassing that I also talk to them. ("Come on, where are your nice new shoots? You're going to grow up big and strong and pretty like your sister, aren't you?")

57) Get a haircut. Having awesome hair is a sure-fire way to put you in a good mood, and you'll feel the difference whether it's a striking new look (as one of those "dramatic changes"), or a mere trim. Alternatively, have a deep conditioning session. You don't need an expensive hot oil treatment – nab some olive or coconut oil from your

kitchen. Afterwards, your hair will feel so swishy and soft you won't be able to stop stroking it.

58) Play a musical instrument. You can get hold of them pretty cheaply second-hand, then find a local teacher or watch tutorials online. Not only can you learn to make pretty sounds, but getting completely engrossed in finger placement is an excellent distraction technique if you're feeling tense. If your friends are also musos, you'll get a kick out of jamming together.

59) Keep a journal. You don't have to force yourself to write in it every day – it shouldn't feel like a chore. Use it when you need it for getting your problems out of you and onto the page. (Mine has seriously saved me THOUSANDS in therapy bills.) A diary is a far better listener than a friend because it will never interrupt, judge you or tell your secrets to anyone else (if you hide it well, that is). The added bonus is that it provides life perspective – you'll read it in years to come and think "I was worried about *that?*" You'll find embarrassing moments which occurred with people whose names you've completely forgotten, and "disasters" which meant nothing two weeks later.

60) All those boring chores you've been saving up for the weekend? The laundry, the grocery shopping, the bed-changing and vacuuming? Do it all in the evenings during the week. It'll take less time, because you *have* less time. Then your weekend is free for relaxation, just as it should be.

61) Wear your super-duper new shoes / party dress / silver trench coat even if there's no occasion for it and you'll be horribly overdressed for the office. You might fall under a bus tomorrow and never have worn your best outfit! The same goes for the precious jewellery you never wear because you're afraid it will get lost or damaged. It could get stolen from your house – just take pleasure in using it right now.

62) Go out and see some live music. It doesn't have to be your favourite genre – the enthusiastic atmosphere and the quality of the sound will make it a night to remember even if folk / jazz / blues isn't your thing. Dancing is irresistible when you're watching musicians who are having a riot up there on stage.

63) Write a list of all the things in your entire life that you're proud of. Your model village won first prize in the school art contest when you

were five? It goes on the list. You can make pancakes without looking at a recipe book? That's some outstanding stuff right there! When you're feeling challenged, remember all the times you ended up achieving exactly what you set out to do. Those obstacles might have seemed insurmountable, but you *did* manage to pass your driving test, or get into that school, or wallpaper a room without any help. You'll be able to do *this* thing too.

64) Slather yourself with scented lotion before you go to bed, and wake up silky smooth and smelling magnificent.

65) Do what you're proficient at... and then try something else. You don't have to start too many things at once; if you take up drum lessons, join a tennis club, and learn to code websites all in the space of a few weeks, you'll end up overwhelmed. Instead, balance out the stuff you're already familiar with (so you can luxuriate in NOT being a beginner in at least one area) but keep pushing yourself to try new skills. How else will you find out what other talents you might have?

66) Wear the biggest sunglasses you can, all the time. You may look a bit of a dope, but when people can't see your eyes, they're the ones who feel strangely nervous. Wowser.

67) Volunteer. Whether it's doling out soup at a homeless shelter, teaching adults to read, or doing some shopping for your elderly next-door neighbour, nothing makes you feel fab faster than knowing you've made a difference.

68) Buy some gorgeous crystals. You might not believe they have any magical qualities, but they look really pretty and there's something pleasing about the smooth roundness of a pebble, especially when it's pink.

69) Have a cheeky weekend away. It's not quite as extravagant as booking a fortnight's holiday, but they do say a change is as good as a rest, and a weekend is just long enough to feel like a real break. I once took a trip to Liverpool purely to check out an exhibition at the Tate; listening to the warm Liverpudlian accents made it feel like an exotic foreign land, even though I was only a few hours' drive from home.

70) Bake some bread. It's so satisfying to knead out all your problems and the delicious smell will lift your sprits in no time.

71) When your friend sends you that special tea / chocolate / face cream that you can't get locally, don't be afraid to use it up. Treat yourself, and enjoy every bit of it.

72) Figure out the non-negotiables in your life. Could you deal with never travelling the world, if you raise lovely children instead? Will you be heartbroken if you reach your deathbed without ever having worked at NASA? Decide what's a) essential, b) important, but you could live without it if you really had to, c) something you'd kind of like, and d) something you're indifferent to and don't care if it never happens. You might realise that society has suckered you into pursuing the aims that are the least important to you. (No, I don't want a house in the suburbs, thanks. I'll be saving that money to start a tiger sanctuary...)

73) Now you know your goal, figure out a way to get there. Whether it's saving £5 a week for the next three years, putting your studies on hold so you can volunteer in India, or spending money on a dating site so you can meet a decent man – there's one action you can take that will be the first step towards your target.

74) Join a choir or visit a gospel church: singing is a natural way to boost your mood, and belting out show tunes with a group is even more fun than your usual solo efforts in the shower.

75) If you find yourself short of friends, there are lots of ways to find new ones. You might find yourself chatting to someone at your ballet class, or a fellow bungee jumper (because you're being so brave about doing all that stuff that scares you). There are meet-up clubs for virtually anything, all listed on the internet. Keep it legit by joining official groups who meet in public places, preferably in daytime, not by calling that guy from a shady pick-up website.

76) Take a small child to a farm or petting zoo; it will make your day when you get to see the first time a toddler touches the soft wool of a tiny lamb, or gets a snuzzly kiss from a donkey.

77) Do a favour for your future self. Maybe you could hide a £10 note in a coat pocket that you'll have forgotten about by the time winter rolls around (make sure it's a coat you really like and won't throw out in your wardrobe-clearing craze). Or you could do your taxes before you have to, then when the dreaded deadline looms and you finally sit

down with a calculator, you'll find that it's already done. Cheers, past self!

78) Print out one of those lists of books you should read / films you should watch before you die, and then tick them off as you go. You'll end up being more cultured than a courtesan of ancient Greece.

79) Take some time to experiment with makeup, hairstyles and clothes. This is an awesome way to spend a girly night in with friends; you might not be brave enough to try bright red lips or purple eyeshadow in public, but home is a different matter. There are so many tutorials online that you can learn intricate techniques for changing the entire look of your face with some well-placed warpaint.

80) Get a massage. Grab a deal on a voucher website, or try your local college for a cheap option. (So far, I've avoided doing this because I fear the inevitable awkward moment when I'll bump into the student in our (small) town shortly after they've had their hands on my naked, oil-covered body.)

81) Keep a note of funny things you've done or overheard. I write everything down in a notebook if it makes me laugh – I recently spent an hour with a pal having hysterics at all of my past embarrassing moments. We also read aloud from diaries we kept when we were twelve, which was equally hilarious. Apparently "my BFF is being annoying today" and "X is trying to take my friends away" are universal complaints for pre-teens.

82) Grab your favourite people and share out that amazing vintage bottle of wine you've been saving for a suitably special occasion. Carpe the damn diem – *today* is special! (And you'll feel silly if you wait too long and it's turned to vinegar.)

83) Put your favourite quotes on display as a constant reminder to think positively. It doesn't matter if they're on a poster, printed out in ornate script from your computer, or written with crayon on a scrap of card: make them visible.

84) Go to a farmer's market and get some delicious locally produced cheese, vegetables, meat, or honey. You're supporting small businesses and being environmentally friendly too – it's stupid to buy potatoes flown in from another country when they're being harvested within a mile of your home.

85) On the other hand, you could create your own vegetable garden; growing your own food is like printing your own money. It's also one of those activities which helps you to unwind; as the saying goes, "Gardening is free therapy, *and* you get tomatoes." If you end up with huge piles of fruit you could do swapsies with your friends or neighbours, leaving everyone with a community-minded glow and delicious home-grown organic goodies.

86) Hang out in the library or a second-hand book shop. You never know what treasures you might find there, and it's a delightfully mellow place to check out what's on offer and sniff the old book smell. Libraries are so wonderful I can't believe everyone doesn't use them. FREE BOOKS! What could be better?

87) Buy yourself a box of chocolates. A big bar is pretty yummy, but somehow an array of exquisite little morsels feels more special. Maybe it's the luxury of not having to wait for someone to give you something that's traditionally seen as a present. Self-gifting all the way, baby!

88) Go to a museum or an art gallery. I always used to conscientiously work my way around the entire exhibition, until I realised that looking at stuff I'm not really interested in is a waste of time. Now I just focus on what I like (basically: dinosaurs, the wackier side of modern art, and ancient Egyptian jewellery) and I end up with a stimulated brain and a less exhausted body.

89) Give someone one of those Princess compliments – something absolutely sincere, heartfelt and unexpected. They will sparkle with joy (even if they don't show it) and that will make you sparkle with joy too.

90) Don't bulk-buy your beauty products. Is it sad that I find it exciting to use a new moisturiser or shampoo? Your old one works OK – but who's to say that a different one won't be even better? Try a new scent and a new texture – variety is the spice of life.

91) Go to a movie in the middle if the day when you have time off during the week. Matinees tend to be cheaper, and indulging in an afternoon show somehow feels delightfully naughty.

92) Have a retro day: put on your mum's old records and have a swinging good time to the Beatles, The Cure or Madonna (depending on how old your mother is).

93) PLAN your future treats. Scientists tell us that while taking a holiday makes us happier, we're actually in our highest spirits beforehand – when we're looking forward to the fun we expect to have. (If the holiday involves living in a tiny caravan, the idea of it is almost guaranteed to be more enjoyable than the reality.) So make some plans for next weekend, get a restaurant reservation, book those tickets early, and start anticipating happy days.

94) Go through all your old toys that are taking up space in the attic. You'll revisit lots of memories, meet some friends you'd forgotten about, and maybe find something to donate to a kid who'll like it as much as you did. (Alternatively, you could find your beloved old cuddly lion and bring him to his new home on your bed. Not that I did this.)

95) Take a drama class. If you're shy, it will build up your confidence. If you're already addicted to the smell of the greasepaint, the lights and the applause, getting involved with an amateur dramatics production will be a real scream. Even if you have no intention of acting professionally, drama provides plenty of life lessons: keeping your cool even when you know everything is going wrong backstage, the ability to think on your feet and improvise, and how to empathise with all sorts of characters.

96) If you want that disgustingly unhealthy but mouth-wateringly shiny glazed donut, just eat it. Make sure you wring out every ounce of ecstasy to make it worth your while.

97) Have a girls' night out and try a new place – it could end up being your new favourite. Spend a warm summer evening at a bar or restaurant with a roof terrace, watch the sunset and feel glamorous.

98) Change your bed sheets. Sliding into fresh sheets feels sublime, and starching your pillow cases so they're lovely and crunchy is optional but recommended. If you do this early in the day you may not be able to resist the temptation of having a little cat nap; there's something so luxurious about getting all comfy in your bed while everyone else is bustling about. Fools.

99) When you're feeling stressed, soothe your soul via the wonders of the internet and watch some heart-warming videos to calm down. It's impossible to stay in a bad mood when you're watching pandas amuse

themselves on playground rides, or a baby giggling hysterically because paper is being ripped up.

100) Have a get-together to celebrate a TV event. A big sports game, the finale of a series you love, or a marathon of an old favourite; it's entertaining to watch with pals so you can dissect the action as it happens. If you like dressing up, make it a costume party (come as your favourite character), or lay out the red carpet and make it a posh A-list bash with everyone in their tuxedos and gowns.

101) Sit on a beach, watch the waves and realise that the universe is unimaginably huge, and you're in it. You're part of the family that lives here – the stars, the rocks, the trees, the animals, the people. We're all here together. Fantastic, isn't it?

COMPLETELY RANDOM TIPS FOR LIFE

"Don't say you don't have enough time. You have exactly the same number of hours per day that were given to Louis Pasteur, Michaelangelo, Da Vinci, and Albert Einstein." H. Jackson Brown

(Yeah, but they didn't have to self-tan, pluck their eyebrows or keep up with what happened on TV last night, did they?)

Here are some final hints and tricks to help you navigate the Princess life:

- If your idea of "me time" is a shopping trip, getting a manicure, or putting slices of cucumber over your eyes while your face is covered in a mud mask, good for you. If you'd rather spend the afternoon killing zombies on the computer, reading a book about Carl Jung, or watching ice hockey on TV, that's cool too. You don't have to fit into the stereotype that because you're female, "relaxation" means beautifying yourself – there are a limited number of hours in which examining your pores can really be interesting.
- Lots of us play a game with ourselves, saying: "When X happens, *then* I'll be ready to do Y." If you're always waiting around for the ideal conditions, you'll never get anything done. Seize the day and go for it – having a bash at something and learning from your mistakes is better than never starting at all because you're afraid it won't turn out perfectly.
- Shakespeare summed it up: "Neither a lender nor a borrower be." It's easy to forget a loan and your friend might be too shy / polite to remind you about that tenner you owe them, then end up resenting you. I've had disasters with lending out everything from cake stands to sleeping bags – when someone says "Is it OK if I borrow this? I'll bring it straight back", it's inevitably been six months before it gets returned. These days I only lend books to people who've proven themselves to

be utterly reliable; if anyone else asks I say "Sorry, I don't lend books, but I bet the library has it." Alternatively, if you're feeling generous and decide to let your friend borrow something, photograph them holding it and just delete the picture when it's returned. Ultimately, the secret is to only lend what you can afford to lose.

- Carry a tiny book of matches (the kind you get in hotels) with you at all times. Striking a match gets rid of unpleasant odours which can occasionally be found in bathrooms. Need I say more? Never again will you fear your boyfriend having to hold his nose if he goes in after you.

- Lots of people have a "timeline" in mind for their life: the age when they want to get married, have kids, retire. The best advice I ever got was to forget all about this schedule. Why try to squeeze your life into a totally artificial construct based on meaningless rules? You'll end up doing stupid things, like randomly marrying the guy you happen to be dating when you're 29 because your self-imposed wedding deadline is age 30. Despite people hotly debating the "correct" age to tick off life's milestones, it's different for everyone – there's no right or wrong answer.

- Leading on from this, we all know that age ain't nothing but a number; you can be 14 and wise, or 70 and stupid. However, the frontal cortex area of your brain – the bit which deals with judgement, decision-making and impulse control – doesn't fully mature until you're 25. So on the plus side, you have a great excuse for all the crazy stuff you've done thus far. On the other hand, it might be a good idea to hold off from making any of those life-changing arrangements, like marriage or children, until your brain is fully-equipped to deal...

- Keep in mind that procreating isn't compulsory. It's your decision, and it has nothing to do with anyone but you and your partner – even if your parents want to have grandkids and your friends are all having babies. Why do some people have the bizarre idea that not having children is "selfish"? If you told them "You know, I don't really fancy being a train driver," it would just be considered a personal preference. Likewise, raising small human beings either strikes you as a cool way to spend your time or it doesn't. Incidentally, there are thousands of children in foster care who would love to have a forever family, so if you do like the idea of experiencing parenthood, you might also want to consider adopting.

- Don't let anger get the better of you. I know people in the movies are always punching holes in walls and throwing plates of spaghetti, but the upshot of using these as stress-busters is that you're still furious afterwards, and you now have an extra mess to clear up.

- Before you sign a lease to share a house with your friends, have an in-depth talk about your expectations: will guests always be welcome at any time? How will you divide household chores? Will you buy basic groceries from a shared kitty or keep your food supplies completely separate? There's a lot more to it than just picking a pal you get on well with, and communication is the key.

- Drugs = bad idea. Seriously, nobody in the entire history of the world has ever actually *improved* their lives by taking recreational illegal substances, even if they seemed fun at the time. Psychoanalyst and author of *Women Who Run With the Wolves* Clarissa Pinkola Estés defines addiction as "anything that depletes life while making it 'appear' better". Compulsive behaviour sucks away our time and energy, make us less healthy, and prevents us from living life to the full.

- If you're trying to give up a bad habit, don't think of it in terms of "forever". In the throes of nicotine addiction or a strict diet, telling yourself "I'm never going to indulge again" could push you over the edge. Just think "I'm going to get through the rest of TODAY" and it will feel easier. The same goes for life after an addictive relationship, too.

- If your confidence is based purely on the way you look, you're setting yourself up for a) years of fretting about how to appear perfect, and b) anxiety / despair as the wrinkles inevitably set in. (Not to mention the fact that the world is FULL of pretty girls – you're going to have to dig a little bit deeper if you want to stand out in the crowd.) Base your self-belief on what's in your heart and mind; you'll never lose your inner beauty.

- Before sharing some scandalous news story or conspiracy theory on Facebook, check it out on www.snopes.com. That way you'll avoid looking silly when somebody else posts a link to the truth, and you won't have contributed to the giant swirling pool of misinformation on the internet.

- You don't have to take on board what someone else considers "wisdom". Sometimes, other women give terrible advice. This may or may not be because they've already made decisions they regret and hope somebody else will do the same so they'll feel better about it.

- Embarrassment is a completely pointless emotion. If you've done something shameful and fear you'll be ridiculed for the rest of your life, distract yourself until the feeling passes. Going over and over it in your mind is a waste of time when you could be doing something fun instead.

- Things that fall under the "Life's too short" category: parking with geometric precision (as long as it's in the space, nobody cares about the exact alignment), watching unfunny comedies that everyone else finds inexplicably hilarious, and matching your pairs of socks. Oh, and one more: not ordering the chocolate-fudge brownie you've been looking forward to, because nobody else wants dessert. Stop asking for permission ("Is anyone else going to have a pudding?") and start getting what you want.

- If you have an annoying cough and it's going to embarrass you when you're in a quiet room full of people, try minty chewing gum: it takes away the tickly feeling in your throat.

- Don't hold back because you're afraid of hurting someone else. If your best friend wants to be a cheerleader and you make the team but she doesn't, don't feel guilty. If you end up earning more than your sister, it's not a betrayal. Your success might be an inspiration for someone else, while limiting yourself to avoid upsetting the balance doesn't help anyone. Equally, rather than being paralysed by jealousy when someone else is coming out on top, use it to spur you on to greater things. Some of our best achievements will be triggered by envy at seeing someone else fulfilling our secret ambitions.

- Regularly back up everything on your computer and phone, and keep your data storage device somewhere totally different from your everyday electronics. I'm still haunted by the story of a guy who was burgled and lost the lot because he kept all his external hard drives in the same room with his laptop.

- Keep an overnight bag packed with a spare toothbrush / moisturiser / knickers etc. That way you'll be ready to go at a moment's notice in an emergency (in a dystopian future where you're on the run from the government, for instance), and in regular holiday situations, you'll have everything you need in one bag and you won't forget something vital like deodorant. You'll also avoid that annoying situation where you can't finish packing because you need to brush your teeth / apply your makeup one last time before you leave.

- Find the lesson in everything. Instead of smacking your forehead and saying "What was I thinking?" try to find out what you were *learning* instead. Your best teacher is your last mistake.

- When you move into a new place, get the locks changed. You never know how many of the former inhabitant's friends have spares.

- No matter what stressful life experience you're going through, there is probably at least one moment every day which is *utter bliss.* Sneaking in an episode of your favourite TV show as a break from exam revision. The peace that descends when the kids are finally in bed. Sinking into a hot bath. The secret of a happy life is noticing and appreciating these little snippets of euphoria.

- We're brainwashed to think that hating our lives is normal. Radio announcers gleefully declare that Wednesday is "hump day"– you're halfway to the weekend and that means a 2-day respite from your job, woohoo! Holiday companies entice us to "escape from it all". But what are we trying to escape from? Our lives, which we've built. If we don't like them, it's a sign to change them, not bury our heads in the sand and count the days until we get a break. We have this idea that one day we'll *get there* – we'll reach the pinnacle of our existence and from that moment on, everything will be perfect. But the truth is, you'll never be completely satisfied, because human beings aren't designed to sit back and be complacent. We're always on the move; aspiring to new accomplishments, making stuff, searching for answers. When you create a lifestyle that you truly inhabit instead of trying to duck out of, you meet challenges with enthusiasm and you're excited to see what will happen next.

EPILOGUE

"It had long since come to my attention that people of accomplishment rarely sat back and let things happen to them. They went out and happened to things."
Elinor Smith

So, there you have it. The master plan for feeling beautiful, the tactics for dealing with tricky customers, the blueprint for enhancing your prestige: The Princess Guide to Life. Are you feeling royal by now?

You may be more like a Princess in a fairytale than an ordinary human being, but that doesn't mean you have to hang out in a tower waiting to be saved. We talk about wanting to change the world, and we often picture this as a lofty goal reached only by superstars, politicians and billionaires. The truth is, no matter where you are or what you're doing, you're making a difference just by existing. Every action you carry out will either make the universe a better place or a worse one.

We can all vote for the principles we believe in, protest against injustice and inequality, and use our money to support ethical businesses. Maybe you'll also help your brother when he's going through a rough patch, cheer people up while you're packing their groceries, or be a great mum – it all counts. Even if you're currently penniless, ill, or housebound, without lifting a finger you can still send out your very best *vibes.* You never know the influence you might have until you try.

At the opposite end of the Princess scale we have the kind of people who make the world that little bit crappier than it was before they got here. They don't care about anyone but themselves, so they'll happily drop litter, leave their dog's poop un-scooped, and shatter the peace and quiet with loud music or endless public phone calls (and react with hostility anytime they're challenged). When someone is this self-centred, all these little things add up and have a negative impact on the lives of everyone around them.

Being a Princess takes a lot of effort. We could take the easy route; blame others for our problems, focus on the bad side of everything and everyone, and spend more time worrying about the state of our makeup than anything in the real world. But where's the fun in that? It's not a satisfying existence and it doesn't do anybody any good – least of all us.

Princesses root for other people to have success because great things happening to one person is a joy to be shared. We set goals and work hard to reach them. We share glory instead of claiming credit for every achievement, and we're grateful for every day. We won't always get it right, but we can fake it till we make it, asking ourselves "How would a wise / strong / brave person handle this situation?" – then doing that.

If other people want to be grouchy, aggressive, or manipulative, it's up to them – you just sail past with a cheery wave, straighten your tiara and keep spreading happiness everywhere you go. And instead of asking yourself "Who's going to let me do all the epic stuff I want to do to change the world?" ask yourself this: Who's going to stop you?

Now get out there and start Princessifying the planet!

Acknowledgements

"The writer must believe that what he is doing is the most important thing in the world. And he must hold to this illusion even when he knows it is not true."
John Steinbeck

First of all, a shout-out to the best family in the whole world: Daisy, Chris, Nicole, and especially JP. Thank you for a) putting up with me, b) giving me SO MANY helpful suggestions, and c) being amazing.

My two BFFs, Anna and Jasmine: You rock!

Anna, thank you for the *long* chats encompassing everything from books and the craft of writing to the Law of Attraction... and of course, for providing me with top-notch entertainment!

Special thanks to Jasmine for your unwavering support and encouragement. When I was moaning about how long the whole process was taking, you looked at me incredulously and said "You're writing a *book*." I kept remembering that when I was buried under piles of rubbish drafts, feeling sorry for myself, and it helped a lot.

Thanks to everyone who encouraged me along the way, whether in person or via the magic of the internet – you have no idea what a difference you made.

Thanks to my silent writing partner – the park. Where would I be without my daily walk in the woods?

And massive thanks to the entire team at JC HQ. Y'all are awesome.

Aut viam inveniam aut faciam
I will either find a way or make one.

If you liked this book, please consider writing a review to let others know about it. You can also join The Princess Guide to Life newsletter to get updates about new releases.

Check out www.princessguidetolife.com for more details.

ALSO BY ROSIE BLYTHE

The
Princess Guide
to Being a Cat

Rosie Blythe

PREPARE TO BE WORSHIPPED...

If you've ever envied your cat's effortless grace, slinky walk and power to command a room, this is the book for you.

Rosie Blythe (author of self-help manual *The Princess Guide to Life*) reveals how being a Princess is a lot like being a cat; it's all about quiet determination, intoxicating eye contact, and enjoying each moment as it comes.

Feisty moggies have long been noted for their independence, mysteriousness and self-possessed cool. By following their poised and purry example, we Princesses will discover:

- The importance of rejecting anything which doesn't meet our high standards (contemptuous sniff optional)
- How a little mischief can liven up your workplace
- The art of dealing with failure (an inevitable side effect of making bold leaps of faith)
- Why trusting your instincts is essential
- The secrets of kittenish flirting

Attitude is everything, and channelling your inner feline is a sneaky shortcut to feeling more confident, chic and sensuous.

So follow the red laser light of your dreams, relish every mealtime and allow the wisdom of our fluffy overlords to inspire you to a life of curiosity, playfulness and magic.

And if anyone tries to feed you drugs, give them hell.

The Princess Guide to Being a Cat is part of the official Princess Guide to Life series, aimed at smart, sassy and stylish women (and fabulous men).

www.princessguidetolife.com

Lightning Source UK Ltd.
Milton Keynes UK
UKOW04f0629181115

262987UK00001B/159/P